PRAISE FOR *THE GIRL AND THE TIGER*

"After so many years spent working in India it is a magical experience to be so viscerally transported there by Paul's writing. Through Isha's eyes we walk beside tigers and elephants, in a beautiful and tragic journey through India's threatened jungles. This is an important journey that I highly recommend you must take." (Steve Winter, photojournalist, *National Geographic*)

"Rosolie's gripping novel examines the complex relationship between nature, man and animal, subtly foregrounding the chief concerns of the present. The numerous characters in this novel and the intertwined nature of their journeys are powerful in reality, as well as metaphorically... Only someone with an enormous love for nature and the talent to be able to see in details can produce a work of such merit." (Vivek Shanbhag, *Ghachar Ghochar*, NYT Critics' Top Books of 2017)

"...A 21st century *The Jungle Book*." (Lorraine Thompson, WritersKitchen)

PRAISE FOR PAUL ROSOLIE

Paul Rosolie is also the author of *Mother of God: An Extraordinary Journey into the Uncharted Tributaries of the Western Amazon* published by Harper Collins

"Rosolie writes with intrepid curiosity and a passion for ecological preservation." (*Booklist*)

"Rosolie is a gripping storyteller. . . . His enthusiasm for the wilderness and his ability to convey it poetically makes him an exceedingly persuasive advocate for conserving what's left of the natural world." (*BookPage*)

"Rosolie's solo adventures in the heart of the Amazon jungle, up close and personal with giant anacondas and jaguars, are gripping. And his dedication to preserving one of the earth's last wildernesses is where he really sets himself apart. *Mother of God* is an awe-inspiring read." (Bear Grylls)

"Thanks to fastidious journal-keeping that preserved a wealth of detail and emotion, Rosolie delivers an old-fashioned jungle adventure, one with rare immediacy and depth of feeling for the people and creatures he encounters." (*The Wall Street Journal*)

"His vivid writing immerses you in his adventures as he explores an ancient pristine forest where no white man has been, where he encounters amazing creatures, and experiences the relentless power of untamed nature…There are parts that will haunt you, scenes you will never forget." (Jane Goodall)

"Rosolie's powers of description are so vivid and engrossing that readers will be swept along in his passion." (*Publishers Weekly* (starred review))

THE GIRL
AND THE
TIGER

PAUL ROSOLIE

OWL HOLLOW PRESS

Owl Hollow Press, LLC, Springville, UT 84663

The Girl and the Tiger

Library of Congress Cataloging-in-Publication Data
The Girl and the Tiger / P. Rosolie. — First edition.

Summary:
A girl's crusade to save a Bengal tiger cub becomes an arduous journey across the changing landscape of modernizing India in search of the wild jungle.

ISBN 978-1-945654-31-2 (paperback)
ISBN 978-1-945654-32-9 (e-book)
LCCN 2019939332

Cover Photograph: Andrew Parker, Spectacle Photography UK
Cover Design: Ashley Conway
Interior Elephant Illustration: Isha Ela Chinniah

For the last tigers, the elephant herd,
and the wild creatures
who made our world.

PROLOGUE

The moon was setting and the night birds finishing their song when he woke. In the twisted branches and crowded silhouettes of the pre-dawn jungle, he did not rise but waited for the rustling below. His tree bed was made of dry leaves and a bamboo frame—it was more of a nest than a bed, really. He stretched, yawned, and curled into his warm blanket as heavy steps and the clink of wet chains came from below. A thick trunk slithered up the tree and reached eagerly into the bed. Large nostrils probed about the boy's face, drawing a river of air inward. He pushed it to his shoulder and rested his cheek on the prickly whiskers and tough wrinkled skin.

"*Namaskara*," he said, and the elephant below flapped its ears.

Thimma stood in the nest bed, stretched, and slid down a vine onto the elephant's back. Straddled on the great neck, he leaned forward to kiss the domed head and rub it roughly with his flat palm. The elephant rumbled and started down the path with the chain-clink of great strides. Rubbing the sleep from his eyes, the boy spoke gentle directions as they went so that Hathi knew when there was a branch or turn. With his feet behind the elephant's ears, he would tap this way or that, indicating direction. The blind elephant searched ahead with his trunk as the two went swaying through the jungle morning.

When they reached the river, the white herons and egrets took wing. Mist was rising around the rocks, and dragonflies still slept on dew-bent grass blades. The elephant lumbered in so that his feet, and then shoulders, and then head were submerged.

The boy stood up on the elephant's back so that it looked to the birds like he was walking on water. Only the elephant's trunk poked above the surface, taking great breaths as the giant below

explored the riverbed amid schools of fish. When he reached the
shallow center of the river, the boy stepped down onto the gravel as
Hathi reemerged from the water. With one command from the boy,
the elephant lay down, always to the right first, as he was a righty
in all matters of trunk and tusk. For nearly an hour the boy
scrubbed the mud from the wrinkled skin of the elephant. Behind
the ears, the great legs, and under the tail as well. They bathed together in the warm jungle morning on the day that began it all, the
day that changed their lives, the day that changed us all.

What I know is that Thimma was orphaned at the age of nine. I
never met his parents. What I know is mostly from what transpired
after those placid jungle days. I know that his father had been a
construction worker for the Forest Department, and when he died,
his son was left with his sole possession and source of wealth: a
forty-year-old, semi-wild, completely blind elephant named Hathi.
And so Thimma took his father's place on the giant's neck, working for the Indian government hauling teak, clearing roads, and
catching other elephants.

When I met Thimma, he was living alone in the jungle with
Hathi. Sometimes he took jobs at temples closer to the city. I've
never seen such a relationship between a human and an animal.
Never seen such loyalty or trust or love. The elephant was thankful
to the boy and knew that if the boy and his father had not cared for
him, he would have died long ago in the wild. The Law of the Jungle is unforgiving, but also numinously complex. The honeyguide
bird leads the badger to the hive so that the strong badger can break
open the honey, benefiting the bird and the badger. A boy and an
elephant become each other's keepers. I suppose if these things are
possible and permitted, the Law of the Jungle then must have been
waiting through the ages for the day that a young girl would become mother to a tiger.

I've known many of the people—human and animal both—in
the pages ahead. Thimma used to scold me for feeding lumps of
jaggery to Hathi. Later, when his trunk rummaged across my desk
knocking over books and coffee mugs, I learned why. It took all
my strength to push that giant proboscis away. Arun the sage was a

trusted friend, and it was through him I crossed orbit with the legendary Ramana Gowda. JCB Vijayan earned his name and then some because he bulldozed what could have been beautiful. He was to blame for the Battle of Ramachandran when Hathi and Thimma were parted, and all the fire and madness that followed.

But the most miraculous creature I met was Isha.

I knew her before it all happened. In those days there were no legends about her whispered through the countryside. There were no grand epithets. No one in the countryside had heard of *Hulidevathe* or *Ishamma*. She was just a spindly, uncageable little thing that the animals loved. Back then, when she had turtles or barbets or trinket snakes in her hands, it was her parents that called her the Saint of Small Things.

Outside of the throbbing magic of India, none of it would make a lick of sense. Even for India it is a stretch. Maybe that's why I doubted it. I was in South America on resupply during a long expedition in the Amazon when I received an email from Isha titled "A Question about a Tigress." I remember sitting in the 4 a.m. darkness, hands to my head, in complete turmoil. I considered abandoning everything and rushing across the world to help. But the realist in me, as I would have called it, was assured that her parents and the Forest Department would work it out. My attempted pragmatism was, in hindsight, a terrible underestimation.

When it hit the newspapers, they said people would talk about it for generations, the way an elder remembers a millennium comet or a five-hundred-year flood. It would be written into the story of our age for people in the distant future to read, like hieroglyphics. They would marvel that one so young could have reached across the nearly opaque boundary between species. We thought it would hold and spread and grow to change everything.

Instead what happened is what always happens to the unexplainable and fantastic: it was rejected. It was simply too much for any rational person to believe. But make no mistake—it happened. There are ashes and scars and bones to prove it. And so, the only justice that can be done is to tell it—just as it happened. It all began on that day, many miles from Thimma and the elephant Hathi, in a village outside of Mangalore, when Isha met a tiger.

1

THE COBRA

It was a monsoon morning in her fifteenth year when Isha walked barefoot on a red dirt road. The Mangalore sun was peering above the horizon and warm light filled the hallway of tall palms so it glowed and sent the girl's shadow out slender behind her. She carried her *chappals* in her hand so that her feet could feel the cool red earth. A peacock cried out from somewhere in the mist. The world was beautiful and quiet. She walked slowly, her satchel over her shoulder, as the sun warmed her face. Inside the satchel was a book she was excited to read and the money her grandmother had given her with instructions to buy *mosaru*. It was a pleasant first day of exile.

Isha did not miss the *jing-bang* madness of city life. And she did not miss the oppressive confinement of school. School was a prison she had worked hard to escape. Here, beneath the tall palms in the warm morning, there was no one to keep her captive; she was a triumphant outlaw. She did not know that being sent to live with her grandparents for the summer was just a tiny fraction of the exile she would soon experience, or that the events of that morning would forever change her life.

On that day, it began as so many great stories do: with a snake.

Across the misty countryside the world was still waking. Outside a house nestled in the lush plantation, a woman hunched before the door, drawing on the ground. She held her sari up with one hand, and with the other deftly dropped white flour into a series of dots and lines to create an intricate and auspicious *rangoli* before the door, just as her mother and her mother's mother had done. Isha waved but the woman did not see.

Some distance down the road, a group of boys were shouting.

The young cobra had fully intended to cross the road and reach the safety of the grass before anyone noticed. But the village boys had it surrounded in moments. They shouted excitedly, kicking at it, blocking its way so there was no escape. In retaliation, the young snake stood up, opened his hood, and hissed loudly at the boys. This scared them and intensified their excitement.

From a distance Isha could hear the boys yipping and shouting and saw them jumping excitedly around *something*. As she ran down the road, the boys seemed to strike the ground with sticks. When she arrived panting, the young cobra's back was already broken and bleeding. Even with its body ruined, the snake stood defiantly, hood spread, mouth opened wide, ready to fight until the last.

"Stop it!" Isha shouted, tears welling in her eyes.

One of the boys gave her a hard shove so that she fell backward, and inside her satchel she heard her glasses crack. She covered her eyes as the boys turned back to the snake and rained down a drumbeat of blows.

When Isha rose, they were prodding at the lifeless body of the snake.

"Why would you kill it?" she asked quietly in Kannada.

"What do you know, yah? *City girl,*" the boy who pushed her said threateningly.

Isha's eyes would not leave the body of the snake. She said nothing.

"Can you not speak, yah? Is that why they kicked you out of Bangalore *city girl* school?"

They were laughing as Isha began to leave, miserable for the snake and frustrated with herself. As she moved away, the boys turned their attention back to the body of the snake. Isha's eyes were dark and full of tears. The sadness she felt turned into frustration and boiled into anger with dizzying speed. She wiped her eyes, turned, and with two running steps shoved the boy so hard he fell forward, flat onto his face.

He sat up and checked his palms. Bits of blood beaded through the gravel where rough clay had scraped. The other boys were swearing and whooping in surprise. The boy stood and sped after Isha, her long legs already wheeling behind her so that her hair was wild with the wind that now blew through the tall palms. She knew that if the boys got to her, they would beat her badly. That she was a girl would grant her no amnesty.

She ran her fastest but the boy motored after her like a hornet, flat hands slicing the air. The other boys galloped behind. Isha knew that she could not outlast them for long, so like a rabbit evading a fox, she began to weave. She turned off the road and ran past a house and into a backyard. Dodging through drying clothes and sliding under a drinking cow, she leapt out of the yard and into another lane where children were playing. Behind her the boys crashed into children, disrupting their game and causing screams. Isha didn't look back after a man on a bicycle carrying milk cans fell onto the street to avoid hitting her. The boys leaped over him and continued to gain on her.

Through jolting top speed vision, she saw a coconut cart beside a tree. She leapt onto it and with two quick steps leapt again, catching onto the tree. With arms hugging the trunk, she placed her feet flat, knees splayed outward like a praying mantis, and began inch-worming her way up.

The boy leapt onto the cart behind her, but his weight rocked it over and he fell. Coconuts rolled everywhere, and the vendor was furious as the boy stood undeterred and jumped to try and grab Isha's foot. She climbed steadily, tongue-out concentrated on nothing but going higher. The boy shouted obscene things from below and Isha, no breath to reply, turned and spat down at him and kept climbing. Now he was coming up after her.

Near the top of the tree she came into the thick green fronds where bunches of coconuts hung. Here the wind rattled the palms, and the ground seemed miles below. The boy had made it about halfway up the tree, almost thirty feet in the air, but he wasn't a good climber and was coming slowly. Just in case, Isha reached for a frond from the next tree, hand-over-hand climbing out as far as she could, before swinging her legs over to the neighboring tree.

Far below, villagers were gathering and pointing. The boy was struggling badly now. And when he looked up to see her in the next tree over, his eyes widened with exasperation. His feet skidded on the bark. He clung to the tree with eyes shut tight. Isha wrapped her legs around her tree and slid down ten feet until she was level with him.

"What's your name?" she asked him.

"Pankaj."

"Give up, Pankaj."

He was breathing loudly and beginning to tremble.

"Slide down or you'll fall. Please," Isha said with pity in her eyes. With that, she slid nimbly down her tree, gently alternating her feet and hands like a backward monkey.

On the ground, the other boys were yelling now, completely absorbed in their leader's battle against gravity. Men had come from the fields and stood looking up, shading their eyes, tying their lungis, laughing. Woman had come, some holding babies, some with firewood or water pitchers. High in the tree, Pankaj could no longer hold. Isha stood behind the crowd as his grip gave out. He skidded down the trunk until he fell and hit the ground. She pushed through the people to where he lay crying and holding his broken arm. He was alive and crying, screaming up a storm. She ran away down the street as fast as she could so that no one could see her smile.

If it had not been for the cobra and the fight with those boys, she would not have been so anxious to leave the village that she forgot to do the one thing her grandmother had asked her to do that day: buy mosaru.

In the evening when Ajji sent her once again, it was with strict instructions to buy mosaru from Mr. Chikkanna and come home. Nothing more. Isha bought the two packets of mosaru, thanked Mr. Chikkanna, and turned toward home. It was just growing dark and the stars were soft in the sky where giant fruit bats flew silently towards the east. She was walking hurriedly when she noticed the gathering crowd in the distance.

The men were standing beneath the yellow streetlight just out-side the village, their white clothes glowing against the night. Beedi smoke and apprehension hung in a heavy cloud about them. Nervous hands retied lungis, wiped mustaches, contoured hollow cheeks. A man with one leg leaned heavy on his staff. They were speaking quietly, pointing, gesturing toward whatever lay on the ground amid them. Some held their hands clasped behind their backs, others folded their arms or had hands on their hips. All of

them, at one point or another, turned nervously to the outer darkness.

Isha was no match for her own curiosity.

She came barefoot silent. One hand held the other's wrist at
her back. A single finger held her chappals. The men were five
deep, and she wove quietly between them, a forest of gaunt bare
legs. Someone was passing out leaf-rolled Ganesha beedies, and
the air smelled of sulfur and tobacco, cheap rum and death.

These were the men of the earth. They were the labor class
who cut laterite bricks from the ground or plucked areca nuts from
tall palms. They were the coracle fishermen, the shepherds, the
men who knew the land, and not one of them could fathom what
was before them.

The brown-and-white goat lay with its eyes bulged and tongue
out in the dirt. Blood spotted the inside of its ear. Isha peered at it
as a man with a white stubbled face flexed the goat's leg. He
looked up and said it was fresh. The other men agreed. The man—
Isha thought he must be the owner of the goat—checked the udder
and anus and mouth; he pressed on its belly and ribs. He stood,
shaking his head. There didn't seem to be anything wrong with it
other than that it was dead.

"Perhaps it was choked in a fence," one man offered. The
owner replied that there were no fences to his field, and the struggle would show on the skin. A young man with curly hair
suggested that maybe a car had hit the goat.

"What car drives in the fields, you fool?" a fat man said, raising a hand as if to slap the man for asking such a thing. There were
chuckles.

"Maybe it has eaten something bad," a younger boy said.

"No," said the owner. "Goats can eat plastic bags and wood
and whatnot without a hiccup. What could she have eaten? None of
the other thirty goats has gone ill."

"Could it have been lightning?"

There was a chorus of speculative grumbles.

"This goat doesn't have any burn holes," one man said.

"It was a tiger!" the young, curly-haired man said in his deepest voice.

The fat man slapped him. Now the men laughed in earnest.

"What? Why not?" the curly-haired man said, throwing up his
arms.

"Eh! A tiger would have eaten the goat, you fool!" the fat man bellowed.

"There have been no tigers in fifty years!" an old man said and scowled with a dismissive wave.

"*Idu*, this thing, what is it called? A leopard then! What about leopard?"

This idea brought a crescendo of consideration. Isha watched as they continued talking and smoking, arranging their crotches and sipping tea, as groups of men do. A few women in saris had gathered on the fringes. Someone had lit a fire. In the flickering orange light, a cow that was tied nearby began to shift uncomfortably. The men took no notice. Something mysterious had happened, and it whispered to their primal selves, so the fire and tobacco and talk made them scared and bold at once in the growing night. No, a leopard would have slashed it to bits; there would be teeth marks on the throat, they agreed.

Isha moved backward through the crowd, eager to shake the feeling of the mystery. It was dark now and there were no lights on these village roads. She would be walking home alone in all that darkness. Ajji had sent her to the shop over an hour ago. The two mosaru packets sweated in the warm night. She hurried across the center of the village, making for home.

The shopkeeper, Mr. Chikkanna spotted her and called out, "Isha, you are still here? Aren't you going home to Ajji's?" She nodded. "You go down this way." He motioned to a different road. "Go to the end, go left at the *vana*, it is a shorter path. You better get that mosaru home fast." She thanked him and went.

What could have killed that goat? she wondered as she walked. It didn't look sick and there wasn't a scratch on it. The more she considered it, the more the shadows seemed to throb with the terror of unknown things. She directed her thoughts in another direction and deliberately wondered how Pankaj and his broken arm were doing, and if the pain had made him feel any remorse for the snake he had killed.

She reached the end of the road where she was to turn left, as Mr. Chikkanna had instructed. Looking back toward the village, she could still see the men around the dead goat, beneath the streetlight, beneath the stars.

Now the trees joined over the road. She kept her eyes wide to drink what light there was. She held her chappals and walked soundlessly, hastening to outpace the fluttering fear. The trees grew bigger, and the sounds louder: the chirping of insects, the calls of night birds, the sonic screeches of bats. Squinting, she made out a small pooja area, a prayer altar with flowers and a statue of a seven-headed cobra. Numerous pillars of vine and tree stood all around in the great darkness. Her mouth opened as her eyes rose to see the immensity before her. The great banyan tree of the sacred grove stretched over her in the dark.

Then birds and bats became silent. Even the frogs stopped their chorus. She took half a step back. Then another.

She was no longer alone.

Isha crouched. Her heart felt like it might rupture, the way a rabbit dies from fear. She could not move, and for some minutes concentrated on vanishing completely. On some new frequency in the dark, she could feel another presence waiting. Then the sound of breath as a muscular shadow slipped through the ultradark. It came like a nightmare, shapeless and immense, heavily silent so that there was no telling of it except for the vibrating air. Eyes like two green moons flickered in the blackness; blue smoke breath curled in the cool air. It stood in the soft moonlight, looking toward the town. Everything was still. Then, without a sound, the monstrous thing vanished into the blackness.

Urine ran warm down Isha's ankle. She wanted to run but could not move. For a time, all of her concentration went to silencing her shuddering breaths. Gradually the night birds and frogs timidly resumed singing, and the soft sound of bat wings came into air above. She ran the rest of the way home so fast she barely touched ground.

2

THE TIGER

The tiger had no name. She was born in a forest up the Malabar Coast beneath a blood moon. Her mother, a great long striped tiger of three years, licked her blind new cubs clean as they squirmed helpless. One male, one female. The tiger's first weeks of life were spent blindly suckling beside her brother on the warm, white-striped stomach of their mother. *Mother thunder breath, mother wild eyes.* Those were her first memories: the smell of the earthen den and her mother's giant, godlike form curled all around—her soft fur rising and falling with warm breath, licking her clean, rumbling songs of the jungle into her new ears. Though the cub was new to the world, and her mother only a few years older, they played in the sunset of a story many thousands of years old.

There is a myth that there was once balance in nature, but balance, like peace, is an exception to the norm in the world of men. It is deliberate, and paid for in blood. In the old days it was the tigers that kept what balance there was: they stopped the boar from tearing up all the roots and killing the trees and kept the deer from grazing until every last sapling was gone. It was the charge of the tiger to ensure that the other predators—brother wolf, sister leopard—did not become too powerful and eat up the deer and boar and birds and other small things. Even the elephants respected the tiger.

When the rivers were young, the elephants created the jungle by carrying seeds and tearing up trees—gardening the world that all creatures called home. The tiger never hunted men back then because the men were stupid and slow. But when they stood up and began building and clearing and laying waste to the jungle, the tiger took them, and the elephants trumpeted and stomped the men's small villages and crops. And so man was added to the list of creatures beholden to the tiger, and for a few millennia there was balance.

Then came the great retaliation. The clans of men grew into cities, and then from cities into civilizations. Like water, harmless in puddles and streams, deadly in the monsoon flood. Men became the flood, a plague species. They ceased acting like apes and began conquering like ants: militarized, industrialized, systematized. They forged into the world, burning and cutting until the jungle no longer surrounded them, but they surrounded it. Man, who had once cowered by fires to escape the shadows of the night, burned everything so that there would be no shadows to fear. In a centuries-long fever dream, they carried the flames that lit the shadows, and slaughtered the old gods. They played the game not just to triumph over their adversaries, but to annihilate them; not to win the game, but to end it. Marching on into a new world of their own making, with never a backward glance to the old truth.

The jungle was burned so badly that the elephants fled. Men caught them and climbed onto them and beat them until their minds broke and they became slaves. Then the men rode out in great numbers atop elephants with flames and drums to find whatever forest might still shelter a tiger so that they might kill it. The tiger, once the ruler of the deserts and mountains and jungles of the Old World, became a fugitive. Then from fugitive they were pushed further, killed one by one over the years, until the tiger, greatest of all beasts, became a ghost, skidding and clawing to cling to the light on the precipice of the greatest of all deaths, the final darkness of extinction.

For the first year of her life, the tiger followed her mother's tail, or would wait with her brother beneath the leaves while her mother searched the forest for prey. Humans were everywhere, and there was little more than dogs or goats to steal. The deer were gone, the boar and the bison were gone. When she dreamed, the young tiger dreamed of vines and leaves, of turquoise streams through ancient trees. She dreamed of butterflies to chase and great herds of elephant and deer. She dreamed of jungles she had never seen.

But when she woke there were never more than a few trees on windy hillsides. The lights of men were always close. The streams were full of trash, the water brown. They traveled by night for months and rarely were safe. When the mother was caught in a wire snare, the young tiger watched as the hard metal pulled the striped flesh down, exposing muscle and bone. She watched as her mother became savage before men's lights hurried through the forest. She had cried out when her mother slashed at her to go. She had been running when the shot rang out through the forest. A week later her brother was shot for killing a cow.

For half a year the tiger made her lonely exile by night. Across the countryside, past thousands of homes, farms, roads, schools, train yards. No one saw the great, gaunt, orange cat the size of two men. No one noticed the stripes in the sacred shadows. Not a whisker, not a tail. They did not know what moved through their yards and across their streets while they slept. They never thought to think that a striped anachronism, one of the old gods, walked unseen among them. The old ones had forgotten; the children had never known. A great thing from an age almost passed, searching for a last place where the deer were plenty and the rivers ran clean.

For days and many more miles there was no forest, just the dismal, empty leftovers: the bushy narrow edges of fields, thickets, and overgrown bushes. All that was not man's village had been grazed, paved, or burned. The deer were gone. The bison were gone. The elephants had been starved or run out or chained.

One lean week she managed to kill only two bandicoots and a gamy old turtle. But taste and variety were luxuries she could not afford. Still it wasn't enough to caulk the furrows in her ribs. By her second year, she had grown as much as she would. She was small for her kind, half the size of the snow tigers in the cold north but with a skeletal frame larger than the smaller tigers of the archipelago. She was still far longer than any man was tall and was the weight of two—despite being nearly starved from months of nothing but mongoose or peacock and other small game.

She followed the old elephant maps, trails that had been hammered out by the herds since the first sunrise. These were nearly gone, blocked by roads and farms. The few elephant families that remained spent their nights in panic, hurrying across roads in the glare of oncoming truck lights. Walls they could not climb had blocked the way to the forests they knew, where there were rivers and sweet leaves. Many mornings the herds would stand humiliated and starving, their trunks plucking through the trash mountains on the edges of towns.

The one time the tiger saw them, the herd was moving through farmland. She stood at the tree line as a herd of twenty moved through a grove of jackfruit. The elephants were silent—ears flapping, giant padded feet, swinging tails. Mothers hushing the calves with urgent trunks while others reached up to pluck the huge fruit. Then the dogs started up and the farmers woke. Gunshots flashed, children banged pots, boys ran in to hurl balls of flames that burst onto the backs of the herd. The elephants trumpeted and screamed, flaring their ears in panic. The young males charged in while the cows hustled away the young. The tuskers were full of starved rage and put on an impressive display. But they knew well how fights with men ended, and so they fled with the rest of the herd after roaring out their rage to the night. An entire field of bananas was crushed as they went.

The tiger melted back into the trees.

A lonely week later, she came to the small province in Mangalore where the tall palms made beautiful hallways and the areca nut plantations covered the earth. The villages of men were nestled among copious palm plantations. It was there that she finally, after a week of no other game, had slap-killed a goat. But before she could even lift it, a stray dog spotted her and raised an alarm that sent the tiger running for the protection of the plantation trees. She had looked back from the cover of darkness, a cool hatred blooming in her.

She stood panting in the woody poles and pillars that dripped from the great banyan tree's branches, her eyes glowing hungrily in the darkness. She stalked through the lantana along the edge of the road towards the village. For a time, she watched the men, hoping that later in the night when they slept she could steal back her kill. But she also knew that the men would never leave it. They were more clever than monkeys.

She stalked back along the shrub line to the shadow and shelter of the great banyan tree. As she entered, she paused, her ribs rising and falling, her lantern eyes the only indication she was anything but a darker part of the night. Crouching there in the bushes was something she had never seen so close.

A girl.

3

WINDOW

Nothing felt the same. Light fell with a different hue. The trees seemed full of whispered secrets. Books became boring. For the very first time in her life, the world had become a magical place for Isha. She knew what she had seen in the night beneath the banyan tree—or at least, she was almost certain.

By morning it seemed like nonsense. It became another of her many deluge-style stories to her grandmother: *So after I bought mosaru I saw these men had found a goat, so I was scared to begin with, and then when I was walking past the grove and standing on the road and there was this huge thing and it saw me and I thought it was a tiger but I wasn't sure—because I know tigers aren't in villages—but it was a tiger and it saw me and I ran and...*

Her grandmother nodded patiently and tried not to let her eyes cross from the speed of the story.

Later Isha watched her grandmother move about the kitchen—her wrinkled face and silver hair in a neat braid. She had been very beautiful, and still was in the way of old things. She had gentle features and kind eyes, and her bindi was always at perfect center. Her sari swayed as she hung pots and placed vessels.

Isha was in the veranda, rescuing butterflies trapped against the screen. She had just captured a blue tiger, which she carefully brought in cupped hands through the kitchen to the doorway. Ajji, almost done making breakfast, instructed Isha to finish and come make coffee. Isha hurried to trap a strikingly green tailed jay in her hands and rush it outside.

Inside, she let the milk boil twice before pouring the fresh coffee decoction into two small cups. Ajji watched critically as Isha showed she could hold one cup high above the other and pour a narrow stream. She bit her lip in concentration as she poured, and then rapidly traded the liquid back to the first cup to repeat the process, right to left, mixing and cooling the coffee and foaming it to perfection. She spilled a little right at the end. When she had finished the pour, Isha ceased biting her lip and looked sideways at her grandmother. Ajji smiled until her nose crinkled and she deliberately blinked, nodding her head forward. She grabbed Isha's head with both of her smooth old hands; they rubbed noses.

Ajji resumed replacing the various kitchen vessels and utensils. The old marble of the counter had faint marks where the items of her kitchen cosmos had lived for nearly a century. Isha observed as her grandmother worked. She placed a jar and then adjusted it slightly. She swept crumbs into her palm and then discarded them and refolded the cloth she had used for the crumbs and placed it over the toaster. She not only knew the proper place for each object, but it was her knowing that made it proper.

Isha held her cup between her palms to feel the warmth and made for the open door. She hoped that Ajji would forget the two hard-boiled eggs she had prepared. Her amma had come up with that initiative in an effort to put some meat on her daughter's bony body.

They sat out on the porch under swaying coconut trees. The palms rocked slowly high above them. A peacock called from somewhere in the distance.

Ajja came through the gate and removed his slippers at the end of the footpath. He came in small steps and neatly buttoned shirt and spectacles. He stood before them with an odd expression.

"No paper today?" Ajji asked in Kannada.

He responded in English. "I don't think I need the newspaper today. News travels fast when my granddaughter comes home."

Isha's eyes widened. She tried to look at Ajja without him seeing, but he was waiting for her eyes. His own eyebrows raised accusingly.

"Didn't you tell Ajji that you threw a boy out of a tree?" Ajja asked.

"Isha!"

"I did not!" Isha cried.

"*Oh devare!*" Ajji blessed herself.

"Then how did his arm break?"

Isha began telling the story.

Ajja held up a hand. "Please slow down, Isha! What did I tell you? You have to take breaths when you speak, use periods and commas—otherwise it is impossible to keep up!"

"So the boy fell out of the tree?" Ajji asked.

Isha nodded.

"Who was it?" she said, mostly to Ajja.

"Dilip's son, Pankaj."

Ajji nodded. Isha tried to remain camouflaged by stillness.

Ajja leaned in. "So now everyone knows that my city-girl granddaughter climbs better than the village boys."

Isha smiled.

"It's not funny," Ajja said, his mustache betraying the smirk behind his teacup. Ajji watched her granddaughter with sympathetic eyes; she knew well the struggle that had sent her to them.

Back in Bangalore, where Isha's family lived, there are thousands of classrooms across the great city. But the birds knew well where to find the girl with the messy braids and a book hidden on her lap. They knew because she had learned their songs. When she whistled they would come to peck at the seeds she had left on the window ledge. She was always seated near the window, always watching them. And so the birds were fed, and Isha felt free, at least in spirit.

When the teachers moved her away from the window, the dull infinity of class became suffocating to Isha. She began sneak-reading exciting books under her desk more often. She loved reading and read all the time, as long as it wasn't for school. To the extravagance of her imagination, school was a perpetual dull rain that soaked and dimmed the light she felt within. So, concealed on her lap, the covers of a book became a vital escape hatch through which she could climb. When the books were confiscated, Isha would resort to craning her neck toward the distant window, hoping to see her birds—the bulbul, the sparrow. They came even when she no longer left crumbs and would cock their heads to see her across the room. She would cock her head back, imitating their language, and sometimes let out a quick whistle. Some teachers tolerated this. Others did not.

When Isha was commanded to look forward, she would launch into a cascading debate that although she was required to sit at the desk and point her face forward, her *eyeballs* were not *commandable*. The shyest girl in the room was suddenly animated with righteous rhetoric. In earlier grades, such fights would earn ruler-whacks to the knuckles. Now, however, they led to detentions, parent–teacher meetings, and psychological evaluations. A teacher's ability to endure Isha's logic depended on the particular teacher's stamina on that particular day. But for Isha the day was irrelevant, as she was bored every day and was ready at any hour to defend the few rights she felt she had. Students, teachers, and birds all knew that when Isha argued, it was with the narrow-eyed ferocity of a fighting mongoose.

Even when she was engaged academically, calamity found her. During a lesson introducing flatworms of the phylum Platyhelminthes, Isha raised her hand and proudly pointed out that many flatworms ate and defecated out of the same orifice.

Behind her, two boys snickered. "Something truly disgusting that only a true nerd would know." They were loud enough for the class to hear them, and so Isha turned around to face them.

"Actually these aren't so different than you," she said. "You eat constantly and when you open your mouth only shit comes out."

The class erupted in laughter. Soon after, Isha's parents were called. So it had always been with Isha and school. She was brilliant and kept excellent marks but was utterly untamable.

On an especially long day, when she had been moved to a desk far away from the windows, a powerful headache settled between her eyes. She discreetly put on her glasses and opened a book on her lap. As the teacher droned on, she read, and with each line was transported deeper into the wild adventure of the tale. By the end of the first chapter, she was so immersed that the classroom might as well not exist.

Suddenly a hand gripped her by her messy black braids and she was lifted to her feet. The students all gasped and the teacher, Nagesh Sir, led her out of the room, down the hallway, and into his office. There, with the large angry man in the small room, Isha was cornered and dazed, slowly returning from the book world to the real one. The headache thumped back to life.

With eyebrows grown long beyond all reason and thick ear-brows to match, Nagesh Sir told her that if she didn't shape up, she would be sent home for good—kicked out of school. Isha cocked her head. Sir's rage and sweaty threats were far above normal intensity. Suddenly, the monotony of the day was broken by the thrill of confrontation. Isha smiled and tried until her eyes bulged to hold back laughing: how absurd it was to yell at a student for reading—*in a school!* Isha held a hand over her mouth, but it was no use trying to hold back the laughter.

With a great fat finger, Nagesh Sir told her how serious he was. "I promise you, girl, if you don't shut up, you are out of here!"

It was a tempting promise for the girl with a love of forbidden things. She stood up and ran to the door. She ran right out of that room, down the hall, and out through the front doors of the school into the white of the outside world.

The next day Nagesh Sir invited Isha into his office. He closed the door behind her. When the lock clicked, Isha felt the blood grow thick in her arms. He walked to his desk with a slow swagger that said, *This time there will be no running.* He sat at his desk. A cloth rested on its surface, covering several small lumps. With an index finger and thumb, he lifted the cloth. There, in a line, were the bodies of her birds.

Nagesh Sir had thrown some rupees to the local street boys, who were talented with slingshots, and now he watched her cry, hand over her mouth, tears shuddering down her cheeks. The birds had only been his warm-up. For the main event, he removed a folder from his desk drawer and placed it before her.

"Isha," he said, "I've asked you too many times to not make bird calls in class. You seem to have a problem with noise. Now, I will teach you about silence."

Isha never told anyone about the birds, or what came next. She no longer looked toward the window and stopped speaking altogether at school. In the months that followed, the school psychologist noted her extreme shyness and startling rage—a quiet girl who, when pushed to tears, would tremble, seemingly on the verge of ripping the earth in two with only her mind. Her parents heard her calling out in her sleep, mumbling unnamed terrors, twisting in bed. When she woke in the mornings, she was unrested, tears in her eyes. Her mother held her and spoke to her, begging her to explain what had changed.

It was not the endlessness of school, or even the death of her birds. She could not explain the larger, more terrible something that had happened to her. She became almost morose and the headaches became migraines that sometimes caused her to run to the wash-room to vomit.

So came Friday when Amma and Appa came for a meeting with Nagesh Sir, though he said many teachers shared his concerns. He read her offences from a list: extreme shyness and unwilling-ness to speak, a fistfight with a boy, reading books during lessons, talking back to teachers, bringing wild animals to school (last month she'd come to school with a trinket snake in her satchel), and, of course, her tearful and earth-trembling rage when her sense of justice was threatened.

Nagesh Sir explained that she was simply too wild for the classroom. He leaned in to Appa, confided that sometimes he felt as if he were trying to teach a monkey. He had studied to become a teacher, not a zookeeper. At that, Isha's eyes watered.

But her father smiled for the first time in weeks. Until that moment, he had played the part of the stern parent and had been united with the teachers. A step too far had severed that alliance and left him feeling like he had been a fool to not realize sooner.

He turned to his daughter. "Isha, are you so miserable here?"

She nodded, unable to speak.

He knelt in front of her. "Nagesh Sir says you are an animal trapped in a children's school." He ran a finger over her forehead and tucked her hair behind her ear. "Is that true?"

Isha looked up.

"Because if it is, then Nagesh Sir should have realized long ago that you cannot ask a tiger to sit in a school desk listening to lessons all day long. Can you?"

Isha offered a shaky smile.

Nagesh Sir looked confused.

"Thank you for your time, Nagesh anna," Appa said, standing and holding out his hand.

The flustered teacher shook Appa's hand. "Where are you going?" he demanded.

Appa looked back over his shoulder. "I'm taking my daughter to *ooru*. I'm taking my daughter to the jungle."

She rode the night train from Bangalore to Mangalore alone. The blue-trim stacked bedding of the train was swarming with bodies. Businessmen clothed head to toe poked at laptops. Emaciated holy men with painted foreheads and long gray beards sat cross-legged and mostly naked, their hollow eyes searching. Mothers worked to settle sleeping children amid the metal thundering and clamor. Women in burqas or saris or Western slacks. Some fed babies or read books or shouted at one another. At each stop the mendicant amputees rolled through the aisles on square roller boards begging, exhibiting the most gruesome parts of their anatomy to elicit a donation—through fear or compassion, it did not matter.

On one side of her berth was a plump businessman clothed head to foot in neatly pressed slacks and shirt with shiny shoes, a laptop bag beside him. He was reading a thick book, and his breast pocket contained a comb and several pens. His round cheeks were freshly shaved and there was a phone piece poised ready in his ear.

Directly opposite her, only two feet away, was an emaciated Aghori nomad. Barefoot, bare chested, and with a long beard, he was a true wanderer. His deep ribbed chest bore necklaces with beads and coarse white hair and small animal skulls. His black skin had been smeared ashy white so that wherever he sat bore his mark. He was finger-nailing the deep crevices of his callused feet and staring desperately at nothing in particular. His long beard and rope locs had never been combed.

The train sped west through the arid plains and then upward into the Ghats. For several hours she watched spellbound as jungled mountains, moonlit and impossibly large, slowly marched by. She woke when the train went howling through the tunnels cut through the mountains and realized she had slept. When she woke again, the mountains had passed, and she lay in the dim light, rocked in the *clack–boom* of the train. Later she clung to the yellow pole by the open door as the sun broke. Rural India sped by in visions: people huddled in the cool morning, egrets on the warm backs of cows in the misty, distant paddy fields.

With the light and the warmth came the chai wallahs shouting, *"Kappee! Chai!"* up and down the aisles. She spent ten rupees on a steaming cup of coffee and a pair of warm Mangalore buns.

In the morning, Ajji and Ajja were at the train station to meet her. She hugged them both and smelled the old love that she remembered since before memories—when the Sanskrit songs her grandmother sang were her world. They took an auto home where she threw her bags down and set out into the lush green Mangalore morning to explore. That was how she came to the beautiful golden palm-pillared hallway of the plantation on the day of the snake and the boys and the tiger.

Two days after the night of the goat and the tiger, morning found Isha sitting with Ajji, hitting her heels against the *katte* bench. Ajji was enduring a long run-on story of just about everything and nothing in the hope that Isha would eventually finish her two hard-boiled eggs. But Isha's mind was far away from eating. Especially eggs.

"Why is the cobra statue by the grove?"

"It's a vana, sacred forest."

"I know it's a forest. But why does it feel so different?"

"It's jungle, *magale*."

"Jungle?"

"It's just the last piece that was never fully cut. You know, Isha, the jungle was once everywhere. All over this town and the next—even over the city—long back. It was very different here when I was a child. Now it's all plantations. But the local people believe that by leaving some they will be blessed—make the gods happy. They also believe that the statue—the cobra god, *naagarde-varu*—will haunt you and take you if you disrespect the vana."

"But how did they choose *that* bit of forest?"

"Because of the banyan tree, *puttah*; it is very old. There are many stories. You must be careful of the *naaga devaru*. You must show great respect before it."

Isha nodded. "So everything used to look like that forest?" Her mind strained to imagine a world of riotous vegetation, thick trees, laced by vines and filled with wild animals. All she knew were the plantations and the orderly rows of silent palm soldiers that inhabited them.

"It was the jungle."

"Were there elephants?"

"Oh yes," Ajji said, waving a hand. "Oh yes! Watchmen used to have to stay up in the trees at night to guard the crops, because when the elephants came to the fields, they'd eat up everything. Sometimes my father—your great-grandfather—do you remember him?" Isha shook her head. "He would wake us up, all the brothers and sisters, and we'd have to run out into the fields at night yelling and beating pots and pans and chasing the elephants." Isha watched as her grandmother's eyes danced with the memories she had not met in decades, of loved ones and times long gone.

"But why did they steal the crops?"

"Because their forest was gone, puttah, and they were hungry. People went into the forest to cut bamboo and to take jackfruit, and also they cut the forest. So the forest became too small for the appetite of the elephants, and they had no choice but to steal."

"And where are the elephants now?"

Ajji was quiet.

"Appa said he was sending me home to the jungle."

Ajji waved a hand. "Pah! Your father really has become a *pukka* city boy! People today will call anything green a jungle. Real jungle is wild. Look at all this!" She swept a hand across the world. In every direction around them were palms—a monoculture meant only to provide beetle nut to millions of Indians who would chew and spit it as *paan*. "It's a plantation; it has rows and was planted by farmers. The jungle is very different. There are giant old trees and jungle animals—elephants, bison, tigers, leopards, giant flying squirrels!"

"Have you ever seen a real jungle?" Isha's eyes were full of wonder and far away.

"No, puttah, but I heard stories from my father when I was a girl."

Neither of them spoke for some time, the old woman recalling the past, the young girl dreaming.

Then, "You had better go apologize to that boy, Isha."

"Yes. I guess I should," she said, trying to look innocent. Leaving her coffee and the hard-boiled eggs, she leapt away.

"Isha, take your chappals. Isha!"

She was already gone.

She couldn't bear to walk. She ran so fast down the red dirt road that her toes were the only impressions left behind. Through the plantation where she'd run from Pankaj and the boys, through the tall palm hallway where men called to each other from the treetops. In harvest season, the men used a rope on their hands and a rope around their feet to scale the trees sixty feet into the air. *A terrifying height,* she thought. Then they used the swaying breeze to grab onto the next tree. They moved from one tree to another through the plantation, many feet above the ground, to collect the nuts.

She emerged onto the road that ran along the river, where fisherman in round coracles rowed the slow current. Panting, she came to the *nagarahaavu,* the seven-headed cobra that stood with half coconut shells and offerings of tulsi and turmeric. She passed it without a glance, her eyes drawn to the great pillars and buttresses of the old banyan tree. Like the stained-glass ceiling of an ancient cathedral, emerald green leaves rained down dappled sunlight. Wind whipped leaves and bits of pollen into the air. The rustle and silence and scurry of birdwings. The world seemed alive and charged as she walked beneath the tremendous branches and pillars. All recollection of apologizing to Pankaj evaporated.

Isha stood beneath the swaying leaves, where beams of sunlight swirled with insects, particles, and wisps of floating seeds. She felt humbled and slightly scared by the depth of shadow inside the sacred jungle grove.

She paused to watch and listen and feel. Birds she had never heard before sang in the distance. Closer by, others skittered up tree trunks, stealing glances at her. One ran up a tree trunk and led her gaze upward. She followed the bird with her eyes and climbed the gnarled trunk after it. Higher and higher it brought her until finally it leveled.

What she discovered was that it had not been a trunk at all, but one of the many woody pillars of the banyan tree. From this height she could see the village in the distance, and the edge of the banyan tree's arms, where the thick areca plantations resumed like a green sea around a single wild island.

She had once read that the banyan tree was the tree of life. The forest people believed that a tiny seed carried by the first bird had been dropped in the forest. For hundreds of years the tree grew tall and wide. Branches stretched further and further out until they could not hold on their own weight and dropped legs for support, branches from branches that reentered the earth. The banyan tree would drink the sun through its leaves and grow. The animals of the forest—from ants to elephants, mongoose and monkeys, turtles to tigers—lived in the tree's protection. Some branches went on to become their own trees. The jungle was born—the great thing that ate itself and lived forever. The tree of life.

When the seasons changed, the tree released its leaves to the ground. Other trees rose and fell. Generations passed, and molars and fur and stems and lungs became the earth. And when the monsoon rain fell, the tree drank the tannin of a billion decaying leaves through its roots. The birth of the world occurred in the branches of the great tree.

Isha's feet easily walked on the wide pathway of the branch. Crevices in the bark held little flowers. Lizards scurried up and down and across the vast limbs. She could not comprehend the various birds, bats, beetles, bees, ants, moss, lichen, squirrels, and other creatures she saw. Everything seemed to find its place on this single tree. Even other trees! They came up through the banyan's matrix, with darker bark or thorns or berries. None of them seemed to be the same. A long yellow snake glided along a branch. Its flowing grace made her heart race.

That summer, she spent long afternoons in the labyrinth of the grove. She spent hours exploring the treetops or reading. She talked to the birds and learned their calls. Sometimes she fell asleep on the mossy rocks until the chill of the dusk would wake her. The monstrous old tree and the grove around it held her like a spell— this relic of what was once jungle. Like the fossil of some giant extinct creature, it thrummed with the ancient energy of a wondrous world gone.

Once a pair of lovers came searching for privacy. Another day some boys came with a bottle of Old Monk Rum. But even when there were no other people around, as was most often the case, she knew she was not alone. Whatever she had been in the presence of that night after seeing the dead goat, she knew it was there.

She spent hours imagining what a tiger would look like or pretending that a herd of elephants was marching through the foliage below while she sat perched on the great branches. Just as the cool dusk woke her before the night, and just as the birds warned her of a cobra crossing the grove, her spine thrummed with the positive charge that there was something fantastic, something important, dangerous—somewhere close. She could feel it.

One afternoon after a morning in Ajji's kitchen, Isha explored the little brook that ran through the grove. She hopped on rocks and caught a frog, then sat on a large boulder. For some time, she did not read or draw or hum. She just sat. She watched tiny fish make ripples on the water's surface.

Also watching the fish was a cerulean king fisher, waiting for the opportunity to pounce. The long-beaked bird wore a brilliant blazer of peacock-blue plumage. With beady black eyes that never stopped scanning, and a powerful, heavy red beak, he was a practicing perfectionist. From the branches he'd watch the small fishes. He knew how many of them there were, and where they were. And if they went somewhere he could not see, he knew where it was they ought to be. They traveled in schools to confuse larger fish. But in a small stream there were no larger fish.

Those fish, he knew, had no concept of him, high above. Their little brains and feeble eyes—even if they could imagine, they could never see. He would take to the air and hover for a time, allowing them to come into range, then in a downward flash of azure lightning, he'd dive. Beneath the water, in the chaos storm of bubbles and fish bodies, his beak would close on his prize; his wings would open, propelling his body upward. He would emerge and retreat to a branch to consume it.

With one such perfect dive completed, and a newly wriggling fish in his bright red beak, he caught sight of the girl and turned so as to land above her. From the branch he sat on, a large green seed was loosed.

Isha watched the seed fall. Shaped like a kite with a flat oval seed in the center, it was designed to float on the wind, to be carried far and wide to start new trees in new places. This seed found little wind to fly on and spiraled down from the branch and over the stream, making one large circle before landing on the surface of the water. Isha watched as it swirled past her and then settled on the side of the streambed. Suddenly her eyes were transfixed by what she saw just inches from where the seed landed. Isha sat rooted to her spot, her mouth opening in wonder.

Below the seed rotating in the water, there was a footprint in the smooth clay of the streambed. An animal footprint. Not hoofed like a cow, but a pad and four fingers, wider and thicker than the largest dog—it was a cat's print. She knew the signature of feline paws well; her own cat at home left dainty brown tracks all over the tub and the floor and the porcelain of the sink. But the tracks she knew were only slightly larger than a coin. This was a cat the size of a cow. The footprint was larger than the base of Ajji's largest coffee pot.

4

TIGER, TIGER

The young tiger watched the girl in the grove each day. She did not hunt until night, and so remained inside the tangled protection of the ancient banyan tree. She watched the girl with caution at first, then with curiosity and even amusement. The tiger recognized the girl was a cub and posed no threat. There is a clause in the Law of the Jungle that forgives the trespasses of the young. A wolf pup and a crow can be friends; a fox and a fawn can play. But as they grow, the predators and prey must separate, as age widens the divide between race and species.

One afternoon while the girl slept, the tiger woke. She half rose and leaned long, stretching her forepaws out one after the other and dragging her back claws against the ground. Then she padded out into the open. The girl was sprawled on a mossy rock in the sun, her chest rising and falling in slumber. The tiger stalked in until she stood over the girl and could smell her dreaming. The blue kingfisher watched nervously from a branch above. Isha turned onto her side, nestling herself into the moss, cheek on her folded hands. Long whiskers leading to the giant form of the tiger were just inches from her. The wind pushed petals twirling in the air, and beams of light penetrated the grove as the tiger stood massive above the slumbering form. But the girl did not wake.

Each night after the girl left, the tiger scented the tracks the girl left. She smelled where the girl had read, where she'd slept, where she'd urinated. As weeks passed, the girl and the tiger grew used to each other. Each existed in the incomprehensible fringes of the other's understanding. The girl did not know whether the tiger was more than a fantasy. The tiger did not know why the presence of the strange man-cub was not more frightening. Each had come to the sanctuary of the grove for their own reasons that spanned the vastness of their evolutionary differences. The grove became the window between two worlds. There was an added benefit that the girl became much like the monkeys that had stood watch for the deer in the jungle. When the girl was about, the tiger could rest carefree in the cover of her hidden den deep inside the banyan tree, for if any intruder entered the grove, the girl would notice first and react.

With the changing moon, the tiger was increasingly confronted with the reality that her time in the sacred grove could not last. For several moons the tiger had felt her stomach widening. She had felt the calm swirl of movement inside her. Now her belly was growing fast and her options were running out.

Months before she reached the grove, after her brother and mother had been killed, the tiger had been stalking through a narrow swath of bramble in the wet steppe of the Ghats. She'd first smelled his marking beside a deer kill. She knew instantly that the scent was that of a new and strange male tiger—the first she had ever encountered.

That day her heart beat fast and she was full of nervous anticipation. She called to him. It was the first time she had ever made such a sound—her entire life had been in silence. Now she bellowed a wanting cry to the night. For hours she called. And then he called back. For hours they called back and forth, navigating closer to one another, until she sang him to her. They met beneath a cycle moon. He was tremendous and muscular and handsome, almost twice her size. When she saw him, she was instantly scared he'd kill her. Besides her mother and brother, he was the first tiger she had ever seen.

Each had become accustomed to feeling like the last of its kind. He bounded up to her and then dropped to the ground. He was playful and submissive and tried to touch noses with her. She held her head high and aloof, but he persisted. He rolled onto the ground and growled and whined and then sprang up and nipped at her and ran off into the forest. She followed. He sniffed her, nudged her, and ran off for her to chase. At last she bounded off

after him, and when they met, she rubbed her chin on his forehead
and kissed him.

Despite the constant danger they both knew so intimately, they
ran together in the moonlit fields, and wrestled in the swaying grass
on the first night. On the second night they murdered a cow together and gorged themselves and slept beside each other. In the
morning they played and fought and he smacked her in the face,
hard enough that she was shocked and fell over. He pinned her
with her back to the grass, her white breast rubbing his. Her snarled
teeth clacked against his and she was filled with the smell of his
hot breath as their whiskers tangled.

Then he spun her over. She was scared and struggled and he
bit her hard on the ear so that she bled. Once she was still, he
calmed and moved his teeth over her neck rumbling deeply. He
bent over her and licked her neck tenderly. Then, growling in her
ear, he pushed inside of her.

It had been six weeks since their romance, and now her belly rumbled with more than hunger. The young inside her shifted and
woke, tiny paws pushing up her skin. She turned back, wrinkle-
nosed, and snarled to her belly. Her womb rumbled with the thunder of a tiger's lullaby and grew still.

She felt the cub's hunger and her own.

Pacing through the palm plantations and up quiet dirt roads,
her soft paws carried her through the darkness. Late in the night, a
distant pack of dogs began fighting. She listened as they yipped
and howled and snarled. Then a lone dog came running down. The
tiger moved off the path as the dog came loping down the road.

She watched from the cover of the grass. The dog would have
passed oblivious to her presence, but she whimpered softly. She
had learned to imitate dogs to draw them to her. The dog instantly
diverted its course, drawing nearer to investigate. Her belly to the
ground, the tiger was ready. The dog came closer, sniffing the air.
She did not dare do the call again for fear that at such close range
the dog would recognize it as counterfeit. She stayed quiet.

The dog wagged its tail and then yawned, a symptom of the
fear it was feeling. It stood for some moments drawing rapid

breaths through its nose, investigating the air that bore an unfamiliar heavy scent.

The nervous dog took a step closer, then another. The tiger exhaled slowly so that a long sound came from her jowls, and the dog cocked its head and raised a paw, listening. The tiger's paw slapped the dog across the face so that the dog's skull snapped from its spine and it fell to the ground, dead. There was no mess. Just like the goat. She had not protracted her claws. Her mother had taught her that. She smiled the way tigers smile—inside. She smiled for the small feast and in remembrance of her mother.

The grown dog was several times smaller than the tiger, and she carried it easily in her mouth as she went down the road beneath the tall slumbering trees. Part of the road was wet, and she avoided the puddle. Soft mud left tracks, and humans could find tracks. She knew better than to leave them. So she walked in the center of the road between the tire trenches, the driest, highest part where there were no muddy puddles to record the print of her paws. Her mother had taught her that too. No one saw the monstrous striped tiger pacing down the road with a rag-doll mongrel hanging from its jaws.

She gave birth in the dead of night. Her sides contracted increasingly throughout the day until she crawled deep inside the shelter of a thicket and lay gasping. Eyes wide, she had pushed in growing intensity until she felt the warm release. She licked her two tiny, squirming, blind young clean, her tongue palpating them to life. Then she ate her placenta and slept.

In the weeks that followed, she nursed often and hunted street dog, goat, and peacock by moonlight, always returning to the grove to rest and care for her new young. She had to keep herself strong if her offspring would survive. Producing milk required her to nearly double her intake of prey. And with time, every available animal in the area became hers. And still the men did not come for her, did not even know she was among them.

She knew that this little grove could not be her home much longer. Growing young meant she would have to move her den. She'd have to carry each cub in her mouth and find a new place where they would be safe—where she could leave to hunt without worry of her den being discovered while she was away.

For two summer moons, the tiger spent all day nursing and licking her young, just as her mother had. She felt love, intense love, for what she had produced. *From tiger, tiny tigers.* Small paws played on her. Newly opened eyes, exploring the world, biting her ears and tail. Drinking milk, drinking milk, always drinking milk. Growing and growing. She was god. She was the earth. She was life.

She ate for her young, drank for her young, and would kill for her young, just as her mother had done for her. Her offspring were there because her mother's great-grandmothers of centuries past had given themselves for the sake of their young. The tiger remembered well that her mother had died—and knew viscerally that if she was not shrewd and tough and fierce, she would break the chain, fail her ancestors, and lose the tenuous footing her line had in the world. She was a survival machine, entrusted with the gift of millennia. Just as her mother had given her life, she now gave it. She guarded her young as only a mother can, with the incongruous virtues of ferocity, prowess, and tender devotion. She ate everything that could fuel her milk production. She even ate the feces of her young so that no trace survived to attract predators or indicate to other creatures that she and her young existed.

She did not move her young for the first two months of their lives. As they grew, so too did her stress for the future. They were larger now. Too large to carry. They would need room to explore and wrestle and learn. They could not continue to hide in the den all day and all night. It was only a matter of time before they were seen. On many a night she ranged as far as she dared under the cover of darkness, but found no shelter. And so she would return in the lonely quiet before dawn to rest her head on tired paws and sigh. Food was becoming scarcer. She had already taken the careless dogs from the street, and she had already poached the goats not smart enough to stay with the herd. There was nothing left, and it was time to leave.

Unknown to the tiger and to Isha, the village men had not forgotten the strange death of the woundless goat. The owner of the goat, Veeranna Rai, had brought the goat's body home and spent an entire night examining it. He dissected it behind his house, under a bare light bulb he slung over a papaya tree. He noted the shattered vertebra and the otherwise perfect health of the goat. Days later he noticed his flock was missing another member.

He had walked the dirt roads and the fields patiently, his hands clasped behind his back. The moist earth was conducive to recording footprints, but he found none. For two weeks he walked at dawn, just before the world awoke, to read the wild news of the night written on the earth. He saw the spoor of mongoose, cow, monitor lizard, and even the wide, riverlike trail where a python had crossed the road. When he found tiger tracks, he was not surprised.

His mind had been made up since the beginning. Only a tiger could have delivered such a singular deathblow, and only a tiger could be so clever to remain unseen. He bent down and felt the impression the tiger had left in the sandy road. Thought of his father and the old days. Those men had killed tigers. Now he would kill that goddamn cursed thieving tiger. And everyone would know him as a hero. A legend. He would be remembered as the last tiger hunter.

He stood in the morning and withdrew a pink paper package of Ganesh beedies from his lungi and a box of matches. The green box said *Cheetah Fight!* on the front and had the silhouette of a cheetah fighting an Indian man holding a scythe. Rai nodded, grinned, and lit the beedie. He exhaled a satisfied plume of smoke into the moist morning air.

5

CRUCIFIXION

Early in a nocturnal patrol, the tigress came to the body of a dead calf. The young cow's body was intact, though undoubtedly dead. She found it odd that the calf should be lying so neatly deceased and instantly remembered how her mother had been killed. She searched thoroughly for signs of a trap but found none.

She did not eat the calf but returned to the den. The following night she went back to find the calf still there, the meat already spoiling. She knew there was something wrong with it, something sinister, but her nostrils embraced the intoxicating scent of meat. She touched it with her nose, licked it. As her tongue scraped the taste, her stomach begged her. Her wisdom and experience and intuition warned her, but she could not quiet such hunger.

She ate the calf, all of it. Starting with its hind legs and then up onto its ribs and throat. She pulled out its tongue and eyes and swallowed its soft bones. She ate with her claws deep into the flesh, her eyes closed as if in prayerful thanks. Her stomach was full when she set out to return to the grove. She breathed relief that she was fed, and so could feed her cubs.

Inside the den the cubs were sleeping, the night still young, so she lay out on the rock above the stream, licking herself clean. She felt full and satisfied and relieved. She planned, in the way tigers do, that after her next big meal she would move the cubs away from the grove, no matter the risk. It was time.

Then her muscles seized. She fell over, blinking. She tried to swallow and could not. Staggering to her feet, a feeling she had never felt charged through her stomach and veins. She began retching and coughing but could not vomit. Her body was shaking. She tried to drink, but her throat was on fire.

Isha awoke with a terrified certainty of something she could not name. It was very late at night, but Ajji and Ajja were hurriedly moving around the kitchen. Squinting in the candlelight, she saw her grandfather grab a torch and test it for light.

"What is happening?" she asked.

"Something in town," he said and walked out the door.

"I'm coming with you."

"No, Isha!" Ajja said over his shoulder as he left.

She came barefoot behind him and grabbed his shirt so that he turned. "Please!" she cried.

Her grandfather looked toward his wife, standing in the door. She nodded and he shrugged. That was her way—preferring that her husband take the girl than have her run out after him in the night.

"Get on," he said, holding his index finger at her. Ajja mounted the bike and kicked on the motor on. Isha climbed on behind him and the two sped away into the night, the light from the motorcycle illuminating the trees as they went.

The sounds of frantic dogs made it over the din of the bike. The town was alight, and people scurried and crisscrossed, and other motorcycles were turning on. A great fire burned at each road that entered the town. She held on as Ajja dodged the fire, swerving the bike left and then finding center again. Men screamed and waved at them as they drew nearer, as though she and her grandfather might die at any moment.

"Tiger! Tiger!" one man shouted as he ran toward them.

"What?" said Ajja, slowing the bike.

"There is a tiger, sir! It is killing everyone! You are not safe!"

When the poison that Veeranna Rai had cut into the dead calf began working on the tigress, she panicked. She did not know what poison was or what horrible thing was happening inside her, but she knew that she must leave the grove. As her stomach lurched and her eyes burned, she took a cub in her mouth and ran out into the night.

She had no plan, and the cub was too large to carry. The tiger stopped to vomit, and two dogs spotted her. With the cub back in her mouth, she began running. Soon more dogs came. They barked in the way that dogs do to let man and beast alike know the highest level of alarm. They came from all around, three, four packs. Blurry eyed and panting, the young tigress bounded down the road before a parade of canines. They were rabid in their excitement and brazen from their mega pack that formed so quickly. They nipped at her heels and tail as she ran. But she would not stop. Lights were turning on now in the village houses. Motors were firing.

The tigress stowed the cub in a bush and turned on the dogs, her ears pinned back against her skull, her teeth bared. She slapped one so that it spun several times before hitting the ground. Another, which could not slow in time, ran straight into her mouth. She crushed its skull and advanced on the dogs, and the entire pack of twenty ran as she slashed behind them. But the moment she turned to get her cub, the dogs returned like a tide of teeth. She lifted the heavy cub and ran. The poison burned through her veins. Her vision began to blur and cloud. She fell and then regained her paws. Her cover was blown, and the number of dogs behind her grew alarmingly.

She ran into a plantation, but the long rows of trees were no better than the road. She and the dogs easily moved within the foliage. There was no hiding. Emerging from the plantation she came to the edge of a concrete drainage canal—a manmade channel of running water—and leapt, confident that the dogs would not make the long jump down. And for a time, all they could do was stand above her barking and howling and salivating down at her. Limping up the channel, she crossed into a tunnel and vanished into the darkness.

In the damp interior of the culvert, she set the cub down. Then she collapsed. The cub stood and came to her as she struggled to rise. All she could do was leave him where the dogs could not get him. She had to get back to the grove. She nuzzled his forehead, licked him. Then she ran off down the tunnel. They never saw each other again.

"What do you mean, tiger?" said Ajja to the frantic man while Isha clutched at his back.

"Sir, there is a tiger! With stripes and teeth and claws, killing dogs and cows and many people. You must stay inside the village!"

Thunder tolled in Isha's heart. She stood on the back of the motorcycle with her hands on Ajja's shoulders as he accelerated. She hadn't listened to the voice inside her that knew. Her brain, that thing that had been shaped and trained, had said it was impossible. She could not imagine the great striped cat longer than a cow and as tall as she. But somewhere in the center of herself, she had known the truth for weeks. Her hair and shawl flew wildly behind her as Ajja's motorcycle sped through the night.

Inside the town, Mr. Chikkanna was awake and had half opened his shop as the town center began to fill. Men sought cigarettes; women bought candles. Ajja parked the bike and turned to Isha.

"Stay here. I need to call Ajji and have her bring in the cows." He turned to Mr. Chikkanna and asked to use the phone. Mr. Chikkanna waved him in.

Isha snatched an unattended flashlight and ran down the street toward the grove. As she ran, she let her chappals fall; they were only holding her back from running at top speed. The village lights faded behind her as she went, and somewhere in the distance, the dogs were in a frenzy—undoubtedly they had found tiger spoor. Isha's world throbbed with the sound of her own heartbeat on the silent street. She felt dizzy even as she ran, still unable to process the rushing reality around her. Of one thing she was certain: If there was a tiger, she had to find it. She had to help somehow, though even as she ran she had not the slightest idea how. When she was almost at the grove, she stopped below a lonely streetlight to listen.

They came in a crescendo of racing paws—a rapid panting, baying, snarling din. The pack of dogs overtook her like a flood. They were frantic and savage and surrounded her all at once, knocking her to the ground, biting and barking and crashing into one another. One grabbed her leg, tugging backward on her pant.

Another tore at her ribs as she wrapped her arms above her head. She curled as tight as she could and screamed as the flood of dogs overtook her, bit her, tore her. She lay at the center of the pack, below the streetlight, screaming. And then the ground and air shook with a thundering roar that rendered the night.

The blast boomed from the darkness just before the tiger herself exploded into the frenetic sphere of the streetlamp. She hit the dog pack like a firestorm, rising up on her hind legs and then down with both paws to crush and slash. Swiping left and then right, broad paws sent canine bodies flying. The dogs forgot the girl as a mountain of bright-striped wrath hit them.

The tiger clubbed one dog's skull flat and slashed another so its insides spilled out. One dog leapt onto the tiger's back and bit hard. She tumbled forward to throw it off. Another dog bit her tail and pulled before the tigress turned and clubbed its back with a sickening crunch. She broke them like large insects, a bloodstained hurricane of stripes and fangs and muscle and sinew waging such carnage that the dogs' eyes rolled back, shrieking and delirious, and they bit each other as they fled.

The tiger reached the center of the fray, certain that it was her cub that the dogs were attacking. The girl looked up at the tiger above her and their eyes met for a swirling, suspended moment. The air hung thick with flying dogs and loose saliva, blood splash and street smoke. Bewilderment and tragic realization overwhelmed the young mother.

Motorcycles came like hornets from the dark. A dozen more dogs swarmed in, fresh for the fight. Two dogs hit the tiger at once, knocking her sideways. Another dog snapped at Isha's scalp before the tiger eviscerated it. They all shook when the gunshot broke the air. The tiger's shoulder splashed blood. The dogs fled and everything went silent.

A host of men had formed around the circular boundary of the streetlight. More than a dozen dogs lay dead and dying on the blood-soaked street. At the center of the arena, the tiger stood panting with Isha between its great legs. The crowd was gathering rapidly, incredulous of their own eyes.

The poison was coursing through her body; the bullet hole wept blood.

The tigress fell to her elbows. Her eyes were wide and stunned as she scanned the gathering crowed, snarling. The striped chest expanded and fell with breath. The girl clutched to the safety of her flank. The dogs circled eagerly just outside the streetlight. The men readied their weapons. The tigress's poisoned heart throbbed with love for her young and hatred for every other last living thing. She bared her teeth at the mob, ready for the final fight. But it did not come.

The crowd parted to allow one man into the light. He faced the broken tigress, an ancient rifle in his hands. The tiger's orange coat was illuminated in the streetlamp, and smoke rose from her as she panted. He raised the gun and aimed. The tiger's warpaint face twisted around savage eyes. The man pulled back the hammer, and the tiger snarled a terrible defiant and defeated snarl. For a moment, the townspeople and the tiger and the gunman and the girl were all still.

Then he shot.

The tiger fell to the ground silently in the ringing after the blast. Her yellow eyes were wide and disbelieving as she gasped despite the hole in her forehead. Isha clung to the orange fur of the tiger's side, eyes shut tight with tears and blood. Moths made giant swirling shadows in the rising smoke below the streetlight. Wounded dogs howled on the periphery as the life leaked out of them.

Ajja broke through the crowd and fell onto her. "Isha!" he cried, checking her all over. She was covered in blood, but he couldn't see where the wounds were. Isha nodded and grabbed Ajja and they wept together for a moment. When Ajja stood, he lifted her but she refused to be moved, her right hand clutching the tiger's pelt. "Isha, come!" he said and lifted her. She shrieked so loudly that Ajja and everyone else paused. He had no choice but to let her fall.

She knelt beside the tiger. Her hand moved tenderly on the orange-and-black fur. She stroked the tiger's ear, her eyes moving in awe and sorrow over the impossibly large body, paws the size of dinner plates, the great sleeping eyes.

With her forehead against the warm fur of the tiger's cheek, she whispered, "Thank you."

Knowing what would happen next, Ajja bent down and used every bit of his strength to lift Isha. She protested only feebly as he carried her away through the crowd. As they passed, men drew away like black skeletons in the night. The whites of their wide eyes shone, and their red teeth were bared. They had blood and beast before them. After the years of monotony watching goats chew grass, feeling the sun bake the earth, listening to silence, suddenly that thing in the night that they had always feared was real and conquered before them.

The villagers pushed in around the fallen tiger. They kicked it and spat on it and beat it with poles. Fires were lit on either side of the road. Boys carried eucalyptus poles, tied them into a cross. They rolled the tiger onto it and spread its front legs and lashed them. Then lashed together the hind legs on one pole. The tiger lay with arms spread, white chest towards the moon. The head lolled, so they tied that as well. Then, with great cheering and effort they lifted the tiger, which took twelve men. They carried the corpse on their shoulders like pallbearers. Boys with torches flanked the procession, cartwheeling, shouting, and throwing stones at dogs. Stretched out on the wooden cross and still bleeding, the slaughtered animal was carried through the night as the parade burned south down the road.

Far off, a renewed chorus of dogs rose and, some time later, joined the parade that bore the sacrifice. The hounds ran with heads high, proudly displaying their kill. The men threw rocks at the dogs and swore at them—but the dogs would not give up the bloody pieces of tiger cub.

6

WILD EYES

Long tree branches stretched over the walls. Ajji, Amma, and Isha's sister, Anya, had spent almost a week in the room painting. They had first drawn out the branches that came from the corner of the room and then, outside, collected actual peepal tree leaves. They had done it as a surprise for Isha's tenth birthday. Tracing them onto paper, cutting out the shapes, and then stenciling hundreds of leaves onto the walls. On the ceiling they'd stuck glow-in-the-dark stars.

Unseen in the many drawers were the prizes of a young explorer: crystals, fossils, bones, butterfly wings. The tops of the cupboards were lined with birds' nests and photos of her mother and father and sister. One frame held a magazine photo of a tiger that Isha had cut out the year before.

In the bed beneath the branches, Isha dreamt of a colorless vast plain where stumps and broken trees were desiccated beneath dark sky. Birds fell from the sky like rain. Thousands of them fell, every one of them still. There was a growing rushing sound, gaining and intensifying. A blue-eyed crow landed before her, flapping, screaming, not yet dead. The rushing was deafening now. Nothing was alive. There was no color. Just deafening, nightmare silence.

She shivered awake at midday, clearing tangles of hair that were pasted to her face with sweat. She could feel the sting and ache of dried blood beneath the blanket. Her hand searched over the wounds that had been bandaged. Ajji sat in a chair beside the bed, looking over a book and singing softly. She was not wearing a bindi. Isha could not recall a time when she had seen her grandmother's face without it. Something must be wrong. Something had happened. Suddenly, it all flooded in.

In the blur of her tears, Isha somehow ended up nestled on Aj-ji's lap, enfolded in the arms of the old woman. As she cried, Ajji held her and they rocked as she shivered and sobbed. Ajji sang an old Sanskrit song to sooth her weeping grandchild.

Isha clung to Ajji as she cried. "It didn't hurt anyone," she sobbed.

"I know," Ajji said, rocking her.

"She didn't hurt anyone and they killed her. Why did they kill her?"

Ajji rocked slowly and sang, trying to calm her trembling granddaughter.

Isha didn't know about the poison. She didn't know that the tigress's mother and brother had also been killed. That their home had been burned. She didn't know yet that the townspeople would speak for years of the great tiger attack and all of the terrible things the tiger had done. How it had murdered dogs and livestock, how it had almost eaten everyone in the village. Worst of all, she did not know that the villagers would tout themselves as heroes for saving a girl from the "savage" tiger. All she knew was that the most majestic living thing she had ever seen had been killed in front of her.

She had come so close to something so magnificent, only to be robbed of it. For the first time in her life, Isha had felt like a character in one of the books she read beneath her school desk or on a banyan branch in the grove. Like the boy who discovered a dragon, she had shared a space with something fantastic and magical, something that no one else on earth had done. Just before the dogs overtook her, she had imagined somehow saving the tigress, and the great animal somehow knowing it as it stalked away into the unseen wild.

But none of that happened. Her adventure had ended abruptly, in fangs and blood and tragedy. She had lost her secret wild friend that she'd never really known. It wasn't supposed to be this way.

She cried until she slept. By evening Ajji brought her hot soup and tea. Amma had joined Appa on a business trip to Europe, so they had no inkling of the terrible events. Ajji and Ajja both agreed it was probably best that way. Isha ate and drank in spite of her misery. She felt starved. Her mouth was full of food when Ajji came to the doorway.

"There is someone here to see you."

"I don't want to see anyone."

"I think you should say hello," Ajji said, raising her eyebrows and vanishing through the door.

A young boy walked in and timidly came to the foot of her bed. Isha recognized the boy who had killed the cobra at the beginning of the summer—Pankaj. His broken arm had healed, and he had either left his smug face at the door or lost it all together because he regarded her now with earnest concern and reverence.

"What do you want?" she asked.

"I wanted to see how you are."

She said nothing.

"Is it true you were attacked by a tiger?"

"No," she said flatly, her eyes tearing instantly. She turned her face away.

The boy became uncertain. "Why are you wearing all of those bandages?"

"Because the stupid dogs attacked me." Her voice trembled.

He was thinking. "So you didn't get attacked by a tiger?"

"No," she said. And then realizing there was no alternative, she explained. "The dogs attacked me in front of the old banyan tree. I tried to run, but they caught me." She paused to let the tears pass. When she got control, she continued. "She tried to protect me, but they killed her."

The two were quiet for a long time.

"Madam, why would a tiger protect you?"

Isha hadn't had time to recollect all of last night, but it struck her that she had no idea. Why *had* the tiger saved her? Why had it not just run away into the night? Was it possible that after a summer in the grove, the tiger's maternal intuition had grown to include her?

"I don't know," she answered.

The boy shifted his feet, searching for what to do or say next. "Well, you are very brave," he said, and for the first time she let her eyes meet his. "The men from the Forest Department said they have never seen a girl survive a tiger attack."

"It didn't attack me. And what men from the Forest Department?"

"They came to see the tiger," Pankaj said, looking around the room. "They said it was the first one to come to this area in fifty years. The dogs killed a cub, but they are saying that tigers usually have two or three. Nothing found."

Cubs... Her eyes widened and hairs lifted off her skin.

"How is your stupid arm?" she said hurriedly to steer him in a new direction.

"It's okay, man!" he said with a cool shrug, and Isha suddenly smiled. "Hey, shut up, yah!"

"Pankaj?"

"Yes?"

"I want to be alone"

"Ok, madam," he said.

"And stop that."

"Stop what, madam?"

"Stop calling me madam!"

"Yes m—okay, fine. I brought you something," he said, producing a package. He unwrapped it himself and showed it to her.

"It's a catapult," he said, removing the forked stick with bungee and a pouch. "I used to use it to shoot street dogs." Isha glared at him from her bed and he quickly sought to explain. "If you get caught on the road and there are dogs, you shoot one rock with this and you can take their eye right out! They'll never bother you again."

Isha took the slingshot but didn't respond. She thought of her window birds from school.

"Well, get well soon," he said and left.

For the rest of the afternoon, Isha lay in bed. The doctor came and gave her a painful injection for rabies. Her wounds were many, but except for her leg, none of them were deep. The dogs had not had long before the tiger arrived.

Isha closed her eyes tightly, trying to summon her memories of the previous night—the earthen watercolor whirl of the dogs, the whites of their eyes, the saliva pooling at their paws, their teeth bared. She saw them howling, snarling in their lust for blood. She clutched her bed sheets as she relived the onslaught.

In replaying the scene, Isha was astonished at what was now a part of her memory—a part of her. The tiger seemed to be made of fire. Never had Isha seen anything so powerful, or so beautiful. How she had fought... Then when her eyes fell on Isha...

It was almost as if... she had expected to find someone else.

Suddenly she was running through the grove, but it wasn't the grove, it was the jungle. Her legs were longer, she was older, and beside her was a tiger, bounding in step with her. She turned and went fast, so fast she could not believe it. The tiger became a streak of orange beside her. There was a tap at the window, and the king- fisher flew.

Her eyes opened to the darkness. She was panting. The king- fisher must have been part of the dream. Kingfishers slept at night and Isha knew it. The clock on the wall had four geckoes around it, one on each side, each of the small lizards facing in the direction of time, which Isha took as an omen. Sitting in bed, the tiger's face was as clear in her mind as if she had snapped a photo at that mo- ment. *She had come to the banyan tree for her cub.*

Her legs shifted and she climbed out of bed and onto the floor. Limping across the room, she swapped her pajamas for clothes. She took a flashlight and walked out into the night. Down the road, past *naaga vana*, into the grove. The stream water was cold on Isha's bare feet. The tiger's print was still there in the mud.

The stream flowed from within a thick cluster of bushes and thorns. She followed the water path into a labyrinth of foliage, into the heart of the great banyan tree matrix. Farther above, the gnarled branches spread out like a palace of twisted tentacles. The torch- light showed more tracks now, where the tiger had emerged from the stream and walked through the natural cave. There were deep forepaw impressions where she had bent to drink and a dry, smooth spot where she had lain. Isha was bewildered. She had spent the entire summer in the grove and never found the secret room of wood and vines.

Inside the tunnel of vines and thorns, she walked bent, shining the light ahead of tentative footsteps. Suddenly, ahead were two green eyes.

Isha nearly dropped the flashlight. She pointed it back toward the eyes while she squinted her own. The green eyes blinked at her and bobbed right and left as their owner tried to see around the shine of her light. She moved closer, slowly. The eyes vanished into the darkness. She hastened toward the darkness. Her feet left the water and emerged onto dry ground and into a small earthen cave. She shined the light up the walls and saw nothing. There were tiger tracks everywhere—giant prints from the tigress who had saved her life, and many small ones too. Two eyes reflected light in the darkness. Orange burned stark against stripes and dark- ness in the blaze of the torch. The cub cowered against the cave wall in an instinctive defensive posture—erect oversized ears, whiskers spread, claws protruding.

A wave of realization ran up Isha's spine and out her fingertips. The mother tiger had assumed the dogs beneath the streetlight had cornered her cub. Isha was sure of it, remembering again the unmistakable shock on the tigress's face.

Suddenly she felt overwhelmed with guilt. She wondered if she had somehow caused the tiger to lose her chance of escape, to lose her cubs, to die. But she could not dwell on these thoughts. The cub before her, unmistakably a cub but nearly larger than Isha, was clearly terrified.

The cub was blinking in the overpowering light. Isha turned the torch to her own face and watched the tiger's starburst of green-and-yellow retina gradually dilate in the dark, studying her. When Isha spoke, the little tiger cocked its head at the sound of a human voice.

"Hello," Isha said softly, trying to subdue her racing heart. Its white chest had a v-shaped collar of black and many black bands striped its legs. It crouched in the light, waiting to be killed or fed or played with. She inched closer.

Girl and tiger scrutinized each other. Isha continued to speak to it gently as she extended a hand. The little tiger leaned forward to sniff and tilt its head at the sound of her voice. Isha's hair still bore the scent of the tigress from the night before, and as the little cub breathed the smell of its mother for the last time, it shivered and drew in close. Ever so slowly, Isha put her hand on the tiger's head. The tiger trembled as Isha stroked its oversized ears, and then pulled it into her arms.

"Don't worry," she whispered. "I won't leave you. I won't leave you."

In the morning Ajji woke and turned to her husband. He was sleeping deeply, whistling through his nose like a kettle. But he was okay. She made a sign of thanks to the gods. After the shock and excitement of the previous day, she had been constantly vigilant about his health. Men his age weren't meant for such things. Especially him—he was so soft of heart. She could only shake her head, thankful.

She walked soundlessly to the toilet: washed her face, brushed her teeth, and fit a retainer with one tooth into her mouth. She leaned into the mirror and placed a red bindi between her slender eyebrows. Then she went to her granddaughter's room. The poor child had been shocked, so abjectly sorrowful after what happened and the violence she had seen. The details of what had happened were outside of what the old woman could easily imagine. She would have to work hard to quiet her mind after such trauma. In those morning moments, she was already plotting a recovery plan, a siege of her own warmth: culinary potions and cups of hot ginger tea. She would not wake the child.

Ajji came down the hall, but when she reached the kitchen she froze. There were naked brown footprints crisscrossing the floor. One set was Isha's, the other looked like a cat's paw, but much larger. Black-looking dried blood speckled the floor. The milk jug was gone. There was a roll of tape on the counter. The last length of it had not been cut cleanly and was matted and stuck to itself. Someone was knocking at the door. She did not yet notice the din of chirping from the birds. A soft beam of misty light shone through the back door, left slightly ajar.

Outside, the world was shrouded in mist, as was every Mangalore morning before the sun rose high enough to burn it off. It was cold. The air hung blue-gray between every poised palm leaf, tree trunk, and jewel-laden spider web in the tropical morning. In the dim haze, the old woman walked along the laterite stone pathway, her sari brushing droplets off the fronds of flowers and cycads. There were drops and sloshes of spilt milk on the porous red bricks. She followed the path to cow shed.

The shed was constructed of concrete and covered with ivy. Though the jungle had long ago been cut, the moisture-rich sweltering air allowed plants to claim any space that they were not deliberately eradicated from. This door, too, was cracked open. She wondered at the door, and as she reached to push it, fine gray dust settled on her arm and hand. She looked to the sky. The birds were going mad in the trees and ash was falling like snow. She wondered what was burning.

The door groaned on rusty hinges. Wrenches and spanners and garden clippers hung from nails in the wall above a worktable where clay pots stacked on one another. Against the back wall, Isha hugged a full, squirming blanket in her lap. Striped legs. Paws with black pads. Isha's arm had three evenly spaced lacerations on it; the blood looked black in the half-light. Beside her sat a milky green plastic soda bottle wrapped in copious amounts of tape.

The girl's hair was wild and wet, her black eyes red rimmed from tear-salt and sleeplessness. Amid her protective arms and swaddled bundle, two large amber eyes burned softly in the gloom. The old woman withdrew a step. Her hand went her heart, her eyes at once distant and full of fear.

"What have you done?"

"She won't hurt you." It was barely more than a whisper.

"Devare! Isha, *what have you done...*"

The elderly woman stood motionless in air that was busy with birdsong. The first birds at dawn had called with such urgency that others had come. The sunbirds and sparrows and a paradise fly-catcher hurried to see. Curious crows swept in as kites circled higher above. Soon there were birds in the trees, on the wires and rooftops. Every bird in the village had come.

Ajja came up beside his wife in a lungi and undershirt. His mouth fell open as the blood drained from his face when he saw.

"You can't tell anyone. Please," came the small voice from the darkness.

They heard footsteps from the side of the house and Mr. Chikkanna, from the shop in town, approached looking worried. The shepherds had come into the village early with the report that there were new tracks leaving the grove. Fresh tiger tracks following the footsteps of a girl. The crowd around the grove had grown, and the tension escalated. When they began to burn the grove, Mr. Chikkanna had run to find her.

He came up beside Ajja with a hand raised to remove his hat, but when his eyes untangled the limbs and folds and stripes in the darkness, his hand descended empty. Pankaj was at his hip and swore. The cub yawned and stretched, then huddled into the protection of her arms. After the stress it had gone through, the hours of starvation, and finally being sated with milk and reunited with a hint of its mother's scent, the cub had surrendered to sleep.

Chikkanna blessed himself and knelt slowly but did not enter. For a long time they all stood silent in the swirling din. The bits and shreds of ash fell on their shoulders and noses.

"Isha," the storeowner said gently, sharing a glance with her grandfather. "They found his tracks. The villagers, I mean."

"*Her* tracks," Isha said numbly, eyes a thousand miles away.

"It doesn't matter. They found tiger prints—*tiger prints following the footprints of a girl*. There are rumors; some are saying someone was eaten. Farmers are worried for their flocks. Mothers are keeping their children home from school. The entire village is searching. There is talk of black magic, crazy things. These people are scared, Isha."

Sudden pounding came from the front. Men's voices were shouting. The flurry of feathers as crows flushed. Wild eyes peeked out from the blanket, fearful of the crescendo in the air. Ajja turned worriedly. Chikkanna bent forward and spoke with urgent tenderness.

"Men from the Forest Department were called late last night. They have taken what was left of the body of the mother and cub but are still searching. They've seen the new tracks. I spoke to the chief conservator of forests, KT Chinnappa, myself. He said a cub without its mother would die in days and that they must find it. Most likely they would take it to the zoo. In Mysore, they keep tigers."

Isha shook her head as he continued to speak. "You must understand, Isha, there's no other option. A cub can't live without its mother, and these people," he looked over his shoulder, "they're scared, puttah. I came because I wanted you to know before they come to take her. I didn't know for sure, but when they found the tracks, I was certain they were yours. You've always had a gift." He looked up at the birds swirling and chattering through the ashes in the air. "You've done an amazing thing. You really have. I'll try to convince these men that the Forest Department should be allowed to come and take the cub. It's her only chance."

"No, I'll bring her back to the grove. She needed milk, I only—"

"The grove is gone," Pankaj whispered.

The ashes.

Isha's eyes went to her grandfather. The old man's eyes were tortured. He had seen the fight on the street: the tigress and the hounds. He knew the bond they had already formed, the girl and the cub. The terror in his eyes was from knowing what came next. They would inevitably take it from her. Whether they killed it or sent it away to be locked up, they would take it from her. Distant pounding on the front door echoed heavily through the house into the yard. There was no time. Isha's eyes were full of pain and urgency. Her lips begged him in silence. *Please, Ajja, please.*

The old man placed a hand on Chikkanna's shoulder and nodded to his wife. "Come with me." He let the shopkeeper and his wife go in before him. He wished there were time for him to help her, to take the cub somewhere and release it properly. Where would she take it? There was no time for that now. There were wolves at the door. If the girl could bring home a tiger and call in all the village birds, hopefully she could set it free as well.

He closed the door behind him. *You're a damn fool,* he thought to himself. He paused for a moment to give a meaningful look to his granddaughter. *I can buy you some time.*

The kingfisher from the grove watched, worried, from the window. Voices of outsiders had penetrated the house. She could hear her grandfather stalling. Her heart was suddenly galloping. It had all been building to this. She could see it now. All summer, the grove, the dogfight. Isha could not know the cosmic value of the animal in her arms, or how much struggle and love and blood had gone into its making. The trials of a thousand striped wanderers that came before. She could not know what they sacrificed to survive, or how terribly few remained. She only knew that somehow the cub was hers, and without her, it would be killed, or worse.

She had led the cub out of the grove and back to the house without any plan beyond feeding it milk from the house. And perhaps she had the faint optimism that her grandparents would help. But what could they do? Certainty rushed over her. The teachers had not oppressed her for her antics but her willingness to defy the mad logic of the world. The tiger belonged in the jungle—this much she knew was true. Death by villagers or a life incarcerated were the two logical options. Flesh fleeting before a blade is mercy to what captivity does to a wild soul. But she knew of, could act on, a third option.

There was no help coming. No one alive, human or animal, would help this orphan. The villagers were ready to kill her, and even if by some miracle they spared it on her account, it would never be free. Just like the butterflies she had saved, she knew that if she didn't take action, no one else would. Perhaps it was a dangerous result of reading too many novels. But everything seemed charged and dark and beautifully possible. She had to act quickly before logic hardened back.

A curious paw touched her face. The little tiger's eyes were full of trust and wonder. No, she would not abandon her post. She could not.

"What do we do?"

Isha jumped, realizing Pankaj had been standing in the doorway the whole time. She looked up at him, her eyes burning with wild defiant light.

Somewhere down the road, the ancient banyan tree waved its branches as the leaves rushed upward. The flames leaped at the old bark flesh, every tiny creature fleeing. The tall palms swayed. The grove burned, filing the air with smoke and birds and bits of burning leaves.

Isha raced through the kitchen collecting supplies. Rupees and rushed worries came from stunned grandparents. The girl, led by village boy, hiked with the tiger in tow on a rope taken from the cow shed. Pankaj uncovered a palm-woven coracle, the lone boat at the edge of the river, and helped Isha and the tiger inside. The coracle bore the girl and the tiger down the slow river, through the morning mist, and away.

7

THE ELEPHANT BOY

Most mornings that year, Thimma walked through throngs of people beside the heavy swaying steps of his elephant, using a long switch to guide the mountainous animal away from vendors offering bananas and jaggery to the ever-searching trunk. A river of traffic and animals flowed around them—a deafening current of cars, cows, busses, lorries, cyclists, motorbikes, carts, goats, and barking dogs.

When they reached a sufficiently traveled intersection, Thimma would slide down and sit beside his elephant. At his elephant's leg, the boy was nearly invisible. All passersby could see was the giant elephant, the great incarnation of their adored lord Ganesha. Business men on their way to work, construction workers waiting for cement to dry, grandmothers returning from the grocery store, maids on walks with rich women's children—they all stopped to receive the elephantine blessing. Even the eunuchs, in their saris and lipstick and half-grown beards, gave to Ganesha, praying for whatever things eunuchs desire.

A group of plump women in saris came and held out their hands with coins, and the elephant plucked the coin from each woman down the line. Then they bowed, their palms met for prayer hands. Hathi touched each woman on the back of the head, blessing them. They touched their heart or kissed their hands. Thimma would shoo them away so that others could come, and even then, they barely seemed to see him.

It was noon, and they had been at it since morning. Thimma had grown tired of watching the rushing human safari hours ago. The sun was shining through the mango trees in the square. Orange campaign posters, pasted to trees and sides of buildings, flapped in the wind. Thimma had spent all the previous day on a bamboo ladder painting the elephant in intricate designs of flowers, Hindu swastikas, and ornate *warli*. All done up, Hathi looked like a *pukka* temple elephant, scarcely believable as an animal and much more a god.

Several hundred coins jingled in Hathi's trunk. *Give, give, give!* The trunk came around and Thimma held open a bag. Hathi released the coins and for a glorious moment there was a metallic rushing as his trunk became a living hose spouting metal coins. Thimma closed the bag and slapped Hathi's leg. There were new people waiting to be blessed.

The elephant took a weighty lean forward to reach the outstretched hands of the people. Thimma faded back into the elephant's shadow. He handed the bag off, about three hundred rupees, to a boy named Appu. The bag of coins was traded for a paper bag, which Thimma opened and held to his nose. He breathed in deeply, huffing the vapor. Soon he was drooling, dazed, leaning to one side, and the whole world melted into an intoxicated dream.

Twelve years earlier, Thimma had been born beside the elephant Hathi. That is, he was born inside the thick walls of his father's cow dung and clay hut while his mother glistened and screamed, and Hathi the blind elephant stood anxiously outside. The elephant's trunk squeezed through the gap between the wall and the palm-thatched roof as the boy came into the world.

The small tribal *haadi* of Kolengere lay nestled in the center of a green expanse of southern jungle. The thatched roofs lay like a family of mushrooms beneath the great vine-laced trees. To the west, the Ghats rose like green giants. From their flanks rose the pregnant clouds that watered the land. It was in their shadow that the Kuruba, Yerava, and Betta Kuruba clans all lived. But only the Jenu Kuruba (*jenu* meaning honey in Kannada) still lived so isolated.

Thimma's was a village of honey climbers, basket weavers, and fishermen of tiny streams. It was a village of root pickers, stick collectors, water-carrying women, and weavers. The honey climbers traveled through the dizzy canopy, balanced on branches, and braved the bees. Walking through the tops of the jungle with machetes in their teeth, they cut branches rich with green figs, which they let fall below. On the forest floor stood elephants, thick of trunk and tusk, loaded with the harvest. The men of the forest had worked in this way since time immemorial. Each successive generation of young men took their father's place on the giant's neck.

The few sorrow-eyed oxen they had were shaggy, tenuous beasts. They seemed to know their own impermanence and the hunger that watched them from the darkness. Even the deer sought the safety of the men and stayed close to the village whenever the sun abandoned them. Black-faced langurs, those wise old monkey-monks, and miserly macaques haunted the treetops, scheming their next heist of villager's fruit.

At a time in history when every major city boomed and buzzed with trucks and cars, and the streets were adorned with expensive international-branded storefront windows, as busy men with cellular phones paraded by, the sleepy village that welcomed Thimma remained roadless, phoneless, and as isolated as it had been for centuries. On any given morning, the roofs of the huts were the first to emerge in the early morning's scatterings of sunlight, beneath the blue mist of the trees. The naked backs of the elephants appeared next, veins of dirt caked into their thick skin like old bark, their drowsy bodies still heavy with sleep and staked beside the huts.

The Kurubas would perform a pooja or cultural rituals to pray to the gods, goddesses, and the forest before the annual honey collection. They would pray to the various kinds of rock bees—*hejjenu* and *kaddi jenu*—for all their lives were beholden to the bees that would migrate in from the plains and make large semicircle hives below the tree branches high in the canopy. With smoke torches of green leaves, black skin taut over sinew, baskets for the honeycombs on their backs, they climbed. They would collect some, sparing enough for the bees to regenerate. Kurubas understood that to take all the hives would be suicide.

The men would bring the honeycombs down and separate the honey, leaving its pollen as food for animals, birds, and insects. Throughout the day, the harvesters sang songs about the bees, about the tiger, about the trees—about how the bees collect pollen from different flowers, about how everything was connected.

Anna ne kembare bareyali jenade,
Nodi kuyolu jenana, Kuguru habbina kudimalu
annane arumolad anigaddi, muru molada
muddu sute

When Thimma was six, the Forest Department hired tribal workers to help clear new roads, and the mahouts—the elephant men—would leave for days at a time to work the jumbos in the jungle, hauling teak and clearing trails. Thimma never went to school, since no one in his haadi had any use for literacy. They were people fluent in how mud curls around a paw or hoof, the habits of fish, the stems and roots that bore medicine. He spent his days at home with his mother, singing songs and grinding grain, carrying water, or weaving. In the evenings when the distant trumpet of the returning elephant teams came through the forest, he would race barefoot out of the mud hut, down the forest path.

Out on the main trail, the giants came slowly in a line, six elephants, sometimes ten, swaying and flapping their ears, men on their necks. Thimma would run as they floated by in their line, ears flapping, lumbering sighs, wide padded feet. The hairy, scarred mahouts high on their backs had finished the day's work and were smoking their beedis and shouting their jokes to one another and down at Thimma as he passed by. Hathi, because he was blind, was always last in line, trunk curled around the tail of Krishna, a younger male with impressive ivory.

As Hathi lumbered by, Thimma shouted the command, and Hathi lifted a leg for the boy to climb, bowing his head so that his ear was within the boy's reach. Thimma had to take a running start, up the foot, then the knee, to grab hold of the elephant's ear. His father's callused hand would catch his wrist, pulling the boy up so that son sat before father on the elephant's neck, gently rocking side to side as they continued homeward through the jungle. Atop the elephant, Thimma's nostrils were met with the scent of timber. Hathi's cracked tusks dripped with resin and pulp after a day spent carrying the heavy lumber.

At night, when the elephants were staked, the families of the village played and spoke together, celebrated seasons and fruiting trees. Thimma's house, like so many in the little village beneath the trees, was flanked by the great shape of an elephant, and the sound of flat teeth grinding hay was the rhythm they slept by.

When Thimma was nine, his mother's belly grew. It would be a girl, the elders said. When Thimma's mother hung clothes to dry outside the hut, Hathi's trunk probed about her belly with interest. The elephant seemed to know what was inside and reached for the taut belly and the soft bumping of limbs inside. The baby responded to the tickling pressure of the elephant's trunk excitedly, causing a tumult of jolted movements that delighted elephant and mother alike. Thimma would sit beside his mother as she pounded grain, stoked the fire, or hung clothing from lines, singing.

In the evening they walked on the ceremonial fire. They would distribute *rotti* with pumpkin and vegetable curry. During the festival, the *thammadi* or priest is possessed by the *butha*, or god, and they chanted prayers for good health, good rains, and to keep the forest lush. Wherever Thimma's mother went, the elephant was always beside her, his long trunk reaching out for the baby in her belly.

Thimma's mother told him that Hathi loved him very much and was the source of all the good things their family had, that the elephant was excited for his sibling. In the final month they held a pooja—an auspicious ceremony of choice where flowers and stones were placed on either side of the pregnant woman, and the elephant predicted, based on his choice of item, the sex of the child. Hathi confirmed the child would be a daughter.

That same year, orders came by uniformed messenger. The village was to be moved in thirty days, and the forest was to be turned into a national park for the preservation of animals. It was an official mandate from the government of Karnataka with support from international organizations of which none of the villagers had ever heard.

"And is the forest not already the home of the animals?" they asked. Everyone in the village was perplexed. "It is we who wait nights in the trees to guard against the monkeys, or the wild elephant! And we who shiver when the tigers call! And each night when the deer come in, fearful of the night of tooth and claw, do we not welcome them?"

The *nyaya panchayithi* met around the fire for many nights. They would demand a voice. They would demand a say in their own future. At first it seemed impossible, almost comical. The village had always been there, in the forest, since the eldest man's grandfather was a babe. They would not leave, and they could not be made to leave. They scrambled like ants beneath the sole of a boot—defiant in the shadow, ignorant of the scale of that which sought to destroy them. As the date approached, more messengers came.

The months that followed held more tribal meetings, talk of protest, outrage and of fighting to defend what was theirs. It was defiant, passionate talk, full of promise and met with cheers. Who owned the forest? They did, in their minds.

Outside of the forest, the region was changing. There was an international cement conglomerate interested in the limestone beneath the trees. There were local dam companies salivating to use the cement to build a dam. These interests had conspired to elect a new minister who was well known for his love of collaborative development. A man by the name of JCB Vijayan had promised these and other projects in return for massive campaign donations. Donations that paid, in part, for the thousands of orange posters that hung in the outside villages. *JCB Vijayan*, they read, across an orange banner image of a man in white with a brown vest and curled mustache. *Harness the power of Mother India*. Standing beside him, on the orange flying poster, was a badly produced lion.

At rallies he stood amid vast crowds shaking hands and waving. He spoke of timber and promised the poor villagers a great future he could help them build if they would only use the gifts they had been given. This, however, all took place in the farmlands, on the plains. It was outside the electric elephant trenches, gates, and guarded battlements that existed at the boundary of the jungle. It took place in a foreign world. All the people of the forest knew was that the leaves of the forest were the only thing insulating them from a system of caste and class of which they knew little more than their position far below the bottom. What they knew was that it was their only home.

On the day of relocation, they came with JCBs, bulldozing the houses as the people fled. Hard men with cold eyes and sticks and uniforms cleared out the village. A few of the younger village men tried to fight it and were beaten half to death. After that, everyone went silently. Everything in Thimma's life gradually grew silent.

Buses with dead-eyed drivers came to take them to a place none of them had ever seen. They boarded with what few posses-

sions they could carry—a chicken, a bow, a basket of jackfruit—
and were brought to a hillside where eighteen sparse structures
stood. Not houses, but concrete boxes on a hill. Four walls, one
with a steel door. Each had a corrugated steel roof that was horribly
noisy when the rain fell, unlike the thatched roof they had always
had. Rain that hit the new roofs fell to the hard ground and ran
away, leaving the hill just as dry as it always had been. There was
no forest. There were no birds calling, monkeys whooping—just
hollow wind and silence. The empty hissing of dry grass.

For a few months, the uprooted villagers tried to cope, adapt,
and survive in any way they knew how. But there was no work for
them in this new world. None of them had ever been *employed* before. It took some time before the connection between
employment, money, and food became clear to them. They learned
quickly, though, what modern India thought of tribal people.

One day not long after being moved, Thimma's father staked
Hathi outside the concrete hut and went to the nearest town for
work. But like the rest of the village, his nearly black skin, dark
curly hair, and large feet were like sirens alerting the rest of society
that he was lower than any caste. Even the untouchables sneered—
he was a tribal. No employer would entertain the idea of hiring
him. One even threatened to beat him if he did not "go back to the
forest with the other animals."

And so the uprooted dark forest people began spending their
days silently on the dry grass hill, the wind whipping their curly
black hair. There was no food. There was no forest. In this new
world, one had to work for someone to eat. They stared and sat,
their hunger hardly as painful as the shame and nakedness and silence. Men sipped cheap liquor, or huffed bags of glue. Teeth
turned black, eyes glazed, and skin shriveled. A dazed stupor became the permanent expression of their faces, as though the story
of their lives had left one permanent look of horror etched onto
their very skulls.

The night his mother gave birth, Thimma was not allowed inside. The wind was harsh on the hill. Hathi swayed and grumbled,
his trunk on Thimma's shoulder. Across the hillside other elephants
swayed in the darkness, nearly insane from months of being
chained all day and all night. From inside, the cries of a woman in
labor and then the scream of a new baby. They could not enter, the

boy or the elephant's curious trunk. Thimma was left to sleep outside shivering in a blanket beneath the elephant.

In the morning, the baby was gone. Thimma promised his
mother he would find the child, and he searched all day up and
down the hill and down in the pewter-colored stream. Thimma's
father was absent that day. His mother lay with nothing in her eyes.

Four days later a farmer found the infant where it had been left
in a field. The sun had baked it into a desiccated, mummified little
doll, black skin legs crossed above the stomach and arms spread.

For months after, when they fetched water from below the hill,
the villagers spat at them and pissed in their water. The eyes of the
villagers inflicted the greatest wounds upon the tribals, for they
watched them like vermin. When Thimma's father took his own
life, it was Thimma who found him sprawled on the floor next to
an empty bottle of rum and another of insecticide. Thimma didn't
cry. He cleaned the vomit from the floor, and when he had finished, went to ask his mother what to do next. After seeing her
dead husband, Thimma's mother walked into the lonely field. She
waited outside in the barren open with her palms to the sky for a
week, until the sun dried her the way it had dried her baby.

The orphaned Thimma climbed onto the neck of his father's
blind old elephant and left the barren hillside. For a year, Thimma
and Hathi loafed and lumbered through the back range. In the small
hamlets the boy and elephant were partners in labor. Together, they
made one complete creature, one with eyes and orders, the other
with mass and might to pry four-thousand-pound tractors out of
hopeless mud, to haul thick timber off the dirt tradeways, to demol-
ish houses. Together they could reach jackfruit twenty feet up in a
tree and, with Hathi's rump, could shiver the trunk enough to dis-
lodge the higher pickings.

After the monsoon, they pulsed back to the coffee plantations,
where some mahouts found work hauling downed timber for estate
owners. Although the boy was young for a mahout, the elephant
had worked with his father and so was known among the people of
the borderlands. That currency allowed them hire, and so Thimma
inherited one giant elephant, and the small intercession of his father's labor in a world of hard, hairy men and heavy timber.

Hathi pushed over and moved trees expertly under the boy's
direction. Thimma worked for pittance: just 250 rupees a day. The
men knew he needed the work and would work for a discount due

to his age and the blindness of the elephant. They could in fact find other elephants, elephants that could see, to do the job. On days when Thimma and Hathi were not moving timber, they returned to the forest.

It was not long before men came and tried to take Hathi. It is common in Kodagu for mahouts to poison wild or abandoned elephants, and then collect insurance money from the government, claiming the deceased pachyderm had been their own. As workers who depended on elephants for their living, they were entitled to compensation.

Thimma's mouth tasted of parched copper. He wiped the drool from his mouth and sat up. Hathi had another few hundred rupees jingling in his trunk. The elephant's eyes were dark, and he grumbled long, threatening tones of displeasure, for he hated being kept among the pulsing crowds, standing on the hot street, pinching coins out of eager hands.

The boy stood, thinking of water and a place to lie down. He tried the bag again, but the vapor had cleared. There was no one present to provide the next hit of noxious fumes, to send him back to the time when things had made sense.

He watched, dazed, as two police officers approached on a motorcycle painted yellow with black spots, a pitiful attempt at a leopard pattern. Each carried a polished, segmented cane.

"You, boy."

"Fuck off," he said in English.

"This is Karnataka, you speak Kannada when you address us."

"*Thika muchkondu hōgu!*"

The policemen went rigid. It was one of the most inflammatory things a person can say in Kannada. If the boy wanted to fight, they would be happy to oblige him. They would spend some time on this. People in the street saw the posture of the policemen change, the posture of the boy, and gave them a wide berth.

Thimma was still unsteady on his feet from the glue and did not see the swing before it came. He didn't feel the blow either. With his cheek to the pavement the world spun, his ears ringing. There was a boot on his face as one of the officers held him there.

The other one was fussing, hands raised to Hathi's thick collar. The elephant was nervous, his eyelids fluttering as he shifted menacingly.

Thimma could hear them explaining to a coconut vendor.

"It is no longer permitted to beg with animals in the street. The snake charmers have been removed. This elephant business must stop as well. It is against the law."

The coconut salesman nodded, wobbling his head. Thimma struggled beneath the policeman's boot. Above him he saw the younger of the two officers raise his club. This time the blow landed on the very top of his head, and his arms went around his face and the man's boot, preparing for another hit. Instead, the officer grinned. His teeth were filled with red paan juice, which he gathered into a globule and then hocked.

Thimma's vision went red as the juice splashed over his face. They told him to stay down. The elephant Hathi was grumbling dangerously now, rocking back and forth, protesting as they made to lead him away. Two other men had come in aid of the police. They were tribals or had been at some point. They shouted in mahout speak, struck the elephant's heavy hide with metal poles so that the street echoed with the sound. Slowly, miserably, the elephant began walking.

The boot fit crushingly over his jaw, Thimma watched as the last member of his family was led away. His vision became a montage of chappals and feet and swaying saris. The elephant was gone. Tears mixed with the officer's red saliva, and another blow from the cane made an echoing sound on his skull. Thimma's world went black.

8

EXODUS

A pariah kite's wings lofted across the purple twilight, carrying the large bird down from the mossy forest of the Ghats and over the arid landscape of boulders and shrub below. Expert raptor eyes followed a family of possums crossing the road below. With beaked concentration the old kite noted the location for later. The sun was nearly down in the west. The kite tilted his shuddering tail feathers and turned toward the last orange on the horizon. The largest of the soft boulder mountains passed below. There, in the shadow of the mountain, walked a lonely human girl, and beside her, something large and striped. Riding the wind in a long halo over the mountain, the old kite circled back for a second look.

Isha's eyes went to the tawny raptor above. Twice now it had circled, cocking its head at them, studying with fierce eyes. She scowled at the kite and tugged gently on the tiger's leash. The cub was in a mood to explore, oversized paws flopping on the rock, its nose working between long white whiskers. She wanted to find a cave for them to spend the night in so that they wouldn't have to sleep out in the open the way they had the first night. Up here on the mountain, she was loath to shine the torch light and risk being seen by the villagers in the valley below.

Boulders rose all around her, many of them larger than Ajja and Ajji's house, some of them larger than apartment buildings back in Bangalore. She hoped in a detached way that there weren't bears or crazy men hiding in the shadows of this mountain. Though in the last days, if she had learned anything, it was that the things you are scared of are rarely the same ones that matter.

From the time of leaving the village, Isha had rapidly learned a number of important lessons. One: she had no idea how to paddle a coracle. Two: young tigers become irate when on trembling or uneven surfaces (like a coracle). Three: upset tigers are dangerous. Four: tiger teeth and claws cut through human flesh like warm butter. In the simple act of coaxing the tiger out of the coracle and onto land, Isha had managed to receive a variety of lacerations from the teeth and claws of the frantic tiger that ran up her forearms and hands. Five: fixing the rope to the tiger's neck had taught her how little she knew of knots. Six: trying to walk the cat—which was the size of a large dog but immensely thicker in the legs and chest—was a nearly impossible feat. The young tiger seemed either to fear her surroundings or want to attack them.

She would strain at the makeshift leash to reach the end of a grass blade, a broken stick, and other tips of things. With each new interest the tiger found, Isha would have to use all her strength to not be pulled off her feet. Young tigers, like baby whales, may be small for their kind but remain a strange order of magnitude larger in scale than the world around them. The palms of her hands were raw from holding the rope, *the blessed rope*, that was the most important of all the things she had snatched in the hurried exit from her grandparents' house, that now, just days later, felt like half a century ago.

As the kite lifted off into the sky to wherever kites sleep, Isha and the striped cub continued to skirt the mountainside. They found shelter easily in a high cave among the many boulders. Far below, a small village glowed, and on occasion, the drone of a motorcycle, or braying of a cow, would interrupt the stillness of the air. The shroud of night made them secret in the high silence. Deep within the cave, Isha toiled fruitlessly with grass and matches to make a fire.

The message she had begged Pankaj to relay to Ajja and Ajji before he left was brief but informative. She told them how sorry she was for worrying them but that she saw no other option. In her mind it was quite simple: she would bring the tiger to the jungle. In her mind it was possible, worth trying.

There is a danger that finds a certain kind of dreamer. A reader of adventurous tales and an admirer of heroic deeds will eventually begin to seek narratives beyond the bounds of pages and printed words. Characters racked by fear or the promise of failure or death overcome obstacles in the stories we read. Isha had read so many stories that her mind worked in this way. Heroism was a logical alternative, the only neutralizing agent against the atrocious mundane acceptance that the adult world seemed to operate upon.

Somehow Isha viewed rescuing the cub as compulsory. What would have happened if the hobbits had chosen the *rational* decision to remain in the Shire? What if Huckleberry Finn had listened to his drunken father? Isha knew what would have happened if she had not rescued the cub, and she knew the structure of the adult mind: Allowing the villagers to kill a tiger was *rational* because of lack of a better option. Allowing the Mysore Zoo take the cub was *rational* since no person had ever been able to *teach* an orphaned cub to be wild. Rational structure would funnel events into one of the two horrendous options, she was certain.

She spent these first days lost in analysis of all that had transpired and the reaction it had triggered in her reality. That she was not more frightened was shocking. Instead, she felt wildly powerful. She changed her own narrative, like dropping one book and lifting another. Days ago she had been a little girl, now she was a wild animal. The world looked and smelled different. It was as though she were meeting the sun and rock and grass for the first time. Her fingers would play in the fur of the tiger as she watched the moon paint surreal beauty onto the quiet landscape at depths of the night she had never seen.

Strangely, it was the silence, self-reliance, and agency that she found shocking—not the tiger. To Isha, the wide-eyed cub Kala was no different than the butterflies she rescued—a wild, hunted thing that would perish by flesh or by soul if she did not act. It was the logical consummation of the repeating pattern of her life, an adaptation born many times over, in many instances, where she was unable to accept the alternative to her intervention.

Now out on her own and alone, her own sense of fear was muted by the stories she carried with her, passages etched into a young mind insulated by the hope, charity, and courage that leaped from the written word. She had been protected from the dogs by a wild mother tiger. The death of a great beast ended novels. Her story, her quest, though, was just beginning. Up on the mountain of granite boulders and thorny shrub, she had left the India she knew, the one with cars and horns and crowds and cows, and entered a quieter, grander reality. The safety of her parents, the invisible womb of childhood in which her welfare was the product of the labor of others, was gone. Although fear followed her at a distance, she wrapped herself in pages, in stories of journeys. She would become the hero of her own story; she would guard the tiger and find the jungle. She was certain of it.

Her efforts at making fire resulted in smoke and wasted matches, as well as some charred grass which the tiger found enticing to pounce on. Isha indulged the cub and tussled with her for some time, wrapping the sleep blanket around her arm so that the tiger could gnaw on her. She learned quickly that—just like a tiger mother—she had to discipline the cub with a swift and harsh club to the nose when she bit too hard. That or be gravely wounded by the lacerating teeth and curved claws. The tiger lay on its back, paws clasped over Isha's arm, gnawing and wrestling. Isha spoke to the tiger, calming her, rubbing the white spotted ears with her free hand. Gradually, the paws, which were larger than Isha's face, relaxed, and the tiger lay on her lap.

The cub surveyed her new strange mother in the half-light of the cave. She pushed her nose into the girl where the last scents of Mother and of the grove were still traceable. What Isha couldn't conceptualize at that time was that the olfactory bond she had unknowingly cultivated during a summer in the grove was the reason the traumatized cub tolerated her.

For the tiger, this girl was not as fun to chew as Mother had been. She had no tail or broad paws, and her slaps weren't nearly as hard. The girl's teeth were tiny, and if anything attacked them, it was doubtful that she could defend them. She was not as warm, and certainly not as large or knowledgeable or wise. But she was there, and she was all the young tiger had, one fact the cub understood fully. The cub was still getting used to her curious sounds. Every time she heard the girl's high-pitched warbles, she cocked her head in surprise. The girl spoke two sounds often. It was soft and pleasant. And within days, the little tiger would come to know that when the girl made that combination of sounds, she was talking her. The sounds were *Ka-la*.

After two nights above the small village, they journeyed on, sleeping in caves by day and traveling in the night. Kala was remarkably silent, communicating to the girl in a series of deep groans and whines. She chuffed to say hello or to grab the girl's gaze. These chuffs, or shuddering exhalations, were among the first tiger vocabulary that Isha learned to emulate and utilize.

Isha carried the supplies she had grabbed from her grandparents' home in a satchel over her shoulder. These included blanket, water bottle, milk bottle, flashlight, matches, and Pankaj's slingshot. Her chappals had already been chewed to pieces by the tiger. When Kala's milk supply or Isha's food or water ran low, Isha hiked down to the closest village during the hot daylight hours, leaving Kala tied safely inside the cave.

In the twilight they made their way up the incline of the mountain through sparsely greened boulder fields. Dry scrub of lantana and cactus and lemon grass clung to the rock and sand and cowered beneath monstrous boulders. Near the top of the mountain, the girl and tiger walked beneath these giant monoliths, where the great stones had been laid one atop the other or leaned together, so that many crevices and caves were the labyrinth pinnacle of the mount. She found that as she traveled through the new world of wild solitude, strange things bubbled up from within her—the ghosts of memories, bits of songs. Amputated emotions from a past life that swirled into her in the new a dazzling silence.

After hours of maneuvering through the boulders, Isha paused before the mouth of a cave. The girl and the tiger entered timidly. The beam of the torch illuminated the smooth granite walls, tunneling back into darkness. Isha scanned carefully for bears and scorpions, and then spread her blanket deep in the cave. Dinner was biscuits for the girl, milk for the tiger.

Isha had purchased milk the day before, and it wasn't nearly enough. She was forced to tie the tiger each time she bit off the corner of a milk packet to fill the bottle. The first time she had tried to prepare the meal, Isha had spilled half of the milk as the tiger assaulted her with the anticipatory enthusiasm of a cub, clawing and biting her, fighting for her food.

By now though, Isha was developing a routine. Once the milk bottle was full, she wrapped her arms in the blanket and fit the makeshift nipple into the tiger's mouth. Kala wrapped her large paws around Isha's slender arms and sucked on the repurposed cola bottle and cloth nipple. When the bottle and milk was finished, the massive kitten rolled onto the floor and began devotedly licking the spilled milk from her paws and nose.

Isha watched the little tiger with wonder as she drank the last drops of milk herself and stowed the bottle in her satchel. Once finished preening, the cat came to her. Lying face to face, the girl and tiger touched noses, and both soon fell fast asleep.

Isha awoke first and rubbed her sleep-crusted eyes before leaving the cave and standing on the high promontory overlooking the world, squinting into the light of the setting sun. Far in the distance was a small village, and as evening fell the lights looked like some colony of glowing algae clinging to the vast earth rock. Kala came soundlessly beside her, and Isha sat and put an arm around her. The tiger nuzzled her and mouthed her ear so that Isha had to wrestle her away.

"Kala," Isha sang. "Kalaaaaaa Kala." The little tiger cocked its head and bit her nose softly. Isha pulled back and smiled. "If you like it, Kala I will call you—unless you can think of something better."

The striped kitten pounced on Isha. The cat, chest thicker than hers, bowled her over and stood on her stomach, looking into her eyes. *Hoof!* Isha laughed as the air was pushed out of her. The tiger was heavy. She smeared her hand over Kala's nose, and Kala curled her lips back and bared her teeth. Isha pointed a finger at her and Kala raised a paw and swatted it, and then dove away onto the ground. Isha retaliated with a tackle and the two skirmished outside the cave. When Kala bit too hard, Isha delivered a hard whack to the tiger's nose. The cat paused, stunned, and resumed chewing on her arm, this time more gently.

A shrill whistle came from their right. The girl and tiger froze, listening in the night. Neither had heard such a sound before.

Kala was first to spot the nightjar, an owl-like ground bird, which had perched on a smooth stone some distance from the cave. The tiger crouched until her stomach touched the ground, and then crawled toward the bird. Isha knelt to observe. Kala drew nearer, trembling with anticipation. At intervals, the nightjar sounded a shrill cry. Suddenly Kala exploded, sprinting for the bird, which took flight in a flurry of shed feathers. Kala tackled the stone the bird had just leapt from and tumbled off the other side. She came up confused, looking down at her empty paws.

Isha laughed and watched as the bird fluttered down the hill, and then landed once again. Isha chuffed and bid Kala follow. The tiger hadn't yet figured out the concept of following, so Isha fit the rope leash around her neck and guided the cub down the hillside. When the nightjar shrieked again, Kala's eyes locked on it. Isha released the rope and watched as Kala went slowly beneath a thorn bush, drawing nearer. Convinced of its own camouflage, the nightjar remained stationary even as the tiger drew up beside it. Kala slowly rose above the bird, and just as it spread its wings to flee, she clamped her large paw down, pinning the frantic bird against the ground. It screamed and flailed as the tiger held it down with an immense orange paw, sniffing and watching the helpless struggle.

Kala lay down, grasping the bird between both her front paws, and pulled its head off in her teeth. The screeching stopped. Isha turned in horror, fingers over her ears. Kala chewed the skull and spat out feathers, drawing her tongue against her teeth. She ate the entire body of the bird in a single bite. Isha drew near to watch but Kala looked up at her, eyes glowing in the moonlight, and snarled. Isha backed away obediently. Kala remained on the ground to clean her paws and lick her legs clean of feathers. It was over an hour before she rose, stretched, and came to Isha. The girl held out her hand, and the tiger raised its forehead to meet it.

"Good job," Isha said. The tiger bristled and stretched with satisfaction and pushed into Isha so that she fell off her rock seat. "Okay, let's go," Isha said. They continued on in the night.

In the days to come they traveled in this way, hiking at night and sheltering in the day, with quick forays into towns for supplies of water, milk, and food. The crows and kites and bulbuls and owls seemed to take great interest in the strange pair: a spindly girl and a thick-striped young tiger. One large owl turned his head nearly upside down as he watched them, the girl and the tiger. When the tiger paused to pee, Isha would too. From the tops of mountains they scanned the plains below and dreamed of the jungle. The image of jungle was in the archive of their minds, as it is in everyone's: a crowded, green, busy place full of giant trees and vines and mysterious creatures.

Her eyes searched the horizon, but nothing she could see resembled jungle in any way. Lit by an almost full moon, the landscape revealed only more boulders and thorns. Mountains rose off the flat landscape like rock piles made by some godlike child. Cultivated fields filled the valley, but no towns.

"Do you think there is anywhere that isn't all cut down and eaten up?"

The tiger flicked her tail.

Isha would lead the way and the tiger followed. Her own bare feet and Kala's large orange paws were nearly noiseless on the rocks. While Isha was wayfinding, Kala stalked lizards or mice, slashed the air after moths, and dedicated great care to selecting leaves. As they went, she would sniff and lift numerous leaves in her mouth, but only when she had found the right one would she hold her head high and march triumphantly beside Isha before flopping down, clutching it in her paws, and tearing the leaf to shreds.

They made their way through the nights, and by the seventh night, Isha was certain leaving without a plan had been a very stupid idea. She worried about her poor grandparents, and her parents too. They must be sick with worry. But as they went on through the mountains above the valley, her own basic survival was a more pressing issue. *What am I going to feed this tiger when the milk money runs out? How long can we continue to travel? Where are we even going?*

She would wonder these things aloud to Kala, who never seemed concerned. But these things weighed so heavily on Isha's mind that she became breathless at times.

At dawn of the eighth day, Isha tied Kala and made for a village in the valley below. At the edge of the village she watched as a large man urinated on a pile of sticks and trash. He shook his *thing* and then removed a folded handkerchief and dabbed the tip dry, then tucked it into his pants and replaced the napkin in his pocket. As she crossed the trashy outskirts of the town, where plastic bottles and chappals and tires lay littered, a yellow cobra raced by. Orange banners on trees and compound walls showed some politician dressed in white, a very fake lion standing beside him. Isha shook her head and wondered if anyone in this village even knew what a lion was.

By 8 a.m. she had bought two bottles of water, four milk pouches, and a pack of candles. She drank one plastic bottle and refilled it at the village water tap. Moving on, she bought matches, a backup lighter, and stopped at a tender coconut stand. The man used his curved *machhu* machete to expertly open the coconut and hand it to her, without a straw, and she drank. He smiled as she guzzled the cool liquid. When she finished, she also smiled, and handed it back to the man. He clove it in two and removed the white *ganji*.

Amma had tried to get Isha to eat one tender coconut each day. Of course, Isha found this burdensome and often resisted. Amma had explained ad nauseam how nutritious they were, and how if Isha didn't eat them, she'd have to choke down more eggs, because she was so skinny that it was scary. But her mother was not here, and Isha suddenly felt a longing that made her dizzy. And in the days and miles between those memories, something had changed. Now that her mother was not around, and she was starving, Isha ate the coconut and the ganji with relish and responsibility, and thought, rather proudly, of how happy Amma would be if she could see her diligence. The act of eating the coconut somehow made her feel a warm solidarity to her mother.

"Yes, madam? *Innu jasthi beka?*" *What more would you like,* the vendor asked.

Isha asked him for a two-coconut parcel, and the man expertly macheted the tops off so that only a knife-prick would open them the rest of the way. He tied the pods together using the husk fiber. He included one extra, a soft smaller coconut, and explained that it was his gift. Isha tried to refuse, but when he insisted, she smiled and thanked him and went.

He was a poor man, she knew. Compared to her father and their comparatively luxurious house, furniture, cars, and computers, he was penniless. He made a living from the tree he worked beneath, selling coconuts for thirty-five rupees per customer. It was almost nothing. She pondered this as she went, feeling slightly overwhelmed at the poor man's charity.

With only 820 rupees left, she hiked back to the mountain. The man had called her madam. The way Pankaj had called her madam. The way the washing and cleaning servants her Amma employed called her madam, or *akka*, the respectful term that meant "older sister." Some that called her this were thirty years older than she. No one she knew ever *spoke* about caste, but everyone still *knew*. And even if they didn't know, ages of breeding had ensured the skin spectrum so that even a toddler could tell.

Why them and not me? What had she done to be born to her wealthy, educated mother and father? To deserve the luxurious life she had? Why had Pankaj been born to a family that lived in a house the size of Amma's bathroom, and she into a house with many floors, rooms, servants, and beautiful things? She looked back at the charitable coconut wallah, who barely earned per day what her father paid for his nightly cup of whisky. The beggar and the billionaire, the sick and the strong, all are united in wondering, *Why them and not me?*

The humanity in his smile had warmed Isha and followed her out of the village. She marched with her satchel, bare feet, and coconuts swinging. One of the books she had read under her desk had been *The Adventures of Huckleberry Finn.* Now she felt like a Huckleberry Finn—a runaway, an iconoclast, a *rebel.* She found a stick to serve as a staff, coconuts bouncing together and apart as she went. She sang nothing in particular, an invented adventurous score, and let a wicked little grin creep across her mouth for a time. There were no desks here, no assignments, no etiquette. She could camp alone. She could drop her pants to squat and urinate when the tiger did. She did this with a little grin—*soo-soo* with a tiger. When she stood it was with a brigand's swagger. She was the master of the plains. The tiger mother. At the cave, she prepared Kala's bottle and nursed her.

In the following days, a ridge connecting the mountains meant they need not descend between each peak. The tiger walked beside the girl without the rope leash. Kala had learned that Isha was the source of milk, and that was enough to keep her close.

She fed the tiger by candlelight in caves. They wrestled and played in the darkness within mountains while the sun was awake. At dusk they watched the giant fruit bats and kites swarm the sky. The stars became their compass and the sun their call to slumber.

On the tenth day of travel Isha stole her first goat. With her tongue stuck out the side of her mouth and one eye shut, she launched pebbles with her slingshot so they landed beside a snaggle-toothed old shepherd woman, who looked perplexed at the stones mysteriously reporting around her. When the women went searching, Isha moved in.

"Hello," she said, kneeling beside a black-brown kid. She pet the little goat on the flat, scruffy fur between the eyes. The goat licked and chewed and shivered away some flies. "Come-ma," she said softly and lifted the goat into her arms, searching warily for the shepherd.

It was a beautiful little goat, brown and black with a white chest. It already had little nubs for horns on its head. Before the cave she knelt to compose herself, unsure if she could follow through.

Isha had always been on the side of mercy. The Saint of Small Things, all creatures great and small. Amma said that even a Buddhist would gasp at her commitment to the living, a belief she even extended to mosquitoes. She understood that all things share one common goal: to stay alive. For her there was no divide; her empathy extended to every corner of the animal kingdom. What right did anyone have to separate a creature permanently from its family and take away all their hard work to stay alive?

Amma said she should have been born a Jain, for the devout Jains in their immaculate white garments carry light brooms to brush even the grass so as not to harm a living thing. But she was not a Buddhist or a Jain and had only her mother's vague Hinduism, with its dizzying array of gods and goddesses, and Appa's remnant Kerala-Christian-Catholicism, with its focus on man and God and little else. For Easter one year, Appa had gifted her a beautiful little wood statue of Saint Francis of Assisi, the patron saint of animals. His head was bent and he wore a flowing hooded robe; he held a dove in his hand and there was a fox at his feet. He stood on the bedside table guarding her fossils.

Save the goat and starve the tiger? No, she wouldn't let that happen.

Inside the cave she placed the goat on the ground. Kala stood at attention, fully up against the leash. She pawed the air and fought against the restraint until with great effort and apprehension, Isha untied the rope. Kala bounded up to the goat with laser concentration, eyes wide, nose working. Isha spoke encouragingly and stood at a distance. Kala ran up to the kid and licked it. The tiger nuzzled the goat and tackled it. The goat bleated nervously, shivering on its thin legs. After nearly a half hour, and much awkward tussling, tiger cub and goat kid lay side by side, snuggling. With tremendous relief that became a contented smile, Isha drifted off to sleep beside the goat and the tiger that night.

When morning broke, Isha left Kala tied and hiked down to return the kid to its flock. The shepherd told her that she had spent all night searching for it and thanked her repeatedly. She gave Isha a cloth with five of last night's chapatis wrapped inside.

When waiting out the day proved too tedious, and the cub too eager to play and chew on her already scarred arms, Isha risked moving in the late afternoon. They were moving through high caves that snaked through tremendous boulders on the ridge of a mountain. Somewhere ahead she had seen a patch of green, which she was hoping to find. The sun was boiling hot and Isha felt faint in the heat. Kala's tongue hung long, and she panted as they went. For nearly an hour, Isha struggled with Kala through dense lantana and tamarind trees that provided little shade. But gradually the dry scrub turned lush green. The vegetation opened up and walking became easier as they moved downhill. Large trees with sprawling branches filled the ravine, an oasis of shade and cool air. A stream lay in the bosom of the valley below an enormous temple tree.

Isha was overjoyed. She dropped the satchel and ran toward the flowing water. The tiger's eyes widened with excitement. She ran beside Isha and bounded over rocks and logs. When Isha leapt into the stream, the tiger stopped short. Isha frolicked in the bliss of the cool water while Kala growled and paced at the water's edge, groaning with frustration. She was scared.

"Come in!" Isha called. But Kala would not come. Isha splashed water at the orange cat and laughed. "You are a *tiger*. Nothing should scare you!" Kala's face contorted in an annoyed sharp-toothed growl. But annoyed as she was by the splashing, she was overwhelmingly jealous to be left out of her partner's fun. With wide eyes she reached out a large paw to tap the surface of the water, and then recoiled.

Isha laughed, drew a deep breath, and vanished beneath the water. Kala was shocked. She sat on her hind legs, her oversized front paws flat on the ground, eyes wide, waiting. But when the girl did not appear, Kala cocked her head and chuffed. Then she began to cry. *Where had she gone?* The tiger hopped, paced, and slashed the air with her paw. Finally, with no other alternative and for the sake of her friend, the tiger leapt into the water.

Isha exploded out of the stream and tackled Kala, who was panting and paddling a great deal more than was needed. She laughed and hugged the tiger and splashed her again. The tiger growled and swatted the girl across the face, gently, no claws. They wrestled and shrieked and swam.

Later in the sun on the stream bank, the tiger carefully licked herself after bathing. Beside the tiger, Isha sat cutting her toenails with her knife, tongue out the side of her mouth in concentration. Then she climbed and balanced on the branches of a great tree, gathering mangos and dropping them down to a cushion of leaves she had prepared. Kala eagerly watched the girl above and the falling mangoes. When Isha dropped to the ground, she collected the best mangoes into her satchel. The tiger followed her as they climbed through the sun-dappled forest to the old temple tree and sat beside the stream. Soft, white-petaled flowers with yellow centers floated down to girl and tiger.

Isha spent half an hour peeling the mangoes, and then the rest of the afternoon eating until she felt sick. She tried to feed some mango to the tiger.

"You know," she said, chewing. "You should try eating some fruit. That is the problem with you tigers. You have to eat everything else. If you would just eat fruit, do you know how much easier life would be? Here, try." She shoved a piece of mango into the tiger's mouth. But Kala licked and chewed and spat.

"Too bad for you then. You'll go hungry, and I'll be full," she told the tiger, who already was well aware of that dynamic.

9

LEGENDS OF TRUNK AND TUSK

For two weeks, Thimma slept at the fringes of the city. The deep black gash that crossed his eyebrow had swelled his eye shut. His lip was broken and fat. After two days he managed to steel a coconut from a vendor, which he drank in moments. On the fifth day he managed to stumble to a garbage-filled brown river, where he drank the putrid water. The water smelled of raw sewage, of motor oil. There were dead rats, bits of plastic, and lumps of floating cow dung. But he cupped his hands and brought them feebly to his mouth. For a week after, he continued to sleep on the cold cement, rising often to squat and release hot burning discharge from his convulsing bowels.

When he was able to move better, he begged for food until he had enough in him to walk. Later that day, he waited in the long line of a temple that was giving free food to the poor. Rice and bland sambar were a blessing to his starved stomach.

Next he began asking for directions. Most people had no idea where to find work elephants. Most vendors cursed him and threatened him with hard canes. With his filthy torn clothes, matted hair, and bare feet, he looked like a street child. It was an auto driver named Ganesh who told him the way. And Thimma spent the rest of the afternoon riding on a lorry carrying sand until the smell of dung and sweat and the sound of roaring giants came to him.

It was easy enough to find Hathi. He was chained to a stake beneath a jamun tree with four other elephants. Thimma called to him and the elephant's nose began working, great head rising. From the cover of the bushes, Thimma waved to his elephant friend, and then realized it was pointless waving to a blind elephant. Hathi's trunk was curling and flaring, drawing in the air—he knew that Thimma had come.

There didn't seem to be anyone about in the yard. Thimma ducked under the fencing and took cover behind a water tank. There, he breathed slowly, his hand rubbing the swollen egg over his eye. He prayed to escape this day without another beating.

When the sound of men came from the main compound, Thimma drew lower. Five men, clearly not mahouts, walked excitedly into the yard. Workers and mahouts emerged from shacks and structures as shouting built in the distance. Something was happening. Careful not to be seen, Thimma followed the direction of the excitement.

At the very back of the camp, in a tremendous kraal made of entire trees that had been sheered of their branches and stacked into the shape of a cage, stood the giant: Ramachandran. The elephant stood higher than any other in the yard, or the state, or indeed any known pachyderm in India. He was tied around the legs with ropes as thick as a man's arm. Other ropes came in around his tusks, holding his head in place, rendering him almost immobile in the timbers and lines of his confinement. Only his trunk was free, partly because it was impossible to immobilize, and also to move food and water up into his great body.

The men of the elephant camp knew that even tied in the kraal, with entire trees for bars, the world was not safe from the wrath of the old tusker. At over fifty years of age and eleven feet tall, he was the largest and most dangerous elephant in India. Thimma knew these stories because, like most people, he had heard the stories around the fire at night. But unlike most people, he had met Ramachandran before.

Thimma swore at the sheer size of Ramachandran. The old tusker had grown from an already large elephant to his final form: a violent, wrinkled mountain. The mahouts and workers and bosses were drawing in around the kraal. He could hear bits of what they said. A well-muscled mahout in his thirties wearing only a lungi was climbing the rungs of the kraal. Other men worked the ropes from the outside, releasing the heavy cords. Inside, Ramachandran's throat boomed a long threatening note.

The command was called and ropes fell as the man on top of the timbers leapt onto the elephant's back. The great gate swung open, and everyone present, nearly thirty people by now, ran for cover.

The giant swung his tremendous skull toward freedom. His ears flapped, long tusks almost touching the ground. On his neck, the miniscule human mahout was glistening with perspiration, his eyes dark as he spoke in sharp command. The great joints rolled and flexed, and Ramachandran lumbered out of the timbers, dust billowing around him, orange eyes burning.

"*Baye chalo,*" the mahout called in Hindi. *Turn left.*

Thimma was confused. Ramachandran did not react to the words. With each step the elephant's head swung to and fro, taking stock of the many cowering humans present. He was planning, and that realization sent everyone in the yard cold.

"Left! Left! Go left!" the man shouted in Hindi.

Thimma turned to a young boy who had drawn up beside him. "Why is he speaking Hindi?"

"Two cows and a mahout were killed last month. It is impossible to control Ramachandran. These new mahouts were brought in. They are experts from the north."

"From the north?"

"Varanasi."

"They don't realize Rama speaks Malayalam?"

The trembling boy shook his head.

"Rama was trained in Malayalam." He shifted to look at the monstrous elephant again. "Why would an elephant kill a cow?"

"That elephant hates everything…"

Ramachandran's menacing steps brought him into the yard. Men at distance held onto the chains that came from each of his legs. One by one they skidded forward, lifted off the ground by the unstoppable force of his stride. The elephant was gaining momentum—and not to the left.

A local mahout drew in, shouting and with bullhook extended over his head, intending to strike it into Ramachandran's side. But the elephant was quicker and grasped the man's wrist with his trunk and broke the arm at the elbow. The man screamed as the elephant tossed him to the ground and put a heavy foot on his spine. Others rushed in to help but the great head swung round, the tusks sweeping everyone back as the man flailed beneath the foot that covered his body. A loud snapping and a horrible cry were the last of him, and that was drowned out by the roar of the elephant and the horrified cries of the men. When another mahout came, Ramachandran turned with the jangle of chains, and with the swing of his trunk sent the man spinning through the air and out of sight. Ramachandran advanced to where the man lay in the bushes and bent his head down onto the man's chest, mashing the man's insides out the side of his stomach and his mouth.

Thimma rose and ran back to where Hathi was chained. He threw the heavy chain to the ground and commanded Hathi to lift his foot. Thimma ran up the leg and caught the ear, swinging his leg over the elephant's neck, shouting urgent commands. The blind elephant moved deftly through the yard. Hathi could smell the pathways and knew the need for haste. Thimma was patting right and left, speaking rapidly now. Ramachandran was standing in a circle of men amidst a plume of dust, challenging any to draw near. At his feet was the crushed and folded body of another man he had killed. The earth was stained red. Ramachandran's ears flared, his massive tusks swinging. Thimma closed his eyes, for he knew that if he continued to see, the fear would stop him.

"Forward, forward! Turn, turn, around now! Around!"

Hathi drew past the frantic men, circling behind Ramachandran. Thimma turned him and commanded him to hold the tail, the way elephants in a line do. Hathi's trunk probed the air and found the immense rump of Ramachandran, followed the spine, and curled around his tail.

"Everyone back! Back now! Back, back, back!"

Ramachandran turned now, his trunk meeting Hathi's, and suddenly there was a calming. The giant stood over the younger elephant and the terrified Thimma, but his manner was calm. Thimma spoke softly, in the language of his people, hoping Ramachandran would remember the good days, the jungle days, and know that he was a friend. The fire dimmed in the old tusker's eyes and his trunk worked over his long-lost friend.

Two decades earlier, the jungle was their home. Ramachandran had yet to be named and was part of the wild herd that ruled the edge of the jungle in the Kodagu-Nalkere fringe. He was deep in a mud hole the day Hathi was blinded by another male, deliberately gorged in one eye and then the other.

Ramachandran had hunted down the young bull. He found him in a stand of bamboo. Ramachandran, a fraction of the size he would one day become, was already massive for his years. He lined up the other bull and ran at him, driving his tusks straight through the young male's ribcage and puncturing his lungs so that when they hit, air escaped in a hiss. It took him almost an hour to withdraw his tusks. When he did, he hammered some more abuse onto the gasping youngster, and then left him there to die. He went back to his mother and his depressed and wounded cousin Hathi.

From that day he became Hathi's greatest friend and servant. He led him around, letting the older elephant hold onto his tail, keeping him safe. He became Hathi's eyes. The mothers of the herd saw their tenderness for each other and loved them for it. Ramachandran stayed with the females much longer than a bull of his dominance would. They all understood his devotion to his cousin and the tragedy that had passed.

Leading through the forest, with Hathi's trunk around his tail, Ramachandran would pluck sweet bamboo and jamun and jackfruit and they would play in their own way—nuzzling trunks and pushing against each other. They were grazing in a bamboo forest when Hathi nearly crushed a king cobra. When the snake realized Hathi was bearing down in its direction, it opened its black hood and stood up in the air. Ramachandran saw the defensive snake and the unknowing Hathi, and rushed through the ferns. He came up beside Hathi and grabbed him by the tusk, stopping him just a trunk's length from the cobra. The king cobra stood proudly erect, its tongue waving up and down.

There is an understanding between elephants and the king cobra as old as the rivers. They both know each other's power. An elephant can crush a snake, even the great king cobra, but if it does, it is almost certain to be bitten—and such is the king's venom that even an elephant would be left in excruciating pain, perhaps losing a leg or dying. So Ramachandran had saved Hathi from yet another tragedy, and the two gave the proud cobra a wide berth and continued on into the forest to spend the long afternoon reaching over farmer's fences and plucking fat jackfruit from high in the trees.

They had been captured together.

To prepare for a raid the men, in their villages, would sing for a month straight, and dance around the fires and tell the old stories to harden their nerves. An elephant raid was an undertaking of courage and fire. Surrounding the herd at night and setting flame to the forest, the drummers pounding, the shouting and strain. The tamed bulls crashing into the wild herd, hammering their own kind with the agony of a treason they did not choose. Rearing and screaming, the night becomes a hellish blur. The walls of the jungle become a flickering shadow theater of man and beast, blood, and tusk, their desperate eyes and strained voices howling through the ancient darkness.

Several elephants died in the take. When Ramachandran and Hathi were torn apart in the chaos, Ramachandran killed his first man. He simply grabbed him by the throat and tightened his trunk until the skull broke and released a glut of black and red junk that exploded out the ear and onto the ground. A prick in his rump preceded blackness. When he woke, he was in the same great yard as Hathi. The men had made massive kraal cages, stacked tic-tac-toe to be even taller than the elephants.

Ramachandran's break was the stuff of legend. He had allowed himself to be caught only because he would not part with Hathi. But he had not known what fate was awaiting them inside the elephant camp. Inside the tremendous kraal, Ramachandran bashed against the heavy timber. Men stood at twenty paces, wary of a swift trunk or a hurled stone. Ramachandran headbutted and slashed with his tusks. He pushed his powerful hind side into the timbers, but they barely flexed. For the first time in his life, he was confronted with a problem that power could not solve. He attacked the enclosure until he was bleeding and exhausted. Then the men hurled ropes in. Not one of them dared enter, but they had their methods, and soon each of the giant's legs were chained and pulled taught with winches. He stood with legs splayed, immobile, and only then did the breakers enter.

They were tortured beside one another, though Hathi broke easily. They were far apart so that they could not console each other, or touch trunks, or nuzzle. Day after day they were beaten with canes, hooked hard. Ramachandran kept his head low. He did it for his cousin; he did it for hate. He kept a fire burning within and accepted the break. He made his way as a bruiser—a teak tree hauler, a hammerer of giants, the largest and most brutal employee of the Indian government.

Elephants in south India are traded like heavy machinery, from owner to owner, temple to temple, state to state. In the year that followed, Hathi spent most of his time chained behind a crumbling house at an elephant camp. It was during this time that he learned to hate men. They beat him, chained, him, scolded him. He feared them despite knowing how easily he could crush them. His was a gentle spirit. At the sounds of a man's voice, Hathi's eyelids would wince and flutter, his ears would flare, his tail grew stiff. He learned to take their orders to avoid being beaten and worked with the broken acceptance of a slave. In the long cold nights he would stand there, half dreaming, aching to return to his family.

The mahouts of the camp had little patience to work a blind elephant, and he was traded several times before ultimately being sent to a village in a reserve forest where he came under the charge of Thimma's father. In the tribal village, he received fewer beatings and the work was simple—mostly carrying firewood and wild produce that the tribals cut from the forest. Separated from his herd and still very much a captive, he had at last been returned to the embrace of the jungle, where the air smelled of water and wood and he could hear the wild voices of the forest.

For Ramachandran, the year was less kind. Because of his abnormal size, the hard men of the camp devoted themselves to his taming. With each man who failed or was killed, more came, eager to forge their reputation. He became the anvil against which they hammered their rage—the ancient animal rage of a simian species that had long lost its way. When he refused a command, their hardwood canes fell savagely on the soft place between his eyes where his trunk met his skull.

Within his first month in the camp, however, it became clear that he was too violent and wild to ever train properly. The men of the camp gathered and schemed. He was given a small mountain of opium on the day they brought him before buyers. Ramachandran stood in placid narcotic compliance as the new men inspected him. They assumed that his great size would draw greater crowds to their temple, and that no matter how disobedient he was, they would be able to tame him. One of these assumptions was true.

After the money was exchanged, he was brought to a new elephant yard in Kerala. The mahouts there starved him until the promise of delicious paddy and lumps of jaggery became irresistible to the giant. It was there that he learned the meaning of the Malayali commands. But for Ramachandran, learning to work only provided him the chance to catch the men when their guards were down, when he could inflict the most damage.

Each time Ramachandran killed another elephant or a man, he received weeks of beatings and starvation. When they tried to trim his tusks, he broke the femur of one trainer and mashed another dead against a tree. When he escaped, he was tracked. He crossed into a plantation in Wayanad and spent three days in the jungle. There he fought another male and mated a cow, and then left as the trackers drew near. At the fringe of the forest, he crashed through a farm gate and destroyed an entire banana crop, six *lakhs'* worth in all.

When they found him, they shot him several times. He circled around and used a stick as a club to kill a tracker. It made him happy to crush them—the way a monkey kills mosquitoes. They brought him back eventually. They had chains and guns and firecrackers to frighten him. When he was led back they held him in a kraal, a cage made from whole trees.

Ramachandran feared no man but understood the threat of *men*. No man could have surrounded him and the herd, no man could have driven them into the cages, no one man could have hoped to chain him. He understood this. And so he understood when a local politician came to the elephant yard. He sensed the man had the power of many men behind him.

The politician was dressed in immaculate white trousers and a buttoned Western shirt, with a curled mustache and a brown vest. He was in his early fifties, with gray fringes in his hair. He had rolled up his sleeves and beat Ramachandran worse than anyone ever had. It was a beating that the tusker took inside of the cage. His legs were tied, the timbers were close, and he was already starved. He took it patiently at first, but when the man swapped his club for a spike, the elephant screamed out in real pain.

Ramachandran spent weeks healing from the wounds, and in that time he knew the day would come when the cage would be opened. When he would be the batterer instead of the battered. He bided his time and never forgot the man in white with the curled mustache and the brown vest.

For years and years, he was kept in the yard behind the temple, guarded from public view by densely stacked eucalyptus and jamun trees like a monstrous secret, the chained thing that could not be tamed. Usually an elephant was chained by one foot—he was chained by all four. Trainers threw his food over a concrete wall to where he could snatch it with his trunk, but they would not come near. For years he stood in that same place, swaying back and forth, simmering in rage, and only at times allowing himself moments of misery, of recollection, of pining for his family, for any pachyderm companion. His tusks grew long, so long that they almost touched the ground. The tips made an X in front of his face. He had been abused, beaten, chained, and ultimately weaponized. Only because he was the biggest elephant in five states, and perhaps the biggest in all of India, did they let him live.

One day, he'd thank them for it. His way.

Thimma had succeeded in leading Ramachandran back into the kraal. The terrifying giant would not part with Hathi, and Thimma had had to let the other mahouts close him and the two elephants into the kraal. From Hathi's back, he leapt onto the sheered timbers and climbed down to safety. There he was taken by the collar, lifted almost off his feet, and led to the office of the work yard.

He sat in a swivel chair with no wheels, the armrests rising on either side of him. Several men guarded him for nearly an hour until the sound of a coach came. Several men entered, the leader at the back. Thimma recognized the man from the campaign posters in the city that he'd seen when he had sat with Hathi at the temple. The man's hungry eyes. His thick mustache. His arrogant chest. That stupid lion.

The man, Vijayan, paced into the room and lifted some papers from the desk, which he studied. He placed a cigarette in his lips that another man lit. He drew a deep breath and exhaled. Without looking up from the papers, he spoke.

"Where are you from?"

"Kodagu."

"Ah, I know it."

"Of course you do." *You destroyed it*, Thimma didn't say.

"You have some fine skill with elephants, boy."

Thimma was silent.

"In several months there will be an inauguration parade for my new office. I'd like you to lend your services as a mahout."

"You've won the election?"

Vijayan looked up from his papers now. Thimma kept his eyes on the floor as the man drew closer.

"You will help us with the parade."

"No, I won't. I will take my elephant and I will go. That is all."

"That is not your elephant."

"It is my elephant. He was my father's, and he has been with me my whole life."

"Do you have any papers to confirm this story?"

Thimma's eyes were blank.

"Get out of my office. You filthy tribal untouchable fuck."

Thimma couldn't bear another beating, and he knew that no logic or reason would work in such a room, so he left.

That night, they found Thimma's body limp out by the fence near where Hathi was tied. He was barely breathing. There were paper bags and bottles beside him. The mahouts carried him to the hospital where nurses stretched him on a cot beside dozens of others. They put a drip in his arm and left him in putrid darkness full of the soft beeping of monitors, the coughing and cries of the suffering, the scurry of rats.

In the morning Thimma watched numbly as the man in the cot beside him was inspected. The man's body was thick and well muscled, perhaps in his forties but strong and healthy. The doctor checked the pulse in his neck and found none, then opened the eyelid to confirm.

"He is dead," the doctor told a woman nearby, clearly the man's wife. She sank to the floor in silent sobs. A tall, handsome man in strange robes stood sorrowfully as she clutched his hand.

"What did he die of?" Thimma asked.

The man in robes, a priest, did not answer. He seemed stunned. The nurses had entered the room, and the woman was sobbing loudly. They were trying to take the man's body, and she was begging them to do more. A male nurse came and restrained her, pushing back the man in the robes. The doctor left. The wife was carried out, the body was wrapped, and soon there was a new man in the bed.

"What killed him?" Thimma asked the priest.

"He did."

"Suicide?"

"Yes."

"What did he use?"

"Pesticide. He was a farmer. They are all doing it, thousands of them."

"I know about the farmer suicides. Everyone is dying."

The priest looked down at the dead-eyed boy and realized he might be asking for reasons more direct than curiosity. "What are you here for? The wounds on your face are nearly healed. What happened to you?"

Thimma didn't answer.

The young priest left him.

Late that night when he could walk, Thimma walked to the washroom. There was an old toothless man shaving. Thimma urinated and stood in the flickering bluish light. The tile floor was wet and filthy on his bare feet. He stole the razor easily and walked down the long corridor of suffering beds and out into the yard.

He sat beneath a great old rain tree, with many long arms that bowed out and mingled with the stars above. Thimma watched the sky for a time, and then turned and kissed the bark like a lover. He wished for a bag of glue, or at least some rum. He was too weak to search. He just wanted to sleep, to know nothing. He dragged the razor across his wrist. Little lines released beads of blood. His heart was quickening now. He poised the blade, closed his eyes, and slashed hard. This time the blood came fast, and he rose up to escape it but could not. It was everywhere. He cried out, swore, and tried to hold it in.

In his mother's songs, back when they lived in the jungle and the world was green and full of love, she sang that they would all eventually die and become the trees, the roots drawing them up out of the ashes and streams, become new branches and live in the forest. He knelt and held his wrist over the great roots, slowly fading, until he fell.

10

THE CROSSING

For five days the girl and the tiger flanked the valley on the jagged edge of the escarpment. Their black silhouettes bent forward against the purple dawn and starry skies. They left no tracks. They buried their feces. The man-villages far below were jeweled settlements as distant as alien worlds. Not a man or woman or cow could tell that a girl and a tiger had passed by their farm, orchard, pasture. They did not know, nestled in the valleys, that above them against the stars a girl walked beside a tiger in the night. They would find caves or hollow trees by dawn, when the mosques played *aazaan* and the dogs sang along, howling to the wind and waking the world. Only the owls and night foxes watched wide-eyed as the improbable pair journeyed on.

Isha and Kala walked the arid country that belonged to those wild things on the periphery of the world. The chaotic din of India's busy streets was absent here, for even in crowded modern India, ancient silences remain. Footsteps shifted pebbles that had laid settled for ten thousand years, where the rocks and trees whisper the ancient tongues. On some mountains were old ruins from the time of Tipu Sultan. Girl and tiger took shelter there, where the birds and snakes and monkeys and strange flowering vines were the only tenants of the crumbling battlements. It was the backstage of reality, away from the clocks and screens and traffic lights that guide the human hive, out where the wild things are subject to the wrath and mercy of the sun, the quiet collection of clouds, the trickle of rain.

The moon was setting and the starry universe rotating down, while on the opposite horizon the sun warmed the blackout of the sky. Kala was panting gently beside Isha as they ascended yet another boulder field up the side of a mountain. The girl kept her hand on the tiger's shoulders, which provided unwavering support and forward power. Then Kala stopped and looked down range. Isha searched the shadowy plain. A cluster of dark shapes watched them.

With her cubs beside her, the old mother bear, likely with her last litter, scented the air. She stood like a disheveled woman in need of spectacles, chin raised, nose working. She had never seen a tiger. Her cubs grew silent and drew near, globbing into their mother like little balls of black mercury. The bear family and girl–tiger pair stood for a long moment.

"Come," Isha said into Kala's ear. The ear quivered and the tiger obliged.

That morning they made camp in a deep triangular cave between gargantuan boulders. Isha made a mat of leaves and lay her blanket on top of it. Kala meticulously cleaned her paws and forelegs as Isha worked. Once they had both completed their nighttime rituals, Isha fell onto her back and Kala drew in close. The tiger's face was no longer small like a cub, but flared out on the sides with white fur, and her chin had become a prominent white pommel with long whiskers spreading out on either side of her black nose. Kala lay on her side and rested her head on Isha's chest. The weight of it made the girl breathless. She lay on her back, stroking the tiger's ears, now as large as her hands, until they both slept.

A year earlier, when she was barely thirteen years old, she had found a pair of orphaned squirrels left abandoned after a road crew had pruned a tree outside her parents' house. She cared for them before their eyes had opened, before they had grown fur, religiously feeding them at regular intervals with a dropper, keeping them warm, and ministering to their every need. For weeks she doted on them and guarded them from Faux, the family cat.

One of the pair of pink babies died early on, but the other hung on, and Isha watched while, like magic, the naked rat transformed. His eyes opened, he became furry, with three stripes on his back and a big bushy tail. Isha did her homework with the squirrel quivering in her hair and did chores with him on her shoulder. Once she was certain he would live, she named him Ticki. She would sing to him when he climbed the branches of the rain tree outside her window, and he'd chirp back to her. And if any kites or crows flew near the tree, the little squirrel would race down the branches and through the window, to the safety of Isha's hair.

But while she was at school one day, the maid opened the door to her room, and Faux finally achieved an audience with the prey he had been salivating over for months. The large cat made quick work of the little squirrel, and Isha came home to see her room full of tufts of fur, spots of blood, and a few leftover bone fragments of her beloved Ticki.

Her tears came like rivers, and she shook pitifully. The entire household was brought to its knees with her sorrow. At school her teachers gave no sympathy for her sadness, and one callous relative dryly noted that Isha seemed more interested in "tree rats" than in her family or studies.

Appa came to her when she was reading sorrowfully on the veranda hammock. Street children played cricket in the street beneath the rain tree, and yellow autos occasionally came by the quiet road. He sat beside her with two cups of tea and a bag of green *chakli* and read the newspaper. As they sat, he occasionally stole glances at his daughter, the one for whom he'd coined the name Iron Eyes.

Finally, he said, "Ba," the way you call cows.

They drove for the rest of that day, for the father knew his daughter's love of windows and the world. Her weakness for music. She hung an elbow out the window, chin resting on her hand. A cow nodding down the road to a *tabla* beat. Sitar notes and chai smoke curling through the bustle. There were flocks of women in brightly colored saris. The scent of masala coals glowing beneath gunpowder corn. Her eyes began to dry as her heart swelled to the passing world, and the Hindi songs that played as they went. Tracks from *Dev. D* made her tap her toe as rickshaws wove through blue busses in Banashankari. Later she sang softly to "Ek Lau" from *Aamir*, one of her favorites. They drove through busy streets towards the city fringe, and then sped out onto a highway neither of them knew.

Appa was thrilled by quality of the new highway. "Just look at this road! Look at what a beautiful highway! I tell you, Isha, India is coming along! It has gotten so much better, just look at how well

done it is. I'll tell you—anything is possible in India!" He shifted
to fourth and then fifth and they cruised well over 120 kilometers
per hour with the windows down so that Isha's hair was sent wild.

Then the road ended. Not in any rational way. It just ended,
dropped off onto the sand. It simply stopped like a mirage. They
came screeching to a halt, the car drifting sideways just before
stalling at the end of the asphalt. The music ended abruptly. For a
long moment they sat inside, quietly stunned, as dust caught up and
rushed around them. They both knew how close to disaster they
had come. Outside the car they stood and looked at the barren emptiness stretching before them. The road had been constructed for
miles, and then without any warning, signs, or reason, it just
stopped.

When their eyes met, Isha and her father began laughing so
hard they were bent over. They laughed and laughed and laughed
till their bellies hurt. From that day on their favorite phrase was "In
India, anything is possible."

Such moments of warmth, when recalled, shielded Isha from
the harshness of wilderness. It was a landscape of boulders. The
few other living things—the kites and crows the jackal and dry and
lonely trees—had no concern for her. Her mother's warm laugh,
her father's arms, her sister's constant rivalry—she kept these
memories like candles burning inside her. She mattered there, to
them, in that other world. Here were the sun and the moon and
things of infinite standing, systems and traditions older than her
ancestors, older than her species. Adrift in the great callous abyss
of creation, she yearned for the world where she mattered. Out here
she was nothing but another orphan of reality. The pages of stories
that had insulated her in the beginning had dried and fallen away
like old leaves. It no longer felt like an adventure, and she no longer felt like a hero. She was just another thing that might or might
not survive, a temporary collection of bone and blood and love and
hope traveling across the dark stone. They were creatures of the
fringe, the birds, the foxes, remnants of the once teeming menager-
ie, survivors of a silent apocalypse. And she had become one of
them.

I will teach you about silence.

Isha had bought Kala mutton several times now. She held her
breath by the butcher's shop and tried not to stare at the truth beneath all flesh. The stark white ribs and red muscle that hung from

the hooks on the ceiling. The butcher's blood-stained apron, the flies, the smell of death. She would carry the plastic bag of meat on a stick over her shoulder so that the smell would not hit her. Whenever Kala ate meat, Isha made sure to leave her alone for well over an hour. The tiger would chew the strips of goat meat and crunch sections of bone, then lick her paws and fur with predatory satisfaction.

Though she worked diligently to avoid human contact, she savored the few encounters she was granted while heading for resupplies near the villages. The shopkeepers always found the amount of milk she wanted comical. For water she would find a tap and ask a local family if she could fill her bottle. They almost always permitted her to do so. At one town she bought herself a single chakli for five rupees.

The villagers and farmers in their fields were kind to her and eager to give her whatever would help, despite having so little themselves. One day while Kala was tied in a cave, and she was trying to climb a dangerously high coconut tree on the edge of a farm, the kindly farmer came out, laughed good naturedly, and after talking with her for several minutes, gifted her four coconuts. Another day, Isha met a field-worker woman, skin baked black by the sun, teeth red from decades of areca nut chewing, who gave her cool mosaru and rice to take. It was a priceless gift. Then there were the children and their beautiful young mother who spotted Isha stalking toward the mountains one dusk and ran to her to ask if she was okay, if she needed help, and if they could invite her for dinner. Isha declined but was floored by their compassion.

After three weeks of journeying through the wild, despite only drinking milk and eating several nightjars and a few kilograms worth of mutton, Kala had grown significantly. Her legs had lengthened, her face was longer. Isha suffered the long timeline of her species, which meant that while the tiger grew, she remained the same—and even began to reduce. Her ribs were showing.

Several times thus far, Isha had tried to make fire. She'd never had to make a fire before. Though she'd collected measured sticks as thick as her fingers and piled them neatly, nothing had happened. She held the lighter to them, but they would not catch. A few drops of gasoline, she thought, would be the aid she needed. Finding a mini Fizzi bottle on the roadside, she asked the man at the hardware store to fill it with petrol. There were no petrol bunks or gas stations in the villages, but stores sold it in small quantities.

On her way back to the cave, Isha passed a herd of goats and spent a long moment deliberating. With a wary eye out for the shepherd, she coaxed a goat kid into her arms and made her way to where Kala was tied. She wondered how Kala would react to this goat now that the tiger had tasted mutton.

The answer came at her in a flash of orange muscle and claw. As she entered the cave, Kala broke the rope she was tied to and lunged forward. Isha dropped the goat and fell over as Kala attacked. The tiger's claws were out this time as she tackled the kid, and the goat began screaming terribly as the tiger bit into its leg. Then Kala moved and bit its nose. Then she tore off a piece of its ear. The goat screamed and bled, but all its strength could not overcome the finality of Kala's curved claws now deep inside its skin. The goat bleated and wailed, and Kala sunk her teeth in deeper.

Isha was frantic. Instead of snapping its neck or closing the windpipe, Kala was tearing it apart. Kala held the goat's head to the ground with one paw, while the other held the stomach. Her curved claws were deep beneath the goat's skin. The tiger bit down into the goat's leg, and turned her head to the side, snapping tendons and tearing flesh. She began licking and eating as the goat screamed.

Isha ran at them shouting. Kala turned her hind side to Isha, bearing down on the goat and tearing faster.

"Stop it!" Isha screamed as she tried to fit the stick between Kala's mouth and the goat. She grabbed Kala's ear and tugged.

The tiger slapped her.

It wasn't a hard slap, not for a tiger, but it sent Isha tumbling. When she stood up, Isha strode over and punched the tiger in the nose, and this time Kala dropped the goat and took a threatening step toward Isha, who scrambled backward. She realized for the first time that she was in danger. The tiger's eyes, usually so full of nuzzling cub-like love, were now savage and unflinching. *This is my food not yours, so don't you dare touch it.* Slowly, Isha moved back.

She left the cave and sat outside crying. When the goat's screams became clotted with blood, Isha wretched and fled to where she could not hear the sound. For a long time after, Isha and

Kala remained apart. It was another day before the tiger was done consuming the kid.

In the days that followed, the trail became hard. Isha knew already that their journey was illogical. They had no plan, no direction. But even more urgently, she worried that she could not have Kala thinking she had the upper hand, which she did. The tiger seemed to grow every time she ate. Isha knew she had to create the illusion of power for herself but had no idea how. And besides, there were other things that demanded her attention. As towns were farther apart, water became scarce. They drank from puddles. When there were no caves, attempting sleep through the long hot days was torture. Their milk fund was running low, and their bellies hollowed by the day. Kala took to murdering dry lizards and crunching them discontentedly in her teeth.

They once again hit some small mountains, and at every crest, with every new view, Isha prayed to see green. Sitting dizzily beneath the scorn of the sun, she imagined great trees and rich waterfalls, deep shade and the soft ferns of the jungle. Where was this place she'd heard of but had never been? Her lips were so burned it hurt. This was not the adventure she had envisioned.

One afternoon Isha stood beside a trash-filled river outside a small village, the first they had seen in three days. She watched young men fish. They were friendly and gave her several fish to take. But back at the cave Kala wanted none of the hard, foul fish from the trash river. And so Isha dropped the dry, silver, leaf-shaped bodies outside the cave.

A brahminy kite, a raptor with hooked beak and sharp talons and a proud white head, drifted in with spread wings. For a time it watched, and then streamlined its wings for speed and dove at the fish. Isha dove for cover. Then another kite came. This was a pariah kite. The girl and the tiger watched mystified as the kites circled. But the raptors would not descend near the tiger and shrieked their shrill frustration to the wind. At length Isha realized that the birds were *asking* her for fish.

There is a game that young kites play where they will lift a leaf high into the sky, drop it, and then swoop down to clutch it before it returns to the earth. Isha collected one fish and threw it underhand into the air. The kite turned and, with tremendous speed snatched the fish from the air, swooped out into the abyssal distance to consume the prize on the wing. The next kite approached.

Again Isha hurled a fish into the air. The kite inverted, talons to the sky, then spiraled out wide to consume it. It was magnificent. She fed the raptors until the fish were gone, and the kites were pleased with the girl for learning their game. They studied her with fantastic eyes and trembling feathers. They only left when she did, shrieking their thanks to the wind.

The sun and moon swung around the travelers until they came to where no villages existed. There were no friendly families to ask for help. There was nothing but dying trees bent in ghostly silence. Night fell rapidly. Isha was forced to walk with her flashlight, the dim yellow beam before her. Kala chuffed beside her and nuzzled her in comfort. The tiger had realized before Isha did that, for the first time, she was scared.

One dusk, Isha packed up supplies and untied the tiger. But something had excited Kala, and once the leash was loosed, the tiger rushed out of the cave and vanished into the night. The white spots on the tiger's ears bobbed off, fading into the dark. Isha was left wandering on her own in the general direction Kala had gone. The tentative feeling had grown into queasy dread.

"Where is this tiger?" she whispered aloud through clenched teeth. Isha called for her, softly. "Kala?" But the smallness of her voice was frightening in the vast dark.

At the sound of the girl's voice, he grinned. He was the orphan maker, the corpse worshiper, the limping spotted scrapper with saliva dripping from his smile. The hyena bobbed its head and followed the girl. The long black mohawk of fur above his spine shivered with desire and anticipation. He held his thick neck low so that his scarred and short, brutish nose could work the ground. There was another, his brother, who would flank her.

The hyena brothers were a team of carrion crawlers. They'd split up and scour the night, giggling and talking to each other. When they found something, they hunted together.

The first giggled a wobbling call; his brother sniffed in response in the distance. The girl was walking. He watched her searching, fumbling with the torchlight, pausing to listen. When she paused, the hyena paused. She was not so clever, no. She squatted to urinate. The hyena grinned hungrily from the darkness.

The first hyena crouched and followed behind the girl. She was just there, so close, and still he didn't need to be silent. He was a bone eater. There would be nothing left of the girl. Only a bison's hardware was thick enough to survive his pillaging gnaw. The hyena came close to her. *She doesn't know*, he chuckled to his brother. They didn't care if she heard them, they didn't care if she screamed. Not an animal in the plains would challenge them. Mother birds and foxes huddled their young, the old scrambled away, for he was the reaper of the plains.

Isha wheeled round and gasped. There it was. Wheezing, grinning, dirty gray with spots and stripes and teeth in the beam of the flashlight. That she didn't know what it was made it all the more horrifying. She picked up a rock and hurled it before running. The hyena came loping after her. She could not know that the hyena was funneling her toward his brother. There they would each grab a side of her and pull her apart.

She ran, swearing. She tripped and went down hard onto her elbows, scrambling up just as a messy monster of a thing with glowing eyes and long teeth came galloping in.

Isha backed away until a boulder stopped her. In the trembling yellow light of the torch, the predator advanced. When it reached her, it pushed its nose into her navel and opened its mouth. The teeth were massive. *Knobs of bone. Snapping tendons. The mortal scream of the suffering goat.* Vivid red insides flashed in her mind and sickeningly, she realized she too could be dismantled. Hot breath wheezed onto her belly.

The hyena nuzzled her, looking over her and up at her eyes, at parts of her it desired to taste. Shivering and sniffing and pressing its nose into her belly, it licked her with a rough tongue that lifted her shirt.

A shriek in the dark made the hyena snap around. Kala came bounding, frantic, from the darkness. When it saw her, the hyena leapt into the air and fled a distance. Kala raced to Isha's side. The tiger's eyes were full of urgent things she could not tell. The tiger's shoulder was bleeding, and she pushed in between the rock and the girl just as the second hyena entered the clearing.

The dreadful truth was that Kala had come running to Isha for safety. Now the two cubs, girl and tiger, stood with their backs to stone as the spotted, starving jaw-brothers drew close.

No, the tiger would not save them, Isha realized. Kala's eyes were disks of wide terror. Her ears were flat against her head as she snarled and cowered. The hyenas mocked her for her fear, grinning and clacking their teeth together on the air with a careless and terri-

fying swagger. Isha sobbed and swore without any defense, her
mind racing for a plan. With the flashlight in her mouth, Isha
reached into her satchel. She felt the knife, and then her blanket,
and then her hands grasped the bottle of gasoline.

She removed the bottle and leaned toward the heavy-toothed
brothers. The hyena closest to her winced and snorted at the taste
of the fuel splashed onto its nose. Isha sprayed both hyenas well.
The foreign sting and smell made them hesitate. Kala clung to the
rock. The young tiger had already tussled with one of the hyenas
and had learned enough to be terrified. As Isha leaned back, she let
the bottle gush out onto the ground before her, backing away from
the puddle it made. Then she threw the bottle at the hyenas and
with her back once again to the rock, she found the lighter and
knelt.

Together the hyena brothers came in. They knew how soft her
bones would be. They had their heads low, standing in a puddle of
fuel.

Isha clicked the lighter on and held it to the ground.

The gasoline ignited with a *whoosh*! And the entire clearing
went up in bright yellow light. Both hyenas caught fire instantly
and they leapt and screamed and fled, aflame. Isha ran a few steps
after them, barefoot over the flames, roaring and swearing and
beating her chest.

From that night on, the tiger was terrified of the girl.

Though the incident with the hyenas ended without dismember-
ment, it changed everything for Isha. She was unable to recover
from the terror she had felt. The encounter had focused the possi-
bility that she could actually be eaten, and even worse, never see
her family again. Things were different now. When she had struck
out, she had envisioned that finding the jungle was something she
actually could do. But without a map or a path, they had only wandered and struggled to survive.

That fourth week there was little shelter. They slept beneath
bushes and once in a burned-out train car. Mountains had dropped
off to flat plains. The streams were polluted, and the water thick
and gray. She carried water, but it ran out fast. Once after patiently

collecting from a small trickle, she spilled it. When the bottle fell, she jumped up to save it and slashed her toe on a thorn. She worked with tears in her eyes to remove it from her foot. She slept thirsty.

That night Isha woke shivering. Low clouds thundered and flashed; hail fell in hard pellets. Isha pushed into Kala, and the two huddled beneath the blanket so that the tiger's breath warmed them. The tiger's head was half the size of the girl. With each breath, the tiger's ribs lifted her entirely, and their heartbeats whispered softly to each other through the long, lonely dark. When the sun rose, they sat together warming in the light. Kala was starving and Isha was fevered and distant.

Maybe it was time to find a phone. Maybe it was time to call home. She knew the number, all she had to do was call, and her parents would swoop in. It would all be over. The tiger would go to the zoo, but at least she would live. Wasn't that good enough?

She thought these things as Kala nuzzled her. Isha looked into the wide nebulaic eyes and felt like a failure and a traitor. She cried as she hugged the monstrous striped cat and buried her face in the white-and-black fur of her jaw.

It is time to go home.

11

THE SECOND COMING

She woke beneath the stars, her head rising gently with the sonorous breaths of the sleeping tiger. It was early morning, and the sky was still dark. Isha stood shivering on the cliff, looking toward the east, where the black sky was softening to blue over the hilled horizon. It was night and it was cold and still and quiet. Across some meridian, people of another world were watching a blazing sunset, perhaps laughing, crying, or dying. So many lives the sun would see, so many stories. Could anyone out there imagine a lone girl on a hillside with a tiger, shivering in the dark dawn? The sun limped up a bruised sky, as though what it had seen in other parts of the world had broken its heart.

Isha sat up on the hillside beside Kala, waiting for the sun, dreading what the day would bring. She felt sick with hunger. Amma and Ajji had been so worried about her weight, even back in the world when she'd been healthy. All the hopeful anticipation she had felt months earlier at the prospect of finally growing breasts was ruined as her fingers moved over her own noticeably protruding ribs. She fantasized about hard-boiled eggs, coconuts, *laddus*, and ice cream. To kill the time and hunger, she chewed on a piece of grass. She tried to braid her matted hair. She threw pebbles.

She tied Kala to a bent tree between two large boulders. It wasn't a cave, but it was shelter enough for the tiger from the sun and the eyes of shepherds. She kissed the tiger's nose and told her to stay put. She felt traitorous as she climbed down the steep cliff and tacked down the hill. One final goat. No matter the cost.

Down in the village, the first they had seen in a week, scattered houses had cows and dogs, piles of hay, and water tanks. People were stirring. Wrapped in shawls and caps. Tending to the animals. Drawing *rangoli* on the doorstep. It was the start of a day. Down the path, leaving the small family of huts, was a goatherd and his flock.

This was her mark.

She would feed goat to Kala at whatever cost and then head to town. That was her plan. By midday she had long descended the slope of the mountain. But after two hours of waiting, the shepherd boy watching the flock remained vigilant. The sun had risen and was baking the earth now. Everything was dizzy with heat.

In the distance a great commotion sounded. There were shouting voices and a bell began to ring. The goatherd sat up on one elbow to listen. Then he stood, craning his neck to see the village. He yelled at his goats and waved the stick. They all moved onto their knees and then stood, sticking out their tongues and bleating. The sounds from the village were louder now. So loud that the goatherd started walking toward the sound in curiosity. The girl too abandoned her goat catching and followed.

At the edge of the village a crowd had gathered. They were all focused on something at the center of their midst. Whatever it was, everyone was running to see it. A larger, fairer man in strange monk-like robes was rushing through the crowd of short, dark villagers, begging them to stop. Then he became entangled with a large villager. The two men stood face to face, viciously arguing, their open palms in each other's face as they shouted, spit flying between them. Meanwhile, the crowd continued to grow. Isha guessed it was a fight between village boys. But no, this was something worse.

"Kill it!" they yelled.

And suddenly the air was hot with terror. *Kala!*

Pushing through the legs and lungis and saris and bodies, she broke through the throng and into the center. The bear had been slashed across the face with a machete, beaten with metal poles and sticks, and hit with stones so that its skull was broken and it could no longer stand. They had tied a rope around its mouth, the other end held by one man while two others stood on either side, holding out the bear's arms. Young boys took turns clubbing the bear. One little boy wound up like a cricket pitcher, winding the stick around, and bringing it down on the bear's snout so it broke in a burst of blood. Its eyes were blank with suffering, yearning for death to end the pain.

Isha recoiled in shock and suddenly felt dizzy. She walked backward out of the crowd, past the bodies and saris and lungis and legs and into the inferno beyond. More and more people were running toward the carnage.

It was only when the world flickered and for a moment lost color that Isha wavered and realized she needed shade or water or both. She found a low brick wall to sit on beneath a tree. She was dimly aware that the man in monk robes was watching her. By the time she could focus on him, he was watching the crowd, face stoic, eyes glistening with unshed tears.

He had a messy brown beard and wore a brown cloak that covered his whole body. A hood sat crumpled on his shoulders, and a rope belt was tied at his waist.

As the mob celebrated and leered and spat at the innocent bear, there was a gentle bond between the two quiet mourners—the man and the girl. Two village children ran up to him and began talking loudly and grabbing at his hands. The man could not understand their dialect and spoke in clumsy Kannada, which the children had never heard. He retracted his hand from their grasping.

"They are asking you to join in."

He did not reply but finished shooing away the excited children, and then turned to study Isha. Her tears had left little trails down the dust on her face. There was a dignity to the way this girl wept, he thought, as though she had seen much suffering. He was also intrigued by her perfect English, her aesthetic features, and how incredibly filthy she was.

"Where are you from?" he asked.

"Not here," Isha said. She was suddenly wary of the stranger.

"Not from this village?" he asked. Isha realized that her torn and filthy clothes must have made her look like a street child, but worse.

"No, I am not from here," she said. "Are you?"

He nodded at her sarcasm. "I have a farm twenty kilometers from here, actually."

"Are you a farmer?" she asked.

"No."

"You look like a priest. Like Saint Francis."

The man turned to face her fully, spreading his arms. "These are Franciscan robes."

"Like Saint Francis."

"That's right," he said.

"But now you aren't a priest?"

"No."

"I thought you had to be a priest for life?"

"You do."

"But you aren't one anymore?"

"No."

They were quiet for a long time. He was young and somewhat handsome and had a beard and angular Indian features. But there was something off. No one that spoke English so well and was clearly educated should be running around a village alone in robes. Sure, India is a country filled with naked holy men and all manner of strange sadhus and priests, but in his case, it didn't add up. His eyes were wide with red around the edges. He blinked often, like someone unable to accept what he saw as truth. She noticed that his fingers were shaking slightly, involuntarily. In the distance, a village man was pouring gasoline on the bear. As he did, another man prepared a stick by wrapping it in cloth and soaking it in petrol.

He watched her for a time. She had wild black hair and a scar that ran below her right eyebrow. He asked her how she'd gotten it.

"I fell when I was three," she said dismissively. Then, "I'd like to kill everyone in this town."

"Let's go," the man said, standing. He led her to the shade of another tree where a young girl with one eye sold coconuts. Isha watched as the little girl gestured, inviting them to buy, imploring them really.

"Can I buy you a coconut?" the man asked.

Isha nodded. "What were you fighting with that man about?"

"They called me because they saw the bear, and they assume every animal they see comes from the sanctuary. Like it's the fault of the sanctuary that animals even exist." His fists clenched as he spoke.

"But why did they call you?"

"Ah, they call me for such things—snake rescues, bears, wounded kites. I chase them away or relocate them. My home is a little sanctuary." He motioned over his shoulder.

Isha's mind was full of calculation. She wanted to tell him. She wanted to bare her soul to him. The air smelled of burning fur.

"Thank you," Isha said after a long silence.

"For what?"

"For trying to save her."

The man was unsure of what to say and said nothing. His face was beaded in sweat. He looked up at the sun and then sneezed. They sat in silence drinking cool coconut water.

"There is no hope for this damned country. What can anyone truly know of nature anymore? We have cut and killed everything that once lived. Nature is dead. We are left mourning it like a mother we never knew. Like amputations that never knew from what they were cut. For a while it seemed like things were bad but still holding on. Now it's just a drop-off. And our shadows grow long on the burned earth."

Isha looked around. Was he talking to her or himself?

"Religion has it all wrong too. They say that Jesus was sent to wash away the sins of man. And it is true that he was sent to do it—to save us from our own evil. And that he did it a long time ago and came as a poor man instead of a ruler because God was on the side of the meek and the helpless. And then they crucified him, and he came back, and eventually he left. And now the world has waited. For two thousand years the world has waited. Waited for Jesus to return. But what if it is not *Jesus* that is returning but some other veiled manifestation? What if this time God has wagered, instead of his son in human form, the rest of creation as our trial?"

"Like what?" Isha squinted.

The man put a cigarette to his lips and felt his robes for matches but could not find any. His fingers were twitching worse now. Isha withdrew the lighter from her satchel and thumbed the flame. He leaned in and puffed, nodding his thanks. Isha put the lighter back in the satchel. The man closed his eyes and drew smoke deep into his chest.

"What I'm saying is, what if the second coming is all around us, but we do not realize we are blind."

The man was silent. The girl was silent. The sun was murderous.

Standing up, the man slung a pack over his robes. "Well, there is nothing else I can do here." He stowed the cigarette butt in his pocket. "It was nice talking to you. Take care."

"You too," she said. Her heart was pounding, begging her to say something. Anything. *Tell him.* He swung a leg over a dilapidated old motorcycle. Isha's mouth opened dumbly, the words swelling in her throat.

"Thank you," Isha managed.

"Thank you," he said, holding her eyes for a moment. He did not look back toward the bear. He kicked the bike engine on, shifted to first, and rode away. She watched him go and wanted to cry.

Isha walked away feeling sorry for herself. She had intended to call her parents that day, but she doubted that this horrible village would have a phone. She also felt ashamed to be a person— she wanted nothing to do with her own kind. The loneliness of the trail suddenly seemed like a blessing. Maybe she needed to be away from the world. Maybe it was too cruel for her to be a part of. But despite her morose mood, she knew that if she was not making the phone call, then she still had to accomplish the original goal: find meat for Kala.

Yet as she walked on the scalded dirt road and the wiry skeletons of brush, she felt a growing darkness. There were cows tied to fences, their dried waste burned into gray cakes on the earth. First the tigress, now the bear. Death was the end of every story. She swayed as she walked. She was dizzy and wanted to vomit but could not muster the energy.

A voice whispered from inside her. *You should never have left home. You should have behaved better in school. Then your parents would never have sent you away. You could have been a happy child, safe and at home, loved and happy. Now look at you.* Isha was helpless against this sudden onslaught of doubt and darkness. *Do you think your mother and father will still love you after all the trouble you've caused? Do you think if you die out here anyone will ever find you?* She imagined her mother crying horribly, and her heartbroken father. *You have been selfish, horribly selfish. Think of your parents, your grandparents. They must hate you now.*

Isha felt the weight of years and miles and lifetimes suddenly fall on her. What had she been thinking? How could she have done something so terrible? What if something bad happened to any of them? What if she had lost her chance and could never go back? She had never felt so selfish and unworthy.

The clouds scraped low across the sky in gray waves that hid the sun, the oppressor oblivious to the suffering below. She was certain she had gone against nature. *What made you think of doing such a stupid thing as this? You should have never done it,* the voice whispered. She tried not to think of the wet crunch of the bear's skull or the look of mortal despair in its eyes. She shuddered as she imagined her own skull being crushed under vicious blows.

As she walked she shook her head and tried to clear it, but something was wrong. Her vision was hazy; her exhausted mind wandered. She dreamed that she was dead, her bones brown and fragile in the earth. She would not see her parents again. She had lost that privilege because she had gone away and died and now her body was a secret in the earth, the grass and worms. With the soft voice of infinity, promising everything and nothing of the terrible truth, doubt sank its teeth deep into her. She made her way along the village fringe. In the grass she passed a blind crow, its eyes blue and unseeing. It cawed to her, and she did not kneel. It just stood there on the ground, calling.

She came to where a group of goats were grazing. There were no small ones, so she kept walking. Her steps were wavering. She felt her own head. She was certain she had a fever. Further on there was a shepherd and flock. The shepherd was a boy in his late teens, and he was sitting on a rock talking to an older man. Isha walked numbly around them and before long found a young goat.

For a few minutes everything went well.

She knelt to the ground and called to the goat. It came and she scooped it up. Over her shoulder, she could see the shepherd and the man had not noticed. She took a few steps and then her legs gave out and she fell. Several goats near her bleated and fled a few paces. She swore and, mustering her strength, collected the kid goat again and started walking off.

Suddenly the man and boy were on either side of her. The man grabbed her by the hair and yanked her to the ground. She dropped the goat. He shouted at her and she held her hands up to shield her-self. Her desperate defense only seemed to anger him further. Clutching her hair, he shouted in a crescendo of anger. He smacked her, and she screamed. He struck her again, aiming for her ribs and then her head, holding her up by the hair so that she would not fall. He jerked her head back and slapped her face. He struck again, and it knocked her out cold.

12

THE GOAT THIEF

Isha woke slowly. Her eyes rolled and gradually focused on the face and great hand before her. The hand dabbed a cool cloth across her forehead so that water flowed down her face. She closed her eyes. The touch of the cloth and the hand was tender. It moved across her forehead, down the bridge of her nose, and softly over each eyelid, and then from temple to chin on each side of her face. Isha reached out and grabbed the wrist of the hand the way one lost at sea clutches a float.

"You're okay," a man's voice said. "You'll be alright."

"*Neeru,*" Isha croaked. "Water."

The plastic edge of a bottle met her lips. She drank slowly and with closed eyes and could feel the cool liquid running over the inside of her ribs. She blinked hard and then reopened her eyes, seeing the man with the robes next to her. She squinted. It was just too bright out. The man rummaged in his pouch and removed sunglasses that he placed on Isha's face. She adjusted them. With the sunglasses on, she was able to look around properly. The shepherd who had struck her was some ways off, watching. He held a cloth to his face that was dripping with blood. There was blood all over his lungi too.

Isha nodded in the direction of the man. "Did you do that?"

"Yes, I did." He turned and pointed menacingly at the goatherd. "*Hōgu!*"

"You broke his nose?"

"Yes."

Isha smiled and held up her hand drunkenly. The man gently put his hand on hers and their fingers clasped together.

"What's your name?" he asked, still holding her hand.

"Isha."

"Isha, I'm Arun."

"Hi Arun," she said, smiling through the shades, their fingers waving gently back and forth. The sound of his voice was deep and clear and consoling. His touch was the first human thing Isha had felt in almost six weeks. Her name on his lips was like a prayer. She realized she had not heard her own name in what felt like years. In her fevered, semi-concussed state she felt she knew him, somehow.

Then she remembered Kala up in the cave and felt dreadful panic. Her spirits plummeted. She did not want to hike up; she did not know if she could. What she wanted was to surrender, let this warm, comforting man care for her. But she needed a goat, she needed to hike, and she had to go. She started to rise to her feet.

"Thank you, Arun." Her voice shook.

"What are you doing?"

"I have to go," she said miserably.

Arun watched, incredulous. "You are too weak to go any-where, kiddo."

"I have to go."

"Okay, tell me where you live."

"I don't live near here."

"Then will you come with me to my farm to rest?"

"No, I can't. I have to go."

Their questions went back and forth in a volley of incompati-bility. Arun felt himself growing irritated and held a hand up for silence. Calming himself, he wondered what terrible conflict this girl must be in, what could possibly drive her to such irrational be-havior. There was indeed great turmoil and pain and worry in her eyes. He drew a breath. He would have to do better.

He lifted the sunglasses off her eyes. "Tell me what it is, Isha." The sound of her name was disarming. "Tell me what it is and I will make it better. Just tell me, anything at all. I cannot let you go off in this state, and so just tell me how to help you, and you have my word that I will do all that is in my power."

Isha regarded him for a few dazed moments and then began shaking with laughter. Her eyes closed tight, and she shook until tears ran down her face.

Arun waited patiently, squinting in the sun.

"You really mean it?" she asked.

"Anything."

"Okay," she said, wiping her eyes and grinning drunkenly. She pointed behind him. "You see that mountain up there?"

Arun looked over his shoulder, then back at Isha. "Yes."

"I need to get up there with a goat before sundown."

Arun smiled tentatively. "You do realize you sound insane, don't you?"

"Kinda-kinda"

"Kinda-kinda. Hm. Try *thumba-thumba* (very, very)! You need to get up on the mountain by sundown with a goat?"

"Yes."

"Is this some religious thing?"

"God, no!"

"Good one," Arun said, smiling.

"Good what?"

"Nothing." He waved a hand. "And you can't tell me why?" Isha shook her head. "Of course not," Arun grumbled to himself. He was looking around now, squinting while he tried to think through the dizzying heat.

"Look, you wouldn't believe me if I told you. Please. *Please* help me to the mountain." She paused, and then said, "If you help me, I will show you the most incredible thing you have ever seen."

Arun smiled. "I've seen a lot."

"You haven't seen this."

Finally, Arun held up his hands. "Okay, okay, fine." He stood up and looked around. "Sir, how much for the goat?"

The goatherd's eyes bulged in outrage.

Minutes later Arun piloted his heavy Royal Enfield toward the mountain, the goat slung over his lap. Isha rode behind with her hands holding his shoulders. Her hair and his robes flickered in the brisk wind. When they reached the mount, Arun parked the bike. They climbed for a time, but Isha's legs were unsteady and twice she fell. Arun came and helped her up, joking that she shouldn't delay if she planned on executing him on the mountain before dark. Isha smiled and fell over again. This time he lifted her onto his shoulders.

With the girl on his shoulders and the goat under his arm, he walked. His shadow stretched long across the mountain. Isha thought of Saint Francis with the dove and the fox as Arun panted, drawing deep breaths as they went. When they passed a sturdy

stick, he squatted and took it, leaning on the staff as the hill steepened.

The swallows swooped in and the kites called and swirled
about them. The bats came out early, and the wind bounded up behind them so that it pushed at his back. Isha held gently onto his
forehead as he labored up the mountain. The goat was calm.

When they reached the cliff, he was bathed in sweat and panting. He knelt to let her down.

"Are you okay?" she asked, and he nodded. "Stay here." She
wobbled off into the cave. When she found Kala, the tiger leapt at
her and broke the rope to stand on her hind legs, hugging her
around the neck. Isha fell onto her back as the tiger pushed into her
face, overjoyed to see her. The girl had never been gone so long.
The tiger rubbed her white flared cheek onto Isha, who kissed Kala's nose above her.

Outside in the orange haze of the descending sun, the kites
whistled and swooped, and from the air they watched. Holding
tight to the rope around the tiger's neck, Isha stepped out into the
open.

For a long moment Arun watched. Then a shudder ran through
him and he stepped back. He left them and walked some distance
down slope. He looked up toward the kites, and the sky and the
burning west. He clutched his hair with his hands and pulled so that
it hurt. There were tears in his eyes.

13

SANCTUARY

That first night, Arun slaughtered the goat and Kala ate. He spent a sleepless night alone on the windswept rock outside the cave. He was looking out over the dark range in the morning when Isha came drowsily from the cave just before dawn. She stood, holding her own arms in the chilled morning, raven hair wild around her. The wind rushing over the rocks made the priest into a billowing thing of shaggy hair and wild robes. Purple warmed in the east as they watched in the wind.

"It's time to go," he said.

"Where?"

"Just there at the edge of the horizon, where it's green."

Weaverbird nests hung from the wooden beams of the front porch of the little house. It was a cracked concrete structure nestled in eleven acres of silent boulders, stands of bamboo and acacia, jamun, banyan, and dry ficus. Twisted branches and rare piles of large grassy globs of dried dung indicated the infrequent presence of lone elephants that sometimes came for nocturnal grazing. Arun pointed out the piles, and Isha's eyes were as wide as Kala's at the discovery of them. She knelt and prodded the cylindrical grassy balls, larger than her own head. The tiger sniffed and pawed them. Neither had ever seen an elephant.

Arun had used his mobile to call ahead and clear out the staff that usually worked the grounds. The cook and gardener were given the week off, as were the cleaning staff. Arun provided a heavy rope so that Isha could attempt to tie Kala. He instructed her that if they came into contact with anyone, to pretend she didn't speak whichever language they did. The complicated reality of living in a country with twenty-five national languages and several hundred dialects sometimes had its advantages.

With the tiger unhappily tied to a thick banyan root, Arun led Isha into the modest house. Unsure of what to do first, he led her to the study, where Isha's mouth fell slightly open.

The interior space was a testament of unseen presence, the careful intent of a true naturalist. The bookshelves were dense, the volumes separated by fossils. Ammonites. Large quartz crystals. The bones of things. The walls held framed maps and yellowed handwritten letters—correspondence of mysterious vintage. All of it must have been ordered by a great mind, an apostle of nature, one deeply fluent in natural history. Isha walked past framed butterflies, charted leaves, and artifacts that had been polished and restored, plucked from shore and stream and parts of the world she had never learned the names of. There was the skull of a deer over the doorway, long antlers reaching the ceiling. On the wall beside the study desk was a photo of a handsome man in his sixties with graying hair and uncompromising eyes.

"My father," Arun said. "He built this place. It was his vision." He let his fingers glide over the ancient spines. "He was born in Germany but came to India as a boy to escape the Second World War. Since he was raised during the war, he was always shocked by peace. What was it Milton said in *Paradise Lost*? 'We accept what we see and are not horrified by it.'

"His childhood was a bombed out and frozen Europe with murderous Gestapo soldiers; his manhood was populated by friendly honest farmers of warm, sleepy south India. He spent years crossing Sikkim, in monasteries in Kashmir, and wandering with the Kabir devotees. But when he came to the south, the rolling hills of coffee in Chikmagalur and Coorg, and Kerala's crystal coast—he was home. He loved it here. 'India is where the human spirit flowered,' he would say. But from the start, he was overwhelmed by how quickly humanity was crowding out the other living things of the world. He created this sanctuary and two others. 'A thousand heartbeats are safe tonight'—that's what he'd say."

Isha found it pleasant to listen to Arun speak.

"He spent the last part of his life out in these spaces, a barbet on his shoulder, bent over pruning plants, walking trails. He was an iconoclast, a radical, a believer in the inherent rights of rivers and the sanctity of all forms of life. He loved every little thing in this world. Messengers and promises, he called them. I think he was quoting an essay by Berger..." Arun drifted into silence until a birdcall shook him from the reverie, and he turned to Isha with a small smile. "Anyway. He died three years ago."

Isha looked away.

"But I think he caught the last of old India, when the Brits were still here, just as they were cutting up our last big forest areas. You know he saw five wild tigers in his life?"

"How many have you seen?"

"Only one." He smiled. Isha smiled too—one eye narrower than the other, her tongue poking out from between her teeth.

Her eyes moved over the many ancient items in the room. Arun watched her, producing various artifacts to stoke her wonder: a crystal, a feather, an elephant's tooth. The tooth was so large that Arun had to lift it with both hands, and Isha could only appreciate it on the table, for she could not lift the heavy solid mass of roots and ridged enamel. *How could any animal be so large for such a thing to fit in its mouth?* Her slender fingers played across the giant's tooth, a sense of weightless wonder. She could sense an inner heartbeat in the objects she found, a murmuring from the old letters on the walls.

Old India—the mahout marches, the shikari hunters. She had always imagined what it would be like to see a wild elephant. The wall of books caught her like a tide and pulled her across the room. She stood before them, mouth agape. There were field guides and biographies and dusty classics. It occurred to her that many of them were the ones Arun had grown up reading, bricks in the foundation of the man before her.

When Arun came to the door holding two cups of tea, Isha realized she'd been so lost in the books and photos that she had not realized he left. She followed his head's beckon, and on the veranda he handed her a piping steel cup of tea.

"Is it okay?" he asked. "Usually the maid would have prepared it but..."

"It's wonderful," Isha managed between slurps. She held the cup by the rim so as not to scald her fingers.

Arun was clearly not a man accustomed to company, or, Isha thought, one that should be living without parental supervision. Something was off about him, she was sure of it—but it wasn't something threatening. He was, she was also certain, doing his best to be hospitable. After tea he collected a towel and soap and whatever clothes might fit her. The clothes she'd been wearing were all "threads and shreds."

"Would you like to have bath?"

She shook her head. Arun shrugged with the almost-dumb indifference that only a boy could have. He found her answer curious but of no importance to him personally. Isha had never vetoed a bath before, and it made her think of Ajji. A bath untaken was enough to unravel the poor woman.

The electricity at the remote house came only when it pleased, and so Arun made dinner by lantern light, while Isha sat on the counter, asking him questions and swinging her feet. He chopped onions and ground garlic, filled the pressure cooker with rice, and warmed *parotas*. When the meal was almost prepared, Isha went out to spend some time with Kala. The tiger was incensed at having been tied up. In the new surroundings, she was nervous of threats and eager to explore. Isha brought Kala what milk they had in the house and fed her in the yard. Once Isha untied her, the tiger spared no time on affection, but padded off into the bush and was gone. Isha called after her, only slightly concerned for what she might get up to.

She and Arun ate their supper with their hands on the front porch. He watched as Isha ate like a starving animal, filling her mouth with great piles of dahl and rice and then gasping for air as she chewed. For a long time after they finished, they sat in silence with their own thoughts. A peacock called from somewhere in the sanctuary. As the food metabolized and Isha's brain began to thaw, she realized that she had a million questions for Arun. They rose inside her like lemon soda fizz, so crowded and numerous she could barely choose one.

Arun smiled as she fired them at him, and at length attempted to slip in some questions of his own. He was careful though, to keep the focus light—books, movies, wild animal sightings. Isha told him tales of teachers and fights in school and the trouble she'd had—proud war stories now long in the past. He gathered that she was bright but unsuited for the conformity required to survive the Indian public school system.

"Have you ever heard what C. S. Lewis said about education? He said that the purpose of a teacher is 'not to cut down jungles, but to irrigate deserts.'"

Isha thought for some time and made him repeat it several more. A smile spread across her face.

Working with orphans, some of whom had been psychologically and physically wounded by the world, had taught Arun that the best medicine to lift the weight off a young mind was simple distraction. He once made a boy who had just lost his parents laugh by spinning coins and teaching the boy to do the same. So he held back his own questions of family, future, hardships, and disbelief. It was a decision he congratulated himself on when Isha's narrative eventually came to her parents. For the first time, he saw uncertainty in her. Unknown clouds darkened her eyes.

The lights flickered on. The change allowed Arun to steer the conversation in other directions. Sickle-eyed geckos appeared on the ceiling, crawling inverted toward the glowing bulbs where moths were already collecting. Isha and Arun watched. She narrated the hunting lizards with so much glee. Arun watched her as she pointed.

"Oh look! There he goes!" She watched the geckos hunt like it was a cricket match between India and Australia (though she couldn't decide whether to root for the insects or the lizards). Arun also noticed that every thirty minutes or so, two green eyes would show briefly in the darkness beyond the porch. The tiger was out there, orbiting like some striped planet drifting quietly past.

A mosquito landed on Isha's hand and she brushed it aside carefully, without harm. Arun paused mid-gesture, incredulous.

"You don't kill mosquitoes?"

"Of course not!" Isha said, her eyes wide. "The poor things just want to have dinner and everything on earth hates them for it."

Arun nodded sarcastically. "You're absolutely right."

"So you agree with me?"

"No, no I don't. You are mad. Mosquitoes spread disease."

"I'm not mad—everyone else is. Mosquitoes thin populations, balance ecosystems. They also feed frogs and salamanders at the larvae stage."

"How old are you again?"

"Fifteen." She yawned.

"I can prepare a bed," Arun said, beginning to gather plates.

"No. I have to sleep out with Kala."

Arun seemed unsure. "I can't let you do that—I mean, you need rest."

"You have to remember, she thinks of me as her mother. She's never spent a night alone. Look, anyone else would never have knocked out a goatherd. They wouldn't have helped me—they would have just called my amma or something. I'm depending on you to make the *wrong* decisions. Which in this *ulta* case are the right ones. Do you understand?" Isha finished and immediately realized she'd never spoken so directly to an adult.

Arun grinned.

He found himself gathering the heaviest blankets and a pillow, which he dumped into Isha's arms. He fitted a headlamp onto her head, which slipped down over her eyes. She wobbled out into the night. He thought to ask to help her set up camp but knew by now not to. He remained there on the porch, and later in the study. He found himself recalling the vision of her from that afternoon, silhouette in the sunlight, beside the tiger. Speaking with her arms, skipping, grasping at leaves. Deeper within the room, when the night had come, he distractedly turned pages in his father's old annotated copy of *Joan of Arc*. He flipped through Twain's pages, searching for a passage he could not quite recall but suddenly needed each word of.

He slept half the night with the book fallen open to his chest. *She was a rock of convictions in a time when men believed in nothing... unfailingly true to an age that was false to the core.*

Kala's eyes were wide and full of light. The sanctuary was the wildest place she had seen. The bushes were thick with exciting scents, the tracks of mongoose and civet, the air rife with the calls of birds and the musk of snakes. Years of protection had allowed the vegetation to grow in dense, and creatures from near and far had come to the sanctuary and made it dense with life. Kala trotted along, eager for something to hunt, her eyes opened wide. Sniffing led her to a place where the wet on a tree gave off the heavy musk of leopard. A female. She was young, maybe as young as Kala, and had been in the area recently, perhaps that very day. Kala knew this without truly knowing what a leopard was, since she had never seen one. She bristled all the same and headed out to learn more.

Later Kala found Isha wandering drowsily and singing her name: "Kalaaaaa." The tiger trotted up to the girl, full of new excitement. She had explored on her own, she had followed strange creatures, she had learned new things. The tiger lifted her head and closed her eyes so the girl could put an arm under her wide white chin and kiss her broad nose. Isha rubbed the tiger's ears lovingly. Moments later they were a mound of blanket and stripes and tangled leafy hair, snoring softly together beneath the stars. It was the first time in their journey together that they enjoyed a respite from danger.

Isha woke before sunrise when the nightjars were still whistling and the bats were fluttering in the darkness. She snuggled into Kala's coat and bit her gently. When she woke again, she was cold and the tiger was gone. Isha made her way to the porch where Arun was waiting, a cup of steaming tea with a metal lid placed over it to hold the heat. There they drank tea together, letting the sun warm away the chill of the night as they slowly thawed to wakefulness.

At first they were silent, watching the birds and sipping. Isha absently pulled leaves from her hair. But as her awareness came back to the world and her mind hastened, the banter began. They argued, debated, competed to name birds, and each came to marvel at the flow and familiarity of their strange nascent friendship.

After their morning porch time, Arun returned to the kitchen to clean the steel teacups and vessels. While he was busy she crept into the washroom and filled a bucket. She lathered soap and bathed for the first time in weeks, trying to pour the water over her head in a way that it would not splash on the tile. She didn't want him to know she was bathing, though she was unsure of why. The towel was filthy after she finished, but she was too cold for it to worry her. Her bare feet left little muddy-wet footprints on the red oxide floor when she ran back out to the patio and began warming herself like a lizard in the sun.

"Hey, I'm going into town. Do you need anything from the shop?" Arun asked, handing her dosa on a plate.

"Yes please! A toothbrush. And some paste. And chakli."

"Are you saying that you haven't brushed for over five weeks?"

Isha grinned and tongued her plaque-rough teeth, which pulled the old scar below her eyebrow and made her eyes crazy. "Nope."

"Ugh!" Arun shook off his disgust and made for the door. He noted her dripping hair and clean face. "I see you had a bath though—very good. You look all new!"

Isha made a face. "Oh, also…"

"Yes?"

"I need girl stuff. Erm… pads, you know?"

"I can do that. You want to join to town?"

She told him that she couldn't leave Kala and wanted to spend the time writing some letters home. She agreed to ride with him as far as the property gate. On the way, Arun gave her a tour of the property. He promised to pick up a pile of pears and apples and other fruit. She was dying for fruit. They needed meat and milk for Kala and fresh vegetables for the house.

Isha exited the Mahindra jeep at the gate and went in search of Kala. Arun drove on for town. He had noticed the way she calmed in the seat of a car; her rapid-fire talking ceased. She enjoyed riding, looking out the window, listening as he pointed out birds' nests, rock formations, or remarkable trees. In the days that followed, he made a point of taking her for a drive each day. He instinctually believed it was a kind of relaxation needed for unknown burdens.

On the second day they drove, Arun sighted Kala out in the middle distance.

"Look there!"

Isha folded her legs under to gain more height in the seat. The tiger had no idea she was being watched. She was absorbed in stalking a peacock that was plucking pebbles and ants off the ground. The tiger dropped to her stomach, her eyes fixated on her target. Isha and Arun exchanged a smile. Kala inched closer. The peacock didn't know. Only the tiger's eyes were visible. Her stripes melted with the rest of her into the yellow grass. For tense moments, they waited.

Then suddenly Kala exploded out of the grass. The peacock spread its brilliant tail with many eyes and intricate decorations, and in an instant became many times larger than it had looked moments earlier. Kala skidded on her hind paws and her ears went back. She leapt about-face and ran, the peacock cackling. The fantastic bird folded its sweeping tail and took cerulean wing, like a dragon, pursuing the tiger and then flying up into the naked branches of a tree.

Soon after, Isha grew curious of the old car. Appa's back home was an automatic. She had seen people shift but never understood it fully.

"Why do you have to do that?" she asked, watching Arun's hand work the gears.

"What, this?" He shifted to neutral. "Give me your hand." He placed her right hand on the gearshift with his larger left hand cupped over top. "One," he said, pushing the clutch and moving the shift. He went slowly over the unmade road. He drove for some time, then said, "Two," and guided her hand to the position while holding the clutch with his foot. After some time, he pushed the clutch again, moving her hand and the gearstick forward. "Three."

Isha grinned as she heard the engine change to the speed.

"Okay, now get ready to bring us back down to two when I say so, okay?" He lifted his hand so she was on her own and pressed the break. "Now!" Isha moved the shift down, left, down. Arun accelerated slightly. "Very good!" Isha was exuberant and clapped in excitement.

"Three," he shouted over the motor and crunch of tires on gravel. This time Isha missed the position and the car screeched and shuddered to a stop. She looked at him, wincing.

"I'm so sorry!"

"That's okay," he said. "It happens to everyone."

Each day for a week, their afternoon drives went in this way. Arun meandered up and down small roads and around the border, pointing out birds, searching for the tiger. They drove through the sanctuary, at times speaking out the numbers, at others just shifting in silence.

Arun at first had assumed she was the result of a broken home, perhaps even abuse. What else could spark such an extreme reaction? A girl with a dangerous will. But within moments of arriving on the mountain, after talking to her at length, he had realized that his initial assessment was wrong. No, she had parents that she loved and who loved her. It was clear from her stories. And so it pained him to imagine what they might be going through. Despite her heroic qualities, she was still a child, and it was not impossible that she was ignorant to the suffocating anguish her parents, who-ever they were, must be enduring. He could not yet fathom what he would later conclude—that the windswept plains of a denuded landscape, the howling sound of the nothing that continued to spread, were in fact the winds that stoked her radicalism.

He was explicit on one thing: their time at the sanctuary was limited to whatever time it took Isha to regain strength. If they stayed, he explained, it was inevitable that they would be discov-ered. He could only keep the staff away for so long. Villagers let cows and goats occasionally graze on the fringes of the sanctuary. Sooner or later a farmer would notice and then the whole village, Forest Department, police department, and God knew who else would come. If Kala was seen, or worse, if she killed an animal, it would inevitably spiral into some tragic reiteration of what had be-fallen Kala's mother.

And so he waited with hurried patience while Isha ate, slept, and rested. Already, after only days, she was calmer than she had been. When he met her in the village with the bear, she had seemed like a refugee, starving and dazed. That hunted look in her eyes. But warm tea, food, friendship, and nights of sleep free of worry were quick medicine. She herself brought up questions of what the next step would be. It was a topic that he knew caused worry with-in her, but their developing bond brought with it a resurgence of hope and trust where Isha had given up.

It was easy to imagine their future adventures since they al-ready had a week and a half of histories. Isha would still glow each time she recalled the shepherd's broken nose and how Arun had *rescued* her. When walking the trails or waiting for water to boil, their conversation often returned to the serendipitous meeting and the adventures they had already shared. These legends were the first chapters of their story together. When he prayed at night, he became increasingly convinced that divine intent had brought them together.

There was one day in the middle of the week when Arun had not been able to purchase a goat, which left Kala eager to sniff out some supper from the sanctuary brush. It was dusk now, and the fresh leopard spore she had discovered excited Kala. She followed it for a time until the lights of the house grew far. The tiger turned and trotted back, approaching the house silently. It was quiet. She crouched low and bobbed her head, sniffing. She could smell the man and the girl. She observed them from a distance, noting that Isha was sleeping on the man's shoulder.

Earlier, Arun had removed a floppy book from the shelf on a hunch and come to sit beside Isha on the porch.

"I think you'll like this," he said, placing the book like something sacred in her lap. She observed the artwork of the cover. A cartoon tiger was poised in the air above a small cartoon boy in striped shirt.

"What is this?"

"It's *Calvin and Hobbes*. It's about a boy and his stuffed tiger—who is his imaginary friend—and their adventures. It's wonderful and true. It's comedy, therapy, and the best part of being young, all in one. You won't believe what these two get up to."

They each held one of the large covers. He had allowed her enough time to turn the pages herself and to become accustomed to the artwork. Some stories were a page, others several. Most of them were outside, where the boy and his tiger would build snowmen, or follow snakes, or clash with the neighborhood girl. Arun turned to his favorite pages. Soon she was laughing. Gradually she was shaking her head in disbelief.

"These ones where he is in school..."

"Yes?"

"It's like they are *me* in school! He hates it! It's delightful!"

"I thought you might like this—I always have. It used to be a favorite for me and my..." Isha looked up when he stopped. He avoided her eyes. "It was a childhood favorite."

She returned to the pages. "It's a wonderful book."

"Yes. And isn't it funny that I'm reading a comic *about* a boy and his tiger to a girl who *has* a tiger? I don't think that has ever happened before, anywhere."

Isha grinned. It was the devilish grin that signified delight and made her right eye narrower, her tongue pressed against her upper right canine.

And so they sat. Isha read the lines of Calvin aloud while Arun covered Hobbes and any other characters. Isha especially liked the one where Calvin made a village of miniature snowmen and then planned to sled down through the village and destroy it like a monster. Arun's favorites were the ones where the boy and his tiger followed a black snake in wonder, or rode their wagon through the woods, or stood beside a tree stump grieving. Sometimes they were quiet. Reading and watching the illustrations, Watterson's pen on the page, black-and-white truth—childhood and philosophy. When it began growing dark, Arun bent his head to check. Isha was sleeping.

A soft brushing brought Arun's eyes toward the darkness beyond the porch. From the blackness beyond burst orange and white. Kala stood in the doorway, taking in the porch. She padded soundlessly through the entrance and up to him. He raised his eyes from his book and did not move. The tiger uttered a shuddering chuff, drew up to his face and sniffed. Arun was a marble statue. Up close the tiger was far larger than he had realized. The tiger turned her head to the side and sniffed down his shoulder and onto Isha's messy head. Then the tiger advanced further, placing a heavy paw on Arun's stomach and leaning in to sniff his other side.

Isha woke and looked up in surprise. "Come here-ma," she said drowsily to the tiger, who pulled back. She would not lie with them both.

Kala busied herself in another part of the patio, sniffing and searching. This gave Arun time to rise and spread a mat on the ground for Isha to collapse onto. He covered her with a blanket and tucked it in around her, her eyes never opening. Kala advanced and Arun backed away through the door as the tiger dropped down and snuggled in against the girl. Arun watched from inside the house for some time. The tiger's great chest rising and falling, Isha's frail frame barely visible beneath the blanket, her little brown arm across the tiger's neck the only proof she was even there.

"I did some reading while I was in town the other day," he told her the next morning. "A tiger won't survive without its mother."

"I know."

"I know you know, now listen." Isha grinned. "If Kala is going to survive wild, it has to be somewhere that she can be left alone and has plenty of food, but also where she can be monitored, protected, and safe."

"The jungle."

"Exactly. Protected jungle—a national park or something. But Isha, these parks are not easy places to penetrate. There are a billion people in India and the Forest Department knows it. They are very strict about keeping people out. And then on the inside, you have tribals."

Arun gave her time to think about what he'd said before telling her his idea. "I have some friends who live in the jungle, you know, mahouts."

"Like the ones who ride elephants?"

"Exactly."

In her excitement, Isha had a torrent of ten thousand questions swell in her throat. They flowed out her mouth uninhibited, no periods or commas: "Wait, wait, wait! How would an elephant help? Would they bring their elephant? Can anyone ride an elephant, or can I learn how? I think Kala will almost certainly be terrified of an elephant, and come to think of it the elephant will almost certainly—"

"*Swalpa chill maadi*, yah? Please choose *a* question," Arun said patiently.

"Okay, but this is not my official question. Are you telling me that you know people that *own* elephants?"

"I am."

"I don't believe that."

"*You* don't believe that people can live with and work with a wild animal?"

"Well I..."

"What is your 'official' question?"

Isha gulped and blinked and focused on finding the most important question. "Okay, so given this idea—and I have a *lot* of questions—but if we do it with the elephant and all and it works—where are we actually going?"

"I was hoping you'd ask," he said with a flourish, and produced a map. "You see that green patch there—between those mountains? That is the Periamangalam range." His finger slashed down the map, over a vast green swath of lines and space where roads and towns were absent. "It's monstrous. There are elephants, tigers, bison, and so many deer that your tiger could become obese if she isn't careful."

Isha laughed. She knelt on a chair with her elbows on the table. Arun was sitting on the table itself, guiding her across the map—their future—with his finger. As he spoke of hope and giant trees and jungle, Isha felt the stress and worry of the plains melt away. The empty caves, the hyenas, the desolation, the lack of a plan—the first part of her journey with Kala had not been easy, and certainly not what she had imagined. But now she saw in the strange lines and gridded spaces the adventure she had *hoped* to be on when she fled with Kala. An adventure with purpose, and one with some warmth and company to it. Most importantly, she thought, looking up at Arun, the jungle really was out there!

Isha looked tormented from anticipation as Arun went on.

"Here's us, and here is the jungle. It's actually not that far. But the one thing is *getting* there. You see the ridges on this?" His finger moved over the map. "This is a topographic map. So like any map you have north, south, east, west." He traced his hands over the compass points. "The ridges you see over the landscape indicate the texture of the land. Where they are wide apart, the land is flat; the closer they come, the steeper the terrain is. Look here, where the lines are very close—this is the side of a mountain. The land here is almost vertical, assuming this is accurate."

Isha watched intently. "I still don't understand."

Arun searched around the room for some aid. Finally, he found it in a piece of lined paper. He folded the paper, some large folds and some small folds, and held it on the table so that Isha could look down on it. The lines appeared widest on the flat parts, and where the paper rose, the perspective stacked them, so they appeared close together. They spent some time making paper landscapes and testing the line theory. She was devoted to understanding the concept, and Arun realized he was unsure how many adults could properly follow topographic detail.

"I think I have it," Isha said after some time, returning to the map and searching it. She pointed to a place where the lines were wide. "So this is flat?"

"Exactly!"

"And this is a mountain?" The lines were densely stacked like ripples in water.

"Yes! Very good."

Isha's eyes reflected a gratifying twinkle as the truth of the map came into focus. The Periamangalam forest was surrounded by a range of steep mountains, the bulk of the forest contained in a single valley. The back of it was like a half a bowl, sharp peaks rising up. Arun explained that those peaks scraped the clouds, catching them, and forcing them to shed their rain into the valley below, creating a legion of rivers and tributaries and a vast jungle below. There it was, on the paper, in dull beige and white, the texture of the challenging landscape.

Arun spoke in muted excitement. "The way I see it, we bring in a mahout to help us with the tribals. But we are going to need someone to get us over the mountains so we can come in the backside of the forest. My father's friend owns a coffee estate here," he said, pointing near the foot of closest mountain to the sanctuary, "and he can be trusted. Once we are over the mountains and inside, Kala will be as safe as she can be. At least it is a place where tigers belong. Then we can start getting some real work done. Get some support, protection, teach her to hunt." He held Isha's eyes with his own. "You do realize that at some point we are going to need help, don't you?"

"Yes, but isn't getting to the jungle the first step? I mean, it's hard for me to imagine all that now." Her eyes were wide as she scanned the map. She had the presence of mind to know she had no concept of what new difficulties might arise within the forest.

"Okay."

They spent the afternoon packing and preparing. Arun phoned his father's friend Ramana Gowda, as well as the Periamangalam Forest Department office and asked a friend to deliver a message. Then he laid out all his gear. As they packed, he helped Isha gather and sort the supplies: a powerful headlamp, batteries, water bottle, kukri knife, a tent, a hundred meters of cord. Clothing, matches, lighter, and medical supplies. He packed food.

Isha followed his instruction like a trained soldier. They swapped trail stories. She told him how fire had saved her from hyenas. He asked why she had been carrying gasoline, and she revealed she did not know how to build a fire. They passed the afternoon among the books and fossils, with warm tea and maps and the distant peacock's call.

It was growing dark out when the lights flickered on. The geckos were already drawing to position, ready for the feast of insects that would come. A gentle *hiss* grew in volume. Cool air rushed in and brought to Isha a smell she had not realized she missed so dearly.

"It's raining!" she told Arun and sprinted out into the dusk. She found Kala watching the sky and twitching as the drops hit her nose and whiskers. "It's rain! You've never seen rain!" she said to the tiger, grabbing Kala's large face.

The rain gathered and grew until it was a steady shower. Kala blinked and flinched as water from the sky hit her for the first time in her life. Isha raised her face to let the cool sting embrace her. Then she ran, and Kala fallowed. The girl and the tiger ran out through the field in the starry twilight. The tiger chased her, massive paws splashing in the suddenly saturated earth, powerful striped shoulders trembling with muscle. Beneath the lone lightpost that stood by the drive, the rain splashed and steam rose from the cooled earth.

Isha turned, soaking, and kicked a splash onto Kala, who flinched and shook and lunged for her. The tiger overwhelmed her and the two wrestled and rolled in the rain. When they stood, the girl and the tiger sprinted, bounding together through the night.

14

THE HUNTER

Isha and Arun set out as the sun fell. Kala stalked beside them, her shoulder blades gliding and slicing under black stripes. For two weeks, Arun had dutifully delivered goats and chickens to the tiger. Kala had watched him from the foliage as he laid the bodies on the ground, searching nervously but never seeing her. When she ate, she could smell his scent on the fur and feathers. She had gradually decided his was a presence she could tolerate, though only at a reasonable distance. She kept Isha between them. And so the three went.

At length, Isha's fingers began to grow stiff from the cold. "Hey, I need to get something warm, I'm freezing. And it's time to feed Kala." Isha dropped her pack and opened it. Arun had provided clothing, chappals, a sweater, toothbrush, and even a sack to replace her filthy satchel. She had spread it out on her bed and stood with her hands on her hips. When she had packed to go on a vacation to Goa, or when she visited her grandparents, Amma had been very strict about folding clothes. She liked them folded perfectly, in fact. But when Isha asked Arun as he sped about the house gathering gear, he told her to pack it however she liked. She spent a great deal of time deliberating the merits of folding.

"Do you *want* to fold everything?" he had asked in a way only a boy could.

"Well, no actually…"

In the end he had come and sat and watched as she packed. He said that there were *folders* and *stuffers* in the world, and that she had better not be a *folder*.

"Why spend so much time folding it up when it's just going to get crushed and wrinkly on its own? We are going to the jungle, not a ball. Just stuff it all in!" This had earned him another one of Isha's special smiles.

He showed her how to fill plastic bags with different types of things. "You have one bag for socks and underwear. One bag for pants and shirts. And one bag for your toothbrush and all that other random stuff. And it's all in different bags so it won't even get wet if it rains. Got it?"

Isha found the blue plastic bag that had her sweater in it. She was already shivering. It was colder here by the coffee hills. The lush green vegetation sent chilled mist into the air.

"Who are we meeting here again?" she asked, somewhat fatigued.

"An old friend. A hunter, actually."

"A hunter?" Isha opened a milk packet and drained it into a large baby bottle that Arun had also bought. Her tongue stuck out as she tried to do it without spilling. Kala flopped into her lap and began nursing at the rubber nipple.

"Yes. He was a close friend of my father's. A few years ago, after my father died and I wasn't doing very well, he took care of me. But listen, as we go into this, from the outset, try to give him the impression that you eat nails."

"What?"

"Just use your eyes on him. He's an old bear—you've got to stare him down."

Kala, finished with the bottle, chuffed ahead of them, eager for distance. For some time they walked in silence. Over the course of the night they talked little, walking carefully instead of quickly.

By midnight they reached the edge of the plantation where a long wire fence clicked with electrical snaps. "Keep out" signs hung intermittently. The sleeping green hills were mossy in the moonlight. Kala's nose rose to meet the thick sweet smell of the coffee flowers that filled the night air. The spore of flying squirrels and civets and wild boar were everywhere. Small creatures ruled the man-made forest. It was not diverse, only a few species, but it was thick and vast and had many places to hide. The tiger stayed close to the girl and the man as they walked down the lonely dirt roads, vegetation rising high above them. Trees appeared ahead and vanished behind in the slow progress of the torch beam.

"You never told me about the boy who owns the elephant."

"Ah yes. He's an orphan from a relocated tribal village. I helped him get his elephant back when it was confiscated."

"Wait. I have so many questions," Isha began, but Arun hushed her. She could tell from his eyes he was lost. They stood for some time consulting the map. The quiet roads led to quieter roads that ran labyrinth through the hills. On one junction a dog found them and began barking. Other dogs in the distance began baying. Isha's heart rocketed. *Oh Deva! Oh Krishna! Shut up!* Arun threw a stone. But the dog just kept barking. Kala was scared and retreated a distance away. Isha's mind was racing as she imagined all of the dogs swarming in, the villagers waking... All of it could end.

She removed the slingshot from her pack, knelt and found a stone. She fit a rock into it as Arun shined the flashlight beam into the dog's eyes. She pulled the band back as far as she could, took aim, and hit the dog square in the nose. It yelped and ran off. For a long moment they stood and listened, then hurried on.

But after two more trying hours, Isha's feet were dragging and she began to trip often. There were so many nameless dirt roads through the tunneling deep vegetation that Arun finally threw up his hands. "There is no way to know where the hell these roads lead. We need light, need morning. I'll make a fire, you can get some sleep if you like. It's going to feel cold here once we stop moving—the air is full of water."

Isha unpacked the pot and water while Arun collected sticks for a fire. He demonstrated how to split them, then ran his knife along the open centers of the shafts, pushing off fairy-light curls of dry fiber, the small kindling required to catch the flame and light the larger pieces. As he worked, his eyes mirrored the small flame until it grew crackling and flashing on the vegetation around them. Kala took to the shadows. Arun wrapped a blanket around Isha's shoulders.

"Warm yourself by the fire. The morning will come soon." He dragged up a log. They spoke softly for nearly an hour, until Isha's eyes could hardly stay open and she lay down.

At the snap of a twig, Isha sat up on an elbow but didn't dare move further.

"Neither of you two fucking move," growled a voice from the darkness.

At the limit of the firelight, behind Arun, was the shape of a man. Shining before him stretched the long polished barrel of a rifle. His eyes were ovals of flame, his spectacles throwing back the image of the fire above his flared white mustache. The barrels of the gun were pointed to the ground in front of him, ready but not aimed. Bent knees kept him low.

"What the fuck are you doing on my plantation?" he said, scanning the darkness as if he believed that at any moment a monster could emerge. He was trembling. Isha locked onto his eyes, holding them with almost vicious intensity.

Arun's arms went up. Isha found his eyes waiting for hers. He shrugged his upheld arms, signaling her to do the same. She rose to sit on her ankles and folded her hands in her lap. It was a polite rebellion.

With arms in the air, Arun rotated slowly so that he could see behind him. "It's me, Uncle. It's us."

"I know it's you, you jackass! What are you doing out here?"

His eyes were visible now, searching left and right, up and down. "My question was what are you doing way out here on my plantation."

Arun stood carefully. He was smiling now, expecting the charade to end and for an embrace to commence. But there was no recognition in the hunter. His beady eyes were fully open, aghast, searching, perplexed. He wore a Nehru cap, a vest, and leather boots. The tremendous rifle was gripped between thick white-forested Popeye forearms. Arun's smile faded as concern clouded over his face.

The hunter entered the sphere of light, heavy boots bringing him beside the fire, where he dropped to one knee. Old leather, or perhaps his joints, creaked when he moved, and he panted like an old bulldog, resting the butt of the gun against the ground to steady himself. His forearms and cheeks were sunburned, crimson in the firelight. Even against the fire smell, the musk of tobacco and dried sweat saturated the space around him. He wore a white mustache that fell from the corners of his lips and rode up his jaws to his ears where a bandana covered his bald head. His chin was bare. Out the side of his spectacles he regarded Isha and grunted as if he was not sure what kind of bird she was.

Arun returned to sit on his log. "Are you okay, Uncle? You look like you've seen a ghost."

"I think I have," he whispered, searching the darkness. The hunter's unkempt eyebrows wove together, expressions bubbling up onto his face and pulling its parts in different ways as his mind raced. His lower lip was trembling below the thick brush of white mustache. Through the spectacles, his eyes penetrated a thousand miles into the fire. Arun's hand came to his shoulder, but the hunter startled violently.

"There's a point when you reach my age," the hunter was panting slightly, "that you start to realize its drawing close, you know? You know that you only have so much left." He leapt up suddenly, rifle pointed toward the darkness.

"The tiger won't hurt you," Arun said calmly. He lifted a stick into the fire.

The hunter's barrel went vertical with a military snap. He rested the heavy barrel on his shoulder and turned, his eyes locked onto Arun's, who kept his hidden and lost in the fire. The hunter gripped Arun's hood the way you hold the scruff of a puppy. "How the hell did you know?"

This new man's nerves were ragged. "I found tracks. Not leopard. *How could a leopard be so massive?* My father shot the last tiger here over fifty years ago. I was certain I was losing it. I was certain of it! I know the difference between a leopard's and a tiger's paw. Okay? I know it. But I thought maybe over the years... Then I started following them. I wasn't daft. They're real. And fresh. I tell you, they are fresh!"

Arun found Isha's eyes: *You might as well...*

"Her name is Kala," Isha said. The fire popped and sent an exodus of embers flowing upward into the black and leaves above.

The hunter turned from Arun to Isha. She was sitting neatly, hands folded on her lap, an uncompromising, slightly mad light in her eyes. The hunter's chin jutted out from beneath the thick mustache, mouth agape with unformed words.

"I told you I had something I needed help with," Arun said evenly, extending a hand to pat the hunter's leg. "You had better pull up a log, Uncle." Arun rose. "And take a good look at that girl. You are about to hear a story that you are not going to believe."

"Pull up a log? It's almost dawn. I have a plantation to run. I don't have time for a story. Do you know how many *lakhs* we have being harvested this year? There's over twenty thousand dollars' worth of coffee beans on the bricks right now."

There was a chuff from within the foliage. Isha rose and slipped into the night between the leaves.

The hunter leaned in. "Okay, who's the mother?"

"What?" Arun scowled. "She's fifteen. You think I could have knocked someone up when I was fourteen without you knowing it?"

The hunter nodded and exhaled through his nose. "Well you two aren't, erm, together are you?" he said with eyebrows raised.

"Oh fuck off! Look, can we at least stay here? If you have workers and dogs and all its going to be hard. Is there any vana area? You have any groves of real forest, at least Isha can tie up the tiger there and—"

"Arun, can you hear yourself?"

"You saw the tracks!"

The hunter raised a cautionary finger. "Don't fuck with me, Arun. Damn the tracks! *Can you hear yourself?*"

Arun turned over his shoulder and owl-hooted to Isha. There was a scuffling sound and then her answering hoot came from the nearby dark.

"He's not buying it at all. Not a bit." Arun kept his eyes on Gowda, though he spoke to Isha.

"I'll try to get her down the road. I'll be at the stream we passed earlier, just down there. It might take time."

"Got it."

Arun led the hunter onto the main pathway. It was a wide dirt track through the jungle-like plantation. At the seam of the valley, a trickle stream chattered softly. A large old banyan tree hung over the palms and coffee. Its lofty branches were holding down the mist so that the entire forest remained guarded and cold. Arun drew his robes up around him. The two men stood on the red dirt in the dim silence. Gowda pulled out a pack of Gold Flakes, lit two, and handed one to Arun. The hunter checked to see that the girl was out of sight, and then allowed his manner to change.

"Come here," he said tenderly, placing his hands on Arun's shoulders. "You sound insane and it's a strange hour, but your eyes are clearer than I've seen in years. It's like a miracle. Honestly, the tracks are nothing compared to seeing you this..."

Arun motioned for silence.

Isha came from the tunnel of the stream. She emerged shivering from the foliage on frail legs, twigs in her scattered hair. For a long time, nothing happened. She stood there, fists clenched against the cold blue jungle gloom. Then the hunter drew back and grasped Arun's arm.

The tiger slipped through the leaves like flowing magma. She stepped out onto the road with broad paws that compressed the moist earth. In three fluid steps she came up to lovingly nuzzle the girl, the *kajal*-black eyes closing, the lower canines unsheathed beneath the whiskers. The girl took a steadying step against the weight of the beast.

The hunter leaned against Arun, his face a scowl of pure unfiltered awe. "That's a tiger. My God. A tiger."

That morning, for the first time since 1910, the Aaney-Betta Plantation was shut down. Ramana Gowda fired his gun in the air in the courtyard, and then again at the main gate. He sent the cooks and the gardeners home and put his foreman in charge of clearing out the plantation workers. There were protests, arguments, shouting, and ultimately more rounds fired to the sky.

"*Out, out, out!* I want everybody out!" He marched and sang and acted like a madman, saluting them as they left. The jingle changed many times during the hour it took him to get them all moving, but the last of it was always punctuated by a blast of the rifle.

> *March, march, march! Oh gadzooks!*
> *The bastards lost the plot! See how he shoots!*
> *Bum ba bum ba bum— (BOOM!)*

During this procedure, Arun borrowed a thick leather belt and a cattle rope, which Isha used to tie Kala to a tree among thick vegetation. He also set up a hammock, just beside the tiger, in which she fell instantly asleep. They both had been worried about the tiger's reaction when the gunfire started, but it had the best possible effect: she dove for cover in the leaves and did not protest being tied the entire day.

While Isha slept, Arun brought the hunter up to speed on the story. They spent the entirety of the afternoon out on the porch speaking. At 5 p.m., Isha came clumsily to them, blanket and mosquito net crumpled in her arms, leaves in her messy hair. She was drunk-legged with sleep. She sat dazed in the warm glow of the setting sun, slightly enchanted by the beautiful setting. Like most of the old plantation houses, it was built wide, not high, cracked with age and grown over with ivy. The artifacts of generations long gone slept beneath the cobweb curtains and bats that hung from the rafters of the attic. But the rooms that were in use had an old splendor, dim and patient. From the floral veranda, the grassy hill dropped off to a panorama of rolling green hills, with mountains huddled on the horizon.

The hunter lit a cigarette and watched the smoke blaze in the sun. He pondered the creature before him in silence. She was not yet a woman, no, but she was not a child. Which was ponderous for him. The man who had escaped from prison in the Andaman Islands, who could speak seven languages fluently and shoot the nose off a mouse at 500 yards, was at a loss with this strange female creature. He studied the girl, grumbling involuntarily as he did.

"You have monstrous feet!" he said, motioning to the Isha's black-and-red stained soles. It had sounded like a compliment before his tongue's publication.

Isha turned to him, face squinting from the brightness. Indeed for her size, her own feet were long and wide and flattened from weeks of walking. She scanned the hunter for material.

"Well, Uncle, you have tremendous everything. And very fat hands."

He nodded, as if she had correctly answered an exam question.

"So, your plan is to take a two-hundred-pound monster like that to the jungle. Very good. *How?*"

Arun was sat forward, clasped his hands. "That's why we are here old friend. We need help."

"What, load it into a fucking truck and drive it?"

"Oh no," Isha said. "Oh no! Kala will tear you apart if you try to make her do something she doesn't want to do, and she's scared of new and loud noises."

"Ha!" Gowda barked.

Arun held up his hand for peace. He rose and vanished through the doorway and emerged moments later with a long rolled map, which he spread over the table.

"Look. The Periamangalam range is only fifty kilometers from here, and it's all plantations in between. If we move at night, we can make it there in a few days. Then we can make it up here," he traced his hand over the topographic concentric shapes of a large mountain, "and once we are inside, there will certainly be no one."

"What about the tribals?"

"I have that planned for as well. I've called a friend of mine, one of my former children at the orphanage, actually. He's a mahout, speaks their language, knows their ways, and can help with introductions. Tribals will never listen to someone not of their own, so he will be crucial. He'll also know the jungle. We'll need him." Arun ran a hand through his hair. "With all the politics with tigers, I'm sure the tribes won't be thrilled."

"Exactly, this is India—there are people living everywhere. Even in the little jungle that is left. What do we say to these people? *Oh, hello! You don't know us, but we are here to deliver a killing machine to your backyard. Have a great day!*"

Isha laughed at his maniacal theatrics. Gowda gave her a covert wink and a slight bow.

"I've told you what she's been through," Arun said.

"Okay! Okay!" Ramana Gowda spoke from under furrowed eyebrows. "So once we are inside the jungle, we stage a re-wilding effort. Is that it?" He looked to Isha who nodded. "Does she hunt? A tiger not taught by its mother will die in the wild."

"She's been killing small things, birds and lizards. I've been giving her mutton."

Arun looked to Isha and then up to Gowda. "So what do you think?"

Gowda rose to his feet and strode across the room, his head shaking. "What can I do? A washed-up old man rotting on his plantation?"

"You know how to survive in the jungle, you are a hunter, a marksman. What we are planning—what we must do to succeed— is dangerous. If the villagers find us, if the tribals are unfriendly, who else could keep us safe? I'm not asking you to train a tiger, I'm just asking you to lead an expedition."

Ramana Gowda growled and paced the room, lost in thought. For some time Isha and Arun watched him in silence. Then his pace quickened, he slapped his leg and laughed, and then clutched his forehead and clawed air in front of him. He was searching the room for something to aid him, a man who spoke with his hands, a conductor in need of a baton. He lifted a fire iron.

"No one has seen a tiger in these parts for a generation. In these hills, all the lads I grew up with are now living on their daddy's farms with an old tiger pelt rolled up in the attic. But it was all in the old days. I'll tell you this—it was a lot more exciting here in the old days. When the elephants would come and we'd go out to chase them off the crops. When the tigers would start calling to each other in the night and all the children would gather in tight. Those were the days, and they're gone. The hills have been silent for far too long. We all wanted to win, we all wanted our crops and babies to be safe. And now what we've done... But this! This is like the old days! When it was all or nothing!

"You, kid," he aimed a thick finger at Isha, "if half of what he's saying is true—if you've really done what he says you have, seen what you have... Then you must be something special. But I still can't work out if you know how much trouble you are in! First off, you think your friend there won't eat you? Once she's grown? Sure, in the early days it's all trust and love and stupidity. Then they grow up, the wild sets in, their eyes drop, and they become killers. Do you know she is going to be double that size in a year? You are tough, but the toughest sparrow can't kill a lion."

"Tiger, in this case," Isha said.

Gowda glared at Arun and turned back to Isha. "I know where you're from. You're from the big city. Maybe you spent some time in the country, and surely what you've done is brave. But do you have a time machine? Do you realize that where you are talking of going there are no roads? There are no cell phones, no televisions. You are going back a few hundred years when you go into such a place. And when you do, the rules change. Do you understand what I'm saying? Those tribals, they still climb trees—steal from bees, raid honey to survive. That tiger could get ripped apart by a bison, or a tusker. Or the worst—a male tiger! Hell, what's her name— Kala—she's three times your size!" The war drums were beating in him. He was boiling over.

"Okay, that's enough!" Arun came up beside him with a glass of golden liquid. "So you're with us?"

The hunter stood panting. Arun lifted the glass up before his nose, so that the biting smell of whiskey hit his nostrils. The hunter's nostrils twitched.

"In or out?" Arun asked, poised to complete the toast. Gowda looked to Isha and then begged them both to wait as he hurried across the room. He withdrew a slender bottle from the cupboard labeled *Crème de Violette* and poured half a finger of the faintly purple liquid into a dessert glass, which he handed to Isha.

"She's fifteen, by the way."

"I can see that for myself, can't I?" the hunter scoffed. "But even if she is just a *pukka kiddu*, you can't leave the leader off the toast for her own expedition!" He bent in with a tender, deep voice to Isha. "It's made from flowers, and isn't that what little birds drink?" He gave her a wink as she accepted the glass and grinned. He straightened up, held out his whiskey. Arun and Isha drew in.

"To the jungle!" The glasses clinked and then tilted back and were empty.

"Now let's get outdoors and find some proper seating. We need to discuss how we're going to get that tiger and little Mowgli here to the jungle."

"Don't call me that." Isha scowled.

"I'm not calling you a boy if that's your issue…"

"Mowgli was a tiger killer. Killing a tiger doesn't make you brave, raising one does. I'm on a whole other level, you see?" She smiled wickedly and inspected her second and final helping of the flowery purple beverage. She contemplated how best to make it last.

The old hunter barked out laughing. "What a brave little homunculus you are! But as long as you're consorting with furry, toothy things, and your hair is that wild, you're going to get that a lot! Have you even ever read *The Jungle Book*?" Isha glared at him, brimming with retort, but Arun put a hand in the air for a cease-fire.

They sat in the sweet humming twilight. Glasses were placed and poured. Gowda paced and spoke and smoked. Arun pulled up a chair and turned it round so his chest was against its back. The men kept on with the whiskey. Isha watched cautiously as they spoke of tusks and claws and bullets and timber. It seemed that the topic of how to transport a tiger required a vigorous recounting of the vast history of wild India. Arun's slim, saintly calm looked different below the lantern light, beside the hunter's thick shadow. He lit his own cigarette and leaned in to argue over a map. She spent some time in the cloud of smoke with the two men and finished her *Crème de Violette*. Arun and Gowda went on in an ever-changing mix of English, Kannada, and Malayalam, arguing over approaches, routes, and gear. So they sat on old cane chairs beneath the ivy while geckos snatched insects near the candlelight.

Isha had the distinct feeling that she was slipping, slowly, and had been for some time. Slipping away from the world she'd grown up in, computerized and gagetized and quick. She thought of her father and his earpiece telephone, electric car, his frequent flyer miles, and wondered how she'd gotten so far marched back through the years. The old hunter, his flasks of whiskey, the hanging plants and laterite stone. The servants, the elephant foot stools in his study. The cars in this man's garage were rusted old metal beasts from the Second World War. His guns, (*he had guns!*) had aimed at tigers in the hands of Mysore Maharajas.

The frogs were calling and the lantern lights flickered. The gentle drumbeat, the torchlight flame. Outside in the darkness a tiger prowled against a long rope, and somewhere out there in the hilly distance, a boy was riding an elephant through the night. Isha finished the last of her violette, feeling drowsy and wild. Oceans become deserts, libraries burn, but the ghosts remain like vibrating fossils, still real.

She was awake most of the night. She and Kala descended beneath the house to where the hills slept beneath a blanket of blue mist while the stars faded above. They huddled together, girl and tiger, as the first birds sang in the world's beginning. The old hunter came at dawn and bid Isha tie Kala somewhere safe and then return. When she had done it and come, Gowda knelt and placed a candle on the ground and pushed it into the grass so that it stood. He paused for a time and watched the sky where the blue burned out the edge of the east. Then he produced a box of matches and she cupped her hands on either side as he lit the wick. Her hands glowed in the soft warmth as the flame trembled in the cool dark.

"Look at the stars, girl. Do you see that one there? Just below the purple one blinking? That one. Yes. A million years ago it was something tremendous, many times the size of our world. It was tangible, real, and *made of fire*. It cast light into the darkness. It burned bright for a time. But what you see now is the light it gave long before our time. The star is gone. What you see is nothing more than the last flicker, only just reaching our eyes light-years away."

Isha watched, silent.

"I don't know if you understand how few of these there are left," the hunter whispered, looking out into the hills to where Kala had gone, "or how close we are to losing them forever. All of this used to be jungle—all of it. My father cut it down, and over to the east and west and north and south other families did the same. It's all gone."

Isha watched the stars reflecting in his spectacles.

"They created us, you know? The elephants, the tigers, the wolves and the bison. There is a reason the first men prayed to them—a reason they were our gods. Back then, when we were still connected to the land, people knew. Do you think we would have been able to breath or build shelter and ships without trees? Do you think your greatest grandmother would have even been possible had there not been fish in the rivers and soil to farm? It's almost absurd to list it all—it's impossible, too. Everything we have comes from them. They were here long before us and raised us on the plains. The bones and teeth and antlers tell the story. We're all the same, made of the same parts. All start off the same in the womb."

He turned to Isha.

"What I'm trying to say is, don't mess this up. It isn't about you. It's about that monster you've adopted. She's part of a much bigger story. The tiger's flame that once burned bright, now but a flicker in the dying light. They are all but gone. I don't know how you came to this, or how you made it as far as you have. It is a thing grand enough to be from the old stories. But I can tell you that the hard part is still coming.

"The only jungle left these days is like a green warzone. There isn't much of it, and everyone is fighting over what's left. The animals, the tribals, the government—they're all fighting for a stake. It's going to be hard for her. And for you. You won't be able to just camp out there the way you have been. It's dangerous, crowded, and violent. It's no joke. Do you understand me?"

Isha nodded.

"You are responsible for something priceless, historically speaking, something fantastic." He shook away the enormity of the subject and turned to put a heavy hand on her shoulder. The stars were kind in his wrinkled eyes. "I'll take you to the Periaman-galam. It's not going to be easy to make it across the countryside—this is India after all. But you've done it so far, and maybe you've got some more luck left in you. But what I want to tell you is what you mostly already know. If we are found out by villagers, or the Forest Department, or even the tribals, it will all be over. And even if we bring her to the jungle, she could have her head crushed in by a bison on her first day. Or be poisoned by some farmer on the second. You have to be prepared for that. Okay?"

Isha looked him bravely in the eyes and nodded. His great hand rested on her head so that their eyes were level.

"Make your effort honorable and if you fail, let the failure be memorable." He nodded, almost winking, and held her shoulders. "Let's finish it."

A vast, symphonic roar sounded and echoed in the distance. The hunter stood. Sheets of blue mist lay across the sleeping coffee hills as a dark shape grew therein. The hunter lifted the candle from the grass and held it aloft, a beacon to bring in the travelers that now approached.

It came like a black zeppelin through the plantation. Wide-padded, callused feet tramping through the dark. Flapping ears high above the bushes; long, slow soundless steps. The shape kept growing and becoming larger until Isha could not believe her eyes at the size of the blue monstrosity among the shadows of the morning. Amid a surreal silence, the elephant drifted in. Isha's heart was pounding; the hunter was stoic, rifle folded in his arms. The elephant came and stood above them, the boy on top shivering and soaked from the dew.

The elephant held out a foot and the boy climbed down to stand before them. He did not speak and took no notice of Isha. He bowed to the hunter, as if he were frightened of him. The world was brightening rapidly in the east.

Isha looked up in awe at the great blind elephant with long, cracked tusks and wide-veined ears. The trunk found her and probed her hand, then up her arm, her chest, her neck, and then to her hair. The pachyderm could smell the tiger and the mango tree she'd slept under, and it could also smell a friend.

The elephant accelerated, long legs undulating under thick wrinkled skin. He swept past them and off around the house. The boy ran beside him, giving direction as the blind elephant nearly ran. Hathi swung his trunk before him like a blind man's white cane, feeling the ground toward an unknown destination. He reached the front door—which might as well have been a mouse hole.

The elephant stood by the small door, ears flapping. Gowda and Isha caught up and shared a look of confusion. Then Hathi's trunk reached inside the house, the elephant's tremendous face pressed against the doorway as it felt inside. Hathi's trunk came back grasping Arun by the middle, lifted off his feet in a powerful and terrifying elephant hug. When the elephant released him, Arun dropped to his knees where Thimma crashed into his arms. Isha saw that the boy was crying. Arun whispered words to the boy, who wiped his eyes and laughed. The elephant stood with them as they spoke, his trunk and tail swinging with pleasure.

"Isha, come," Gowda said softly. "Will you help me get some breakfast going?" They went into the house together.

15

FELLOWSHIP OF THE TIGER

Kala was distraught. Her stripes streaked through the plantation, her nose telling her things she could not believe and did not understand. She leapt up a boulder and then onto a branch of a banyan tree and balanced down toward the center where she leapt to the ground. She was all light footed and hot breathed, snorting and searching, turning down trails and following the musk.

Emerging from the dense coffee to a manmade water tank, her eyes moved over the surface of the small pond. A green bee-eater spread its wings and flew. She bent to the water to drink. Suddenly what had seemed like a boulder began to shift. The tiger stood at attention as the flapping ears and swinging trunk unfurled and great legs moved. Water rushed over the banks of the pond. Kala leapt above the waves of water along the edge of the tank. When Hathi's trunk found the tiger's scent, the blind elephant let out a shriek so sonorous it shook the morning dew off the leaves. Kala leapt ten feet vertical and then sped up a tree to the highest perch that would support her.

Back at the house, Thimma was having his breakfast and eagerly waiting to learn the reason he had been summoned. Arun began the story from the beginning, with Isha's being kicked out of school and sent to her Ajji and Ajja's in *ooru*, and the encounter with the tigress. Thimma listened with wide eyes. Isha was able to follow the story, which Arun was telling in Kannada. When Arun was halfway through, Thimma stopped him with a hand in the air.

"Wait. Where is this tiger at this moment?" His hand went to the chair arm because he knew the answer before he could process the information.

A piercing feline shriek and then a resounding elephantine trumpet blast filled the air. The girl, the tribal, the priest, and the hunter were on their feet and running out of the porch, scattering teacups and potted plants. They sprinted down the path that led to the water tank. There they found Hathi in the water, too afraid to leave. Thimma had to swim out to meet him, talking in calm Adivasi language to sooth the tremendous elephant. The boy sat on the giant neck and rubbed the double bulged forehead. After confirming that the elephant was unharmed, Isha stalked into the plantation to find Kala.

She located Kala high in a tree and climbed up to console her. The tiger had been shocked silly by seeing her first elephant. Her eyes were still dilated, and she had an impish, panting grin. Despite Isha's continued pleading, Kala would not come down from the tree, so Isha returned to the others.

At the water tank, Thimma had begun to wash the elephant. Isha watched enthralled from a safe distance as the boy coaxed the elephant to lie down and walked barefoot over the large ribs and thick skull. The boy had retrieved his brush and worked for nearly an hour scrubbing one side and then the other of the monstrous Hathi. When finished, Thimma chained Hathi to a thick tree with a small mountain of hay to eat.

Isha watched Hathi's trunk swing and clutch hay, which was lifted into the great mouth and chewed slowly and with much smacking and crushing. She moved closer slowly. She had always imagined elephants to be soft, not hard. To be kind and not intimidating. The pachyderm was draped in thick, gray, wrinkled skin, with small dark unseeing eyes. Each tusk was nearly as big as she was. As a whole, the elephant was rough and immense, powerful and dangerous—a great chewing mountain with an alien face and deep, unknown thoughts.

She came closer but paused nervously as the elephant shifted the great heavy chain round his foot. Arun came quietly, and Isha turned to him. He had a knowing smile and handed her two large bananas before walking off. Isha stifled a squeal as the impossibly long trunk plunged over her shoulder and clutched at her hands. One banana fell as the other was lifted up and into Hathi's mouth. Isha knelt and picked up the second banana. The elephant raised its trunk and opened its mouth wide, the pink tongue falling. Isha had to close her eyes as she reached in and placed the banana inside, and then rapidly withdrew her hand as the loud chewing commenced.

Suddenly she was smiling, and ran off to get another banana. The rest of the day she spent patting him on the trunk. She loved the way Hathi's ears flapped when she spoke to him and enjoyed putting pieces of fruit up into the monstrous mouth (though she did so gingerly, fearful that her vine-like arms might get caught in the great vice of the jaw). The great trunk could deftly pluck the smallest morsels out of her hand.

In the evening before supper, Arun and Gowda hauled all the gear that they had spent the day preparing out onto the porch. As Gowda checked off each items from his master list, Arun lifted the item to Thimma, who placed it inside one of two large pouches that hung on either side of the elephant. Tents and hammocks, bags of rice, and sacks of packaged spices and food all went up into the packs. Thimma worked diligently to ensure that the packs were perfectly balanced. Hathi's trunk patiently probed, lifting mouthfuls of grass up into his mouth.

Gowda barked, "Cooking pot! Matches! Blankets!" Arun hoisted each to Thimma's waiting hands. This went on for some time until Gowda lowered his voice to a tone of unique gravity. "Ammunition." Arun bent and tugged at the canvas sack so heavy that it felt sealed to the floor. He swore and turned to Gowda questioningly before bending down to reach into the sack.

What he felt made him pause. He looked up at Gowda with an expression of wonder. "Are these...?"

Gowda nodded.

Arun stood, his mouth slightly open as he considered one of the rounds. The large brass casing was almost the size of his index finger, with a silver lead tip at one end. His eyes narrowed as he studied the hunter.

Gowda went inside the house and returned carrying a long, heavy item wrapped in fabric that was laced with a leather strap—a rifle. He held it in both hands, looking at it as if it held the sum of his life in its parts. He passed it carefully to Arun.

Arun took it with both hands and held it with a curious reverence.

"If not now, then when?" Gowda said. Arun nodded and lay a tender hand on the hunter's shoulder. Isha watched, wondering what momentous thing had passed between them.

At dusk they began. It was an ungainly procession. Thimma cruised forward on the back of Hathi, who moved with the bulk and sweep of an ocean liner. Arun and Gowda each had small packs, the bulk of their gear becoming the elephant's cargo. Two weeks' worth of food, two bottles of whiskey, several bottles of coffee wine (brewed by Gowda), cartridges, medical kit, bedding, flashlight. The men walked at speed without heavy packs, but still they struggled to match the elephant's pace.

To Isha's delight, Kala was cooperating. Arun had prepared a plastic container of cubed goat meat that Isha carried, and Kala, who had known hunger nearly every day she had lived, followed obediently beside Isha in the hope of receiving new morsels. Whenever the tiger strayed, Isha would call to her, flashing the light. When they had traveled alone, Isha had no way to entice the tiger to obey, but with the meat cubes, Kala came rushing back, attentive and ready. Isha withdrew the cool slippery cubes, offering the morsel on a plate of flat palm, as the great mouth opened, and Kala's long pink tongue slurped it back. Isha had to be careful not to let the serrated tongue remove her skin. She wished her mother could see her, for old Isha would never have touched raw meat.

Arun hiked with a staff, despite his youth. Together with the robes, he looked like some traveling sage. He and Gowda argued for hours. Logistics and routes turned to places they had been, people they had lost touch with. Who had grown rich, who had died, rivers that had dried. These varied topics would be volleyed back and forth between their two opposing minds. When Isha wasn't with Kala, she watched the two men, a curious and pleasant realization that with them, she was safe. She wondered, much as she had for meeting Kala, how she could have found these two very people in the vastness that is India.

For two days the elephant lumbered down green corridors beneath the stars through rain showers and sunsets. Most of what they traveled through was coffee estates, which meant they had hundreds of acres of quiet space empty of humans. The cover of thick coffee plants was as high as their heads (save for the elephant). Silver oaks rose from the green substrate with vines of black pepper winding around them. From the light green coffee to the darker silver oak canopy above were the blackened trunks of the tall trees, crosshatched across a world of calling barbets and crows. The intoxicating rich smell of coffee flowers filled their lungs.

At times they would navigate around electric elephant fences, or quickly cross roads, but mostly this was a time isolated in the stunning beauty of India's coffee hills. The few workers they met on the road at dawn or dusk barely took notice of the two men and the mahout boy, who was simply riding his elephant, as one does, from place to place in south India. Perhaps he was a Kodagu mahout on errand for an estate owner, they would wonder, and then forget it soon after. No one suspected that nearby, somewhere in the vegetation, the young, curious eyes of a tiger watched them.

Ramana Gowda, in charge of navigating, held the map. When camp was decided, he set to work instantly. He cleared brush but kept the leaves to furnish soft bedding on which he set the tents. He set lines for wet clothes to dry and worked with an efficiency and pace indicative of experience.

Thimma strung his own hammock in a tree beside Hathi each night. His tribal heritage would not be called upon until later in the journey, and so his was mostly the job of lookout (for he sat ten feet high on Hathi's back) and cargo carrier. Arun continually paused and hooted for Isha, checking on her, badgering her to eat or drink or rest. At night he set her hammock at a distance from the others and insisted that she tie Kala to a tree, leave her, and spend human time by the fire to rest and socialize and recuperate. But Isha often found it hard to detach from the needs of Kala.

On the second night, Arun was unfolding a blanket and staring fixedly toward the forest.

"Let her be!" said Gowda. "If she wants to come, she'll come. Try some of this." He held aloft a cup of Old Monk rum.

Arun sipped and winced restlessly. "She's tired, she needs a break."

"So let her sleep! She'll be fine."

"I don't think you understand. Have you seen her? Her ribs look like a wicker basket. She is several crumbs away from starvation at any given point. And I'll tell you this: you can only mine so much courage from a single person before they become empty. That spindly little *kaddi* has been producing enough to power

Bombay City. Man, there is a kind of tired that only your own bed and a mother can cure."

Gowda nodded and grabbed his crotch. "I've got something *your* mother could cure." Thimma laughed, and Arun rose, shaking his head.

Five a.m. saw them on a long incline of a shallow, cultivated valley surrounded by forest. Arun sat atop of Hathi behind Thimma, while Kala stalked the tree line. Isha marched beside Gowda on the open road.

"Why do you think she hasn't eaten you yet?" Gowda said with an antagonizing twinkle in his eye.

"Why would she eat me when your fat carcass would feed her for months?"

Gowda chuckled and threw a cigar ahead of him and stepped on it.

Isha's eyes were distant toward the tree line now. "I know how dangerous a tiger can be. More than you do." She looked at him to ensure he knew she meant no offense but was speaking frankly. "I've seen it unrestrained. That once she grows up anything can happen. That I can't argue. But right now she is a baby. She's scared of everything, and there is no one to protect her. I don't think she realizes she's so much stronger than I am."

"You've seen a mother tiger's rage."

Isha nodded and looked away.

"There are men who have seen it who can't sleep. They see it in their nightmares and they wake gasping, clawing at the covers. Do you see it in your nightmares?"

"I see things far worse in my nightmares, Uncle."

They were silent while the hunter tried to work out what she could possibly mean. He decided not to push further and changed the topic. "You love her?"

"Very much. We've saved each other's lives. She is my baby."

"Your baby! Ha! She's twice your size. Most mothers aren't at risk of matricidal predation from their offspring, you know. There is an age when she is going to stop being your baby, and you're going to be in very real danger."

"Yes, then she won't be my baby, she'll be my ghost maker. She'll eat all of my enemies and fart their ghosts out into the jungle."

The hunter chuckled and shook his head so that the sweat dripped off his nose. "Do you want to hear a story?"

Isha nodded.

"Up in Nepal on the border of India there was a tiger that ate two hundred people. The villagers were so terrified that they eventually burned down the forest and killed all the animals, and the tiger had to leave. So what it did was cross down into India. The people of the region had no idea, and over the next few years the tiger would occasionally take a person, until this province too had lost over a hundred people."

"I don't believe you," Isha said, defiant but also intrigued.

"Oh! It's true. There were death certificates. And the British kept records of everything."

"So what did they do?"

"What they did was bring in hunters, experts, who were to try and kill the tiger. And try they did. Many men went out into the forest, but they never found the tiger. Only tracks. One hunter would sit up a tree for several days—and on the other side of the province the tiger would carry off some woman from a field. One man actually said the tiger carried his wife off with its mouth around her waist, legs and arms kicking as it ran away with her. This tiger was so fierce, so terrifyingly ferocious, that even when hunters did spot it, they were too scared to shoot it."

Isha's eyes narrowed, incredulous.

"It's true." The hunter continued, panting as he went. "There is no animal on earth as terrifying as a wounded tiger. And those hunters were not stupid men. They knew that if they did not kill the tiger with the first shot, the retaliation would be final. A bear will run when it is wounded. So will a wolf. But if you wound or corner a tiger, its ferocity is awe-inspiring. Especially the females. The tiger will stalk the pursuer, and on foot in a forest alone with a tiger, there is nothing on heaven or earth to save you from that wrath. So many hunters failed, and many more villagers were eaten. The crops were rotting in the fields because people would not leave their houses to harvest them.

"Finally, a local government official brought in some dozen elephants and three hundred men. He also hired a world-famous hunter. They sent the elephants into the forest. They sent the beaters. They set fire to the trees. All of this to push the tiger to a choke point. Only then, with a few hundred men and elephants and a forest fire, did the tiger have no choice but to come into the hunter's rifle. And when he shot her, she came at him, taking several more heavy-bore rounds before going down.

"When they finally got a look at her, they found something remarkable. Back in Nepal when she was barely older than a cub, someone had shot her. The bullet had taken out those long front canines—shattered them. So she was essentially disabled. Missing her greatest weapon. That's why she couldn't hunt real game like deer and boar and was forced to go for field laborers. What I'm trying to tell you is that a *wounded* tiger outwitted the people of two countries and bested a dozen expert hunters and managed to eat over four hundred. It took over a hundred people and a team of elephants to bring her down. A *wounded* tiger!"

For most of their travel, the dense coffee stood just above their heads with the silver-oak trees creating a canopy high above. Winding up the trunk of each silver oak were vines of black pepper. It was all fine cover. They emerged from one plantation onto the bare grassy spine that connected two hills, the lush country of the next plantation sprawled beneath them. Dawn was coming.

"Hey, look," Arun called from Hathi's back. Far below their position on the hill, in the valley where the planation ended, was a small village. The muffled roar of people shouting floated up to them, and a fire burned from the hood of a car. Gowda shot a meaningful look at Isha, who nodded and withdrew toward the tree line they had just emerged from to find Kala and leash her to a tree. The rest of the group followed and made camp just within the cover of the coffee trees on the other side of the hill from the village.

When the sun had risen, Gowda went down to the village to buy a cup of chai and inquire about the fighting. The storeowner told him that seven people had been killed, with deaths on both sides: Hindu and Muslim. Gowda returned to where the rest of the team was hiding in the forest and gave the news. The day would be spent holding camp and waiting for the cover of darkness.

Isha had developed some allergy, and in the mornings would rub her eyes as if she were trying to scrape them out of her skull. Perhaps it was coffee pollen, or the rough old bedding that they had packed for her from Gowda's store room at the plantation. Arun purchased eye drops in a village, and when she began to grind her fists into her red itchy eyes, Arun had her sit down. He placed his thumb and forefinger on either side of her eye and held it gently open. He became suddenly conscious of his own heartbeat. He had done many things for her but this was somehow different. There were little freckles on her cheeks he had never seen.

"Stay still, ya," he said and counted, "One, two…"

The first time, he squeezed the dropper on three, and she blinked just in time so that the drop missed her eye entirely. After that, he learned that he had to hold her eye open himself and trick her with his counting—dropping the solution on the count of one or after three, when she'd least expect it. With each new application, he found new ways of tricking her.

"Now don't rub anymore. Let's go."

On the fourth dawn they came to the ghat. Far above them to the east, a tremendous mountain stood. They camped in its shadow. The vegetation was more than shrubs here, and there were patches of actual forest. These interested Kala greatly, and the tiger set out to explore as Thimma, Hathi, Arun, and Isha made camp downwind of the trees in a grassy clearing. Since the tiger was away, Thimma and Arun set about making a fire, while Isha watched, hopeful of learning the secret. Hathi swayed nearly silently in the shadows, lifting tufts of grass into his mouth.

Isha set up some sticks beside the fire to try and make her own. Thimma watched her with disdain until Arun prompted him to help instead of mock. So Thimma showed her how to shave the first smallest kindling from a dry stick, as Arun had shown her days ago, and prepare the intermediate fodder. Arun translated as he showed her these things, and Isha worked hard to keep up, making a replica fire of her own beside his pile. When he struck the match and the entire pile went up instantly, Isha was impressed with his efficiency and skill.

When she struck her own match, her fire was loath to light. Arun said that Thimma said her pile was too dense, not enough air. She permitted neither of them to touch her pile and struggled for some time in the smoke, blowing and coaxing the fire to take.

When she gave up, dozens of matches littered the ground, and her eyes stung from the smoke.

Arun noticed her blinking and tearing, wiped his hands, and rose to remove the eye drops from his pack. Once again they repeated the ritual of counting, blinking, laughing.

"Okay, now don't rub it all out, ya?"

Isha nodded, the heels of her hands pressed into her eye sockets.

As Arun and Thimma cooked a simple dinner of dahl and ready-made Kerala *parotas*, Ramana Gowda went off into the forest in search of more wood. Isha was sitting beside the bubbling dahl trying to cut her toenails with a knife when two young men approached. The boys were dressed in white with orange bandanas around their necks and several horizontal white lines across their foreheads. Arun greeted them as they stared in wonder at Hathi.

One put his back toward the elephant, looking stern. "You cannot camp in this place. There is curfew in the village."

"We aren't *in* the village," said Arun, "and we'll be gone by morning."

The boy opened his mouth to speak again, but Arun thanked him curtly for his time and sent him off.

An hour later, Thimma made a clicking sound with his tongue and pointed. Three new men approached, all in white Hindu garb with orange bandanas on their foreheads. Arun lifted a long metal pole he had found lying in the grass and hid it beside him.

When the men arrived, Thimma was smoking a beedie. Gowda was sharpening a knife. He stowed it slowly so that they saw.

"You there!" the leader said, pointing at him.

Gowda was slow to rise. "Namaskara," he said amiably. Isha noticed that he stood as though he were a much older man. He squinted as if visually impaired.

They argued for some time, Gowda insisting that they would be gone by morning, but the men were adamant that they leave immediately. The men declared dangerous characters were about, and they could not permit anyone to camp, for safety's sake. Gowda looked around.

"I don't see anyone dangerous around. In fact, there is no one here bothering us except for *you*. And do you always shout when you speak? You sound like a donkey."

"You, sir, cannot be here. You are in—"

He cut the man off again. "Hey, boys, what is this really about?" His eye went to the orange saffron scarfs. Then his hand went melodramatically to his forehead. How could he have missed it?

"Do not worry; we aren't Muslims. You have an atheist, a confused priest, and two children—so no one here is interested in your shit. I'd call you children for the dumb shit you get up to if it didn't so often have such tragic endings. You are fools. And if this isn't *your* land, then we have nothing to talk about. Hack each other apart in peace and stop bothering us."

"Leave now!"

Isha sat up on one elbow. Arun stood like a panther. He lifted the metal bar from the grass and hefted it. Gowda turned and saw him holding the pole and suddenly, she could swear, looked nervous.

"Isha, don't you have to go to the loo?" Gowda said without looking at her.

Isha rose to leave.

"Do not move! No one leaves!" the leader barked.

Arun stepped around the fire and toward the men.

"You sit down, I'll handle it!" Gowda growled pointing a stern finger at Arun. "Drop it! Drop it to the ground now."

Arun let the metal pole fall, but the veins in his temples and the shuddering breaths that filled his lungs were worrying.

The leader stepped forward and removed a baton from his waste. Gowda watched him draw in and didn't so much as smile, as bare his teeth. Then, in the flash of an instant, his hand grasped the man's throat. The sound of impact was shocking. The two other men jumped back. For a time, everything went quiet except for the horrible, muted, wrenching sound that came from the choking leader. To the men, Gowda's face was obscured in shadow, his ears orange in firelight. To Isha and the others, his broad gorilla back suddenly swelled with the breath of rage. His arm had become a teaming mass of pythons beneath the skin as he clutched the throat of the man with oppressive and unaccountable power. The man's eyes bulged with panic.

Arun lifted the metal pole and brought it beside the temple of one of the other two men. "Careful now," he said, an alert and taunting sparkle in his eyes. The man's eyes went from the long pole to the stubby machete in his own hand. He understood fully that he would be beaten to death before he ever had the chance to slash with the small knife. "Just drop it," Arun said with patronizing encouragement.

Gowda held the leader like a suitcase at his side. The man's face was to the sky, his hands clutching at the hunter's wrist, his legs jolting and kicking. Gowda barely noticed as he stared threateningly at the third of the party. If he had thought himself a man, he shrank back to a boy as the hunter stepped forward. The trembling boy dropped his machete to the ground. Thimma grinned in the firelight. Gowda came up to the boy's face so that their noses were almost touching.

"I close my hand and he becomes a corpse." The man's feet were kicking, frantic, shaking involuntarily. He had been without air for quite some time, Isha realized. His eyes were tearing and veins bulged on his forehead. The hunter's hand was as uncompromising as a steel trap. The boy turned and ran.

Gowda snorted and dropped the man to the ground, where he lay gasping. "Thank you for checking on us," he said, lumbering back to sit down heavily beside the fire.

Isha's heart was pounding, partly for the violence and partly because she had learned the power of Gowda and a new side to the gentle Arun. As talking resumed in the hour to come, they all agreed that that was far too close a call. They finished eating, killed the fire, and moved on through the night.

They went silently and Isha wondered. She watched Arun and Gowda marching beside each other. Gowda put two cigarettes in his mouth and lit them both against the wind, then handed one to Arun. The way they spoke, laughed, their motion and comradery, made her smile. She shook her head. What forces had brought her these men? She knew well that traveling alone as a girl of her age, she could have just as easily met danger of the worst kind. When she had first followed Arun to the sanctuary, that programmed suspicion had been present. But now it was long gone. No, there was no worry, not a single droplet or pebble of doubt that she was safe so long as she was with them. They were decent and kind and cared for her like she was their own. In a curious way, these strangers were actually a kind of family that she had not met until now. The serendipity of it far surpassed whatever odds of probability she could consider, and the result was a magical flutter that made her feel breathless, as if, perhaps, her adventure was in fact traveling on the currents of providence.

The next morning, Kala was in a cantankerous mood. Isha tried repeatedly to get her to march, but the heavy cub only wanted to play. As Isha pulled her, Kala leapt up and took her down, and then flopped over to mouth her arm. The large head rolled in her lap. Though she had grown, Kala had retained the kitten-like love of nuzzling, and the puppy-like habit of licking Isha's sweat. The tiger's tongue slipped out between the teeth to lap at her arm, scraping the skin so blood beads emerged. It looked like scrapes she had gotten when she and Anya had raced with scooters and fell onto cement back in Bangalore, a thousand years ago.

Isha swore and inspected the wound, holding back Kala's mouth by the nose. The large pink thing was covered in thousands of white inward-facing barbs, like miniature shark teeth, grasping thorns. Even the tiger's tongue was a formidable weapon, and one that Isha was forced to respect.

"Let's go!" she begged repeatedly, but the tiger was fussing and proud and unwilling to march. Isha spent time trying to coax her, but nothing worked. Kala would lie down, or wander, but simply would not follow. Isha wished for some cubes of goat meat but had none. She looked ahead anxiously, knowing the others had gone ahead, and then back at the smug Kala lying in the leaves.

"I wish I could just whack you hard enough to make you listen!" Isha swore through clenched teeth. She clutched the tiger by the ear and twisted. Kala's teeth emerged as her jowls peeled back in a growl. A swipe of her broad paw sent Isha scurrying away.

Fine, I'm going. Let her come if she wants. Moments later, Isha emerged from the dense greenery onto a well-paved forest road. She found herself face-to-face with four young Indian men. Twenty or twenty-five years old, plump and well-dressed in Western tennis shirts, they were standing beside a modern-looking jeep drinking expensive parcel coffees and taking pictures. They were city boys from Bangalore, techies out for a weekend road trip.

"Hello!" said the one in blue and began walking towards her. He was speaking in Hindi. "What are you doing way out here in the forest? Are you lost?"

A twig snapped behind her.

"Oh fuck!" Isha said, and her hand went to her mouth. She felt sickeningly frozen, the way you watch a vase fallen off a table in the moments before it shatters. She knew what would happen next.

The following fifteen seconds went like so: Kala came trotting out of the trees with her white chin held high, a striped smile on her face. As she emerged, Isha saw the young man's face contort into horror. His hand released the cardboard coffee cup so that it hung in the air as he turned to run. At the jeep, the other boys were already flailing, fighting to get inside the cabin. One fell against the door, pinning it shut, as another leapt over him, clawing into the driver's seat upside down.

Kala found the excitement enticing and trotted after them. The engine turned on and the car accelerated (a hand rather than a foot pushing the pedal). The boy in blue tried to jump on the moving car, but he fell flat on the road. He ran on all fours like a wounded lizard until he fell against the bank at the edge of the road. As Kala drew in, he covered his face and began screaming like a woman being murdered. The tiger came within an inch of the hysterical young man and looked down at him curiously. He screamed again and again, arms over his face. But when he peered through his elbows to see the tiger's proximity, his arms relaxed and his brain shut off. Kala cocked her head to one side, confused at his sudden sleep. Then the car crashed into a tree with a metallic crunch.

Frightened by the sound of the crash, Kala left the sleeping boy and took shelter behind Isha. Isha was still standing with her hand over her mouth. It had gone there for the swear word she didn't mean to say; it remained there to prevent worse words escaping. It all happened so fast. Her hand came off her mouth and went to Kala's neck, which she held tight. In the car, shocked faces blinked and swore.

"Are you okay?" Isha asked in Kannada, leaning toward the smoking car.

"We are okay. Please don't come to us!" came the reply in English. Inside the cabin hands went up in pleading surrender while heads wobbled rapidly. A camera flashed, and Kala recoiled. Isha led her away, past the boy in the blue shirt; he was snoring peacefully in the leaves. The girl and the tiger vanished into the forest.

16

THE CLIMB

That night around the fire, Isha and Gowda argued on the issue of elephants raiding plantations.

"Oh, let them take some, no? Was it so much damage?"

"It was *lakhs* each year! Hundreds of thousands of rupees gone under foot and down those gullets. And when I was a boy a *lakh* was more like a *crore*!"

"Oh God."

"Something had to be done. Everyone was saying it. There seemed to be more elephants than ever. More incidents. The farmers all decided together. That is how it is done in Coorg. Everyone there owns land, and everyone there has respect for the animals, but there is a limit. Another neighboring estate had lost ten *lakhs* of cocoa and jackfruit and coffee. Soon after they cut the forest. They burned the groves and planted the new area. They figured that the elephants would have no reason to come any more since there was no more forest for them to hide in."

"And?"

"And it turns out that there weren't more elephants than ever. It was just that they had lost so much forest that they were being *seen* more often. The jungle was no longer big enough for them to graze, so they had no choice but to raid the plantations. And that is why there were so many problems." He stared into the flames as he spoke. "That was it. They stopped coming. It worked. And for a while the farmers were happy. We all were, because we weren't losing crops. Workers could go out into the plantations without worrying that they'd be trampled…"

Isha watched the hunter. Arun was watching him too.

"But now I remember elephants like I remember the summer nights full of fireflies. They are things from childhood that are gone. Everyone remembers the fireflies, everyone wonders where they've gone. The nights are less magic these weathered days. But for the elephants, we know the reason. We know because it was us. And I'll tell you. Now that I am an old man—nearly an old man— I'll tell you that sometimes I wake up in bed in the night and think I heard them chirping, or that roar. I'll sit up and listen, go out and stand there in the night, look out across the hills and hope. The truth is it just isn't exciting any more. I miss the bastards something terrible."

"No tigers?"

"Not since my grandfather."

"My father saw one not far from the sanctuary. Do you remember? The porcupine?"

"Oh yes. I'll never forget." Gowda nodded.

"Tell, tell!"

Arun cleared his throat. "This was an old, old tiger. He had come through the village. They tried to trap him, poison him. Each year they knew he'd come through because he'd poach the dogs or a cow. You see, the deer were gone, the bison and boar were all gone. The people had hunted them away. So there was nothing for a tiger to eat. And they must travel, as you know. But one day my father got the call that there was a tiger in the village. They'd found him lying in the foliage at the edge of a farm. He was crying, they said. And so they called my father. He went and the tiger was indeed crying, and the sound of it made my father cry. They came close to the tiger, but the tiger only lay there, staring at nothing, in the leaves."

"He let them close enough to see?"

"He couldn't move. He was hurt, dying. They could see that there were porcupine quills in his face and paws. And when he died that night, the Forest Department took him in and performed an autopsy. And what he died of! You know that when tigers get old, their teeth are the first thing to wear down and go. They can no longer go after real prey. On top of that, younger males probably fought him out of whatever forest he'd once lived in, and there wasn't any other forest to go to. It is very sad if you think about it, what would make a tiger go after a porcupine. They found that one of the long quills, as long as ten inches, had been driven straight through his ribs and into his heart. The poor old bugger had nothing left to eat, nothing at all, and so he had resorted to porcupine. He must have been starving. And the stupid rodent stuck him full of barbs and left him there to die."

"Did you see him?"

"Only after he had died. It was enormous. My father, though, he never forgot it. He said it was the most heartbreaking thing to see that tiger's face full of pain and defeat. That was the last one anyone saw." He looked out into the vast green plantation hills. "Until her."

Ramana Gowda had a brisk and exhilarating gift for stories that made you feel as if you'd been there yourself. By now Isha had gleaned from what he and Arun shot back and forth that the depth of wild adventures between the two was vast. She had overheard enough to learn that when Arun was coming of age, Gowda and Wolfgang were at the height of their friendship. Those were the days when Gowda would entertain on the veranda of the estate, where flocks of young aspiring wildmen would gather to drink his toddy, smoke his weed, and hear swashbuckling stories. While Wolfgang was off caring for rare orchids and broken birds, the boys would fill the veranda thick with smoke and drink enough to get their young hearts charging.

Long carrom sessions full of swearing would eventually erupt off the veranda, and Ramana Gowda would take them on bashing rides through the plantation and have them line up glass bottles for rifle practice. More than once the whole crew got into fistfights at the local bars—fodder for future afternoons of backslapping and comparing knives on the veranda.

They worshipped the old lion, unaware that they themselves were pups—destined to become nothing nobler than dogs. They wished to be men like him, unaware that he was cut from different stuff; that the grit and skill he had acquired was forged on actual adventures, work, and experience for which debauchery and mischief could never compare. What were grand adventures for them, to him might as well have been sessions of bridge to pass the afternoon. Gowda enjoyed the stroking of his mane and the good entertainment of being the king. They came and went, the pups. But Arun had always been there, since the beginning and after the end, like a son or nephew eventually grown into a friend.

Isha enjoyed the old stories and enjoyed even more teasing out the details in between. What she couldn't put her finger on was what stood between the days of proud Gowda and an un-robed Arun, and now. She wished sometimes that she could simply dare to ask, *So what happened?* Instead she resolved to work it out on her own, slowly.

"Uncle, can I ask you a question?"

Gowda grunted, his eyes still far off.

"Why are you called a hunter?"

Ramana Gowda pushed the coarse white hairs of his mustache so that they flared out. His eyes met hers with a thrilling earnestness.

"When I was seventeen, eighteen, twenty—young—I hunted through the plantations with my father's rifle. Back in those days we needed to clear the pests, they said. And so I made a name for myself clearing out the land. Guar, dhole, porcupine, leopard. I hunted everything for a few years. I hunted until there was nothing left." He looked down at large wrinkled hands. "The hills used to tremble with the call of tuskers. Aaney-Betta means Elephant Hill, and now the elephants are gone. These hands made the silence."

In those days of travel Isha was often near speechless in response to the care Arun provided. He hung her wet clothes to dry. He reminded her to eat even when she'd forgotten and became cross or distant. She listened to him partly for the luxury of abdicating responsibility to herself, but also because he treated her like a friend and not a child. Along with possessing a staggering amount of knowledge of the natural world, he was the first adult whose empathy was not limited to his own species. He called after birds and helped turtles across roads. He wondered about the happiness of small things. To him, as to her, they were not just rodents or pests with trunks, or venomous dangers, but *beings*. Small beings worthy of respect.

"Most people can't see animals for what they really are," he would say. "They see beauty, or fear, or a pest. They see an object. Most people are so insurmountably human that they cannot imagine sentience or emotional connection in creatures of another form."

"What it comes to," he said one day, grinning, "is the question of whether or not we are smart enough to understand how smart animals are." Then he thought for a while. "Or to register that our smart is not their smart. That it is a dimension we cannot see."

This all made Isha smile. He was speaking thoughts she had never had the power to articulate. He could see the things that only she had seen, and in doing so she felt as though he was the first of her own race capable of seeing her.

At dawn of the fifth day, just as it became bright enough to see, they began the ascent. The mountain stood so large, they were humbled. Ridges and rocky parapets jutted out jagged from the green bulk. At first it was all rocks and stones and giant boulders and thick vegetation. For a time, the four of them rode on the elephant, since the scrub was too wicked with thorns and too dense to allow human passage. The incline increased rapidly, some parts so steep that the narrow pathway began tacking, steep switchbacks taking them higher and higher.

As it steepened, they took to their own feet, for the elephant became unsteady. Thimma's face was a scowl of concentration as he spoke constantly and urgently to his elephant. Hathi's trunk was out in front, searching the terrain and scouting for footholds. Gowda's lungs and legs burned from the climb, and the fact that a half-grown tiger was stalking up the green mountainside made it that much harder for his senses.

By the time Isha reached the cloud layer, the elephant was panting far below and working hard with Thimma to find the way. Arun came behind her, looking like he was going to fall over. When his feet slid and he faltered, she gripped a rock and spread her arms down to grasp his hand. With her help he climbed onto the path. There they both watched for signs of Kala below. But they could not see her.

From this point upward, it was near vertical. They hiked upward on tight switchbacks. Isha's legs burned as they pistoned steadily upward. She looked back, down to the plains. There was a desolate feeling in those plains. It was the feeling of uncertainty, a landscape that did not know itself. It had once been a forest, once been a farm, once been an ocean. She had cried in the caves there and walked through the nights. Now as she ascended the steep, blowing hillside, she wondered at it all. The mountain had always been a mountain; no one had cut the black root braids in its soil or dammed its many veins. It was the windy place above the rest, larger. In the brilliant windswept reality, the plains and the weeks before became a distant dream, a shadow beneath the new and visceral ascent.

It was still early, and above the swirling vapor the sun from the east glowed heavenly in the heights where the mountain seemed lost in the clouds. Isha had to look almost straight upward to see. She remembered staying up late huddled in a blanket with her sister watching an old movie with three cowboys. *The Good, the Bad and The Ugly*. It was long and boring mostly, but they had watched it because they weren't supposed to. And in the end, it was not the movie but the music that had made it worth it. When they finally reached the graveyard, and the treasure, the pulsing piano came in. "Ecstasy of Gold"—the culminating of circumstances, the proximity to glory. As she squinted up toward the dizzy heights, it ran through her. She hummed it, whistled it as she panted, and her eyes danced.

No one back home would believe me. Appa, Anya, Amma— what I wouldn't give to let them see now...

They came to a narrow promontory and she reeled from the plunging distance. The narrow path was little more than a ledge across the face of a cliff. They paused here while Thimma unstrapped Hathi's packs and handed the gear down to Gowda and Arun. But even without the extra cargo, the pathway was perilously narrow for an elephant. Thimma piloted Hathi with scowling concentration. He threw his beedie into the abyss below as Hathi lumbered monstrous feet onto the narrow pathway.

When the elephant hesitated Thimma spoke to him incessantly, whacking him with the stick and urging his feet into the elephants' ears. Hathi chirped and trumpeted with fear. Arun walked with one hand on the wall, he eyes cast over his shoulder, incredulous that the elephant would be able to balance on such a thin causeway. Hathi's right ear and shoulder grinded against the stone as he went. At times the elephant would not move, and

Thimma would strike him with a stick, shouting mahout commands. Isha found it hard to watch and had to hold herself back
from saying, "Hathi is going to fall! Don't hit him so hard!" But
she held her silence.

As he went, Hathi's trunk would sometimes swing left over
the edge to where there was only wind and space. At these times
the elephant would shiver and groan with fear and clutch to the
wall. Thimma spoke urgently to him, instructing him that the path
was right, that left was death—though each of the others privately
wondered if the elephant knew the extremity of his position. Above
them to the right a high wall rose into obscurity; on the left and
below was nothing. A vast cloud snarled in an updraft curl, so large
that Isha was unable to find any human object of analogous size.

Arun called to Gowda, "I don't think elephants were meant for
this."

"Shut up! Dammit! And they're just fine at it. I've seen them
higher. They can climb better than we can."

"I don't know, ya... Even if he summits, think of the way
down, the descent?"

"I'm telling you, I've seen them up on the hills, looking like
insects, way up high. On inclines you'd never think they could
manage. They like the golden grass."

"Oh shit." Arun was watching Hathi inch along the pass.

"Hannibal took an army of them across the mountains!"

"They all died!" Arun said, now nearly looking away.

Hathi's foot misplaced and sent a chatter of gravel of the edge
and down into the nothing. Thimma's lips pursed and his eyes
bulged as the elephant faltered. He spoke urgent reassurance,
pleading with Hathi to hug further right. The elephant's trunk felt
over the edge, finding nothing. Perhaps the wind blew up the scent
of the void, for he moved with slow, deliberate, measured steps.
Arun was soaked from sweated worry, and his lips mimed prayers
as he watched. One wrong move, one collapsing section, would
plunge the elephant a thousand feet.

When Hathi emerged onto surer footing, everyone wiped their
foreheads, exchanging sighs and relieved glances. It took some
time to transport the heavy bags, one by one, across the narrow
path. The last thing to cross was Kala, who had to be lead across
with both Isha and Arun holding the rope. When they were halfway
through, Kala bounded ahead, eager to finish. They let her go, rope

and all. Isha hugged the wall and could feel the wind pushing her
and knew it had the power to sweep her away. When she emerged,
Gowda was busy with Thimma, reloading the elephant's cargo.

Eventually they all stood recovering from the stress of the
crossing, passing water bottles and gasping for air as a cloud overtook them and partially eclipsed the sun. Ahead of them stretched a
vaulted field. A kite swooped over the top of the mountain into the
dim interior of the cloud. *The top of the mountain.* Arun turned to
Isha to see if she had seen it too. She had. He rushed off ahead and
vanished into the mist, taking the mountain with high-kneed strides
through a world of white obscurity.

A minute later his voice came back with electric urgency:
"Isha!"

Again she heard the music she could barely remember, the urgent promise, the pulsing of proximity of great treasure. She broke
into a run. There was not much mountain left above the mist layer.
Isha emerged into a new windy reality where the kites were swoop-
ing and shrieking and the grass was alive like a beast. Arun was
powering up the final stretch ahead. Above him, over the pass, mist
rolled down like ghostly rapids, streaming into the air. As Isha ran,
Kala bounded up beside her, full of wild intensity. Thimma's voice
came calling as he hustled and cried atop Hathi's back. They raced
upward with wild eyes, swinging trunk, panting, sweating, hoping,
clawing toward the sky.

They had climbed the western shadow side of the mountain.

Arun reached the pass first and vanished in the light. The wind
filled his hood and grabbed his robes and pushed him back a step.
He fell to his knees in the brilliance of the sun risen in the east and
blasting out across the world, and for a moment he was blinded.
Then he saw.

"Isha!" His voice came frantic as she ran. "Isha!"

She was sprinting now and crested the pass. She came into the
blinding light and the wind battered her down. She fell onto her
hands and rose, stumbling forward. Arun's hand was still shielding
his eyes when she reached his side.

The terrifying cliff before them was a thousand-foot plunge of
deep green, dizzying before their feet. The wind and distance
sucked the breath out of her as birds whirled around them in the
up-snarling mist. She grasped Arun's sleeve and felt the tears well
in her eyes, and she fell to the ground with her hands over her face.

"Isha!" The wind snatched Arun's voice right out of his lungs. She could not hear him even from an arm's length away. A gust nearly blew her off her feet just as she reached him and he steadied her shoulders.

As the sight of the other side hit her, she sank down and bent to the ground, sobbing with her hands over her face. Arun crouched beside her as she shook, robes billowing out behind him. Hathi bore Thimma over the crest and when the boy saw he began screaming and made a blessing on his forehead. Ramana Gowda dropped his pack and roared with victorious fists in the air. Isha knelt in the yellow grass with tears and wild hair strewn across her face, hands over her mouth, weeping with release for the pounding green panorama below.

A cloud raced along the high wall, hurtling past like a train: unhurried from afar, hurtling up close. The white veil rushed along the cliff, enveloping them so that suddenly they were inside of the cloud. Isha held out her hand as the vapor tufts and pockets of air rushed by. She drew the rich vapor deep into her lungs.

The veil passed and once again the sun shown. The tiger materialized, weaving through the pulsing and swirling yellow grass. They stood at the high pass, the jungle below rich and thick and crowded and loud.

"Do you see it! Do you see it?" Isha screamed to the tiger.

Kala posed on a rocky outcrop, her muscular shoulders rippling her blazing coat. The tiger's face dropped and her lower canines unsheathed as she scented the wind in feline wonder. Burning between the stark calligraphy of her face, for the first time in her life, the smooth plane of the tiger's retinas saw green to the horizon. For the first time, she saw *home*.

They stood jubilant and stunned in the wild brilliant morning amid the birds and windswept wonder of giant clouds that floated high above the vast, steaming jungle below.

17

THE JUNGLE

Wind hurried over the high grass beneath the jagged incisors of the mountain spine; the golden fields undulated as if the skin of the earth had tumbled away from the mountainside to expose the throbbing current of the world. Further down, giant ferns of hopeful green clutched to where the trees could not grow, like refugees from the savage floral battlefield below.

The mirthless green jungle snarled ragged smoke and spat plumes of birds to the sky that chattered and morphed in their shape of millions. Towering even above the canopy, ancient trees gasped in static exaltation; their arms spread to the sky above the stifled wrestling vegetation lashed with vines. The ancient dipterocarps had spent the millennium climbing, sucking life out of death, and drinking the sky. They too would fall and be digested in the infallible march, the infinite cannibalistic churning of the immortal whole.

As they descended, the vegetation rose around them and thickened. Thankfully the backside of the mountain was more gradual than the ascent had been, and Hathi was able to accomplish the day's hike with ease. From the high golden grass, they descended into dense cloud forest. Giant fern fronds consumed them, large enough to make the elephant look like a large beetle. Curled fiddlehead spirals were laden with dew jewels; pinnules captured the moist air that condensed into beads on the fern stalks that ran together down and over the mossy rocks. So many droplets on so many ferns, down miles of moss and rock, were the womb of great rivers. In this world, everything was wet. The ground gradually became a steady trickle; an hour later it had become a stream. By afternoon they reached the lower valley where the stream widened to become as wide as a road. The topography leveled, and the trees became the supremely large vine-covered pillars of true jungle.

Hathi led the procession through a shallow stream, crashing through fallen branches and vines, breaking trail for the others. Ramana Gowda followed next, hacking through what was left with a large machete—a warrior slaying legions of leafy foes. Isha and Arun came last.

Kala had transformed the moment she saw the jungle. There was a quivering new attention in her eyes, a kinetic flow of posture to her stride. Like some astronaut born in outer space and entering earth's atmosphere for the first time, she was home. Her striped ribs drew great breaths of exotic scents. Her eyes were orbs of pure, starving fascination. She stalked low to the ground and held her head high; she licked the dew off of leaves. The smell of her own world electrified her. Almost immediately, she vanished into the green, thrilled by her new surroundings in the most sinister feline way.

By five o'clock, despite the brilliant light high above in the treetops, night had flooded the interior. Gowda and Arun made camp while Isha called for Kala and prepared the tiger's meal.

So it went for the first few days of travel. A small smoky fire kept them warm from the river of airborne water particles flowing through the jungle. The three men would sling their hammocks in a triangle around the fire, while Isha set hers some way off so that Kala would feel comfortable to come close. In the mornings, Arun would give her eye drops and help to feed Kala. At nights they would all cook and sing and tell stories around the campfire.

Gowda read from his copy of Kipling that he had brought from the plantation. In *The Jungle Book*, Hathi was the leader of the elephants, and the tiger, Shere Khan, was an evil, bloodthirsty beast. Thimma would laugh, for he simply couldn't fathom why the animals talked in such stories. Isha detested that he'd made the tiger evil. But none of them could deny the vitality and truth, or the mirror the tales seemed to erect before them.

Twice Isha requested Ramana Gowda to re-read her favorite part of the story, when Bagheera and Baloo and the python Kaa battle the monkeys to save Mowgli. It was after the battle, when they are all reunited, the bear and the leopard are ragged and wounded from the fight and Mowgli sets eyes on his friends and cries, "But, oh, they have handled ye grievously, my Brothers! Ye bleed!"

And Baloo says to the man-cub he loves so dearly, "It is nothing. It is nothing if thou art safe."

They sat in the popping orange light beside the slumbering elephant, arguing over Kipling late into the night.

Kala's pupils dilated as the jungle night deepened. She licked her paws clean, protracted and retracted her claws. From where she lay, there were a thousand new sounds pulling at her ears. Her tail became a restless striped python writhing with eagerness. She rose and padded out. There was some exposed rock where she crept downhill, shoulders high above her spine. As the night shadow grew, her stripes vanished her into the jungle completely. The fresh scent of a stream came to her and for some time she followed it, stopping to lap at the cool water at times, at others stopping to examine the great cylindrical impressions of past elephants in the mud, the ripple of unseen fishes.

There were smells of great monsters. Often she would startle and drop, searching timidly for some giant that she had never met. The scent of deer was everywhere. Barking tiny deer, larger spotted chital, tremendous gray sambar. The tiger found the skull of a chital deer, antlers intact, and spent a long hour inspecting it, licking it, becoming accustomed to its scent. As the first light began to dim the darkness, Kala was chest deep in a stream when something rose from the leaves nearby.

She waded farther into the water and waited. Beneath the surface, her tail moved back and forth eagerly. Her eyes and ears scanned while her nose pumped in information from the rich air. A lone sambar stag, a monstrous animal with long legs and thick muscular shoulders and a proud rack of antlers, came to the edge to drink. The tiger's eyes were disks of anticipation. She licked her lips. Her whiskers touched faintly to the water without breaking the surface.

When she exploded up, the stag released a powerful scream and reared. Kala met chests with the buck and sunk her claws deep into the neck. Her body filled with brilliant excitement as teeth searched for their mark. The two bodies lifted through the air. Then the punch of sharp hoof hit the tiger. Kala's stomach felt a sickening crunch and she was hurled backward, tethered by her claws that ripped out of the flesh. She hit the ground, and the deer gave one more brutal stamp before bounding away.

Kala spent some time on the ground, dazed, thinking about what had happened, breathing through the pain in her middle. The deer was twice as large as she, and more powerful than she had imagined anything could be. She could not understand how anything so large and swift could ever be brought down. Kala stood, licked her paw, and winced as her ribs throbbed where the hoof had hit. She looked back into the jungle and longed dearly for the girl.

One night as the others slept, Ramana Gowda was narrating the jungle's terrors to Isha as they sat by the fire. This was no normal jungle, he said. He'd been to jungles all over the world—the Amazon, New Guinea, the Andamans—but none of them could compare to the jungle of India.

"Here there are bison the size of a van and draped in muscle. Giant deer and tiny ones too. Herds of elephants with unknowable strength. Leopards in the trees. Giant boar in the swamps. Pythons curling through the shadows. This," he said, "is a forest of giants."

To Isha's proposal that the tiger would quickly assume her throne, the hunter had warned that deer and boar have hooves and tusks and antlers for a reason, and that reason was precisely to rip the guts out of an attacking tiger.

Thimma was snoring gently as they spoke, his hammock just beside where Hathi stood. It was late in the night when Arun began suddenly sobbing. His body curled and he began speaking, begging, pleading. Even through the hammock, it was clear he was writhing in unseen torment.

Isha turned. "Uncle, look!"

Gowda was up in an instant and went to Arun. He shook him, held him. Arun's hands clutched the older man's great back.

"It's a dream, it's just a dream," Gowda whispered, his cheek against the boy's head.

Arun sobbed, "I was there, I couldn't save her. I couldn't save her..."

Gowda bent low and spoke in a deep rumble into Arun's ear. Gradually the desperation ebbed and the clutching fingers slid down and away from Gowda's back.

For a long time after, Isha and Gowda sat quietly by the fire. In time, Gowda rose, and when he returned, he sat and laid the heavy rifle cover across his knees. He unwound the sashing that held the fabric and removed the old Winchester from its pouch.

It was his grandfather's gun, he had said, a '76 from America and an antique two times over. He and Arun spoke about it as if mentioning a sacred artifact. It had a black octagon barrel and its wooden parts were some richly marbled hard wood. The handsome aged metal receiver was immaculate. Gowda opened the lever and looked down through the sight. He plunged a single magnum round inside and worked the lever to bring the round into the chamber, and then once more so that the round ejected, spinning, out the top of the receiver. He caught it in an effortless, familiar way and re-placed the precious round into the sack. He had explained to Arun days earlier that you could no longer get rounds for a rifle like this in India.

Gowda's hands moved over the gun, his eyes lost in some deep contemplation. It had sat in a glass case for the majority of his life. As a young man he had daydreamed endlessly of a grand showdown or a great adventure that would warrant its use. But was never in a shootout. In his middle age he had put some fruitless effort into ordering new rounds so that he could at least shoot the rifle for sport within the farm. He imagined that one day he would pass the rifle on to his sons, though he never had any children of his own. In his later years the rifle had become a symbol of finality that watched him from behind the glass.

His fingers played in the ammunition sack for a time so that they clinked and shifted within the canvas. Ninety-three brass magnums rounds. What he had was all he had, and all he ever would.

Isha turned to check on the sleeping Arun. The hunter nodded. "Don't worry, Isha. He's doing well, I think."

"He does seem to love the jungle," Isha said.

"That he does, and his father did too. I think this is good for him."

Isha wobbled her head.

Gowda raised inquisitive eyebrows. "So you saw the sanctuary, no?"

"I did." Isha nodded.

"Wolfgang was a great friend. I helped him build it. He knew so much, and could see the future. He knew it would only get worse, and he knew that if he protected that land, it would become a mecca to small things, a sanctuary of birds and snakes and civets and leopards. And surely, it has." Gowda flipped up the sight and fit the long rifle against his shoulder and aimed out into the darkness. The butt of the immense weapon was wrapped in lengths of leather, padding against the punishing recoil.

"I found leopard tracks when I was there."

"Oh! I've seen them with my eyes! They kill dogs in the village nearby and then carry them to the sanctuary to eat them. When Arun was, oh, about sixteen, he went to climb a tree and found the leopardess in it. You would never know she was up there, a big yellow thing with spots. I swear even once he started shouting and calling, I could hardly see the thing in broad daylight. But we put out chairs that night and watched the tree. Sure enough she came down like a shadow, and we shined a light on her. What a sight."

"You knew Arun when he was sixteen?" This was a chance to build her knowledge of their histories.

"Of course! And younger. I saw him grow up. He was always a good kid. He would never hurt a fly but had a wicked right cross for anyone that did. And smart, he was always a brain that one. I thought he'd do something great for sure."

"Helping kids is pretty great, isn't it?"

"Well it is, I suppose. Not that he's been doing much of that lately. And besides, it's just... not what I thought he'd end up doing. He took Wolfgang's dying hard. But losing Anu just destroyed him."

Isha frowned. "Anu was his sister?"

"He's never talked about her to you?"

"No, I saw her picture at the sanctuary and was too scared to ask. I'm wearing her clothes."

"Good instincts. She was beautiful, wasn't she?"

"She was. But what happened to her?"

"Oh, I don't know if that's something I should tell," he said, holding the detached gun barrel up to his eye so that he could see the firelight on the other side.

Isha lay a hard stare on him.

Gowda stopped working and set the rifle down with a sigh.

"She was fifteen, almost the same as you are now. One evening she took an auto home from a dance lesson in Mysore, but she never arrived." He hesitated but could see she was going to make him say it regardless. He could not hold her gaze and say it, so he picked up a stick and poked at the fire. "It happens every day in this blasted country. Just check the papers. It's unthinkable." He could see her waiting and knew there was no sense delaying the explanation. "Three men took her from the cab that night. She was raped and beaten to death."

Isha's closed her eyes tight.

"That was just after Wolfgang died, and Arun simply couldn't parse living in a world without Anu—or a world where that kind of thing could happen to a beautiful, bright young kid. Worse still was that even though he wasn't there, and there wasn't a thing on earth he could have done, he blamed himself." Gowda was shaking his head, rubbing the white stubble of his face. "What a wonderful girl she was, the most lovely thing. You would have loved her," he said earnestly, meeting Isha's eyes as she opened them a sliver.

"After that he stayed with me at the farm for almost a year. Then he got into the priest work, helping the orphans. After what happened he no longer loved the world. He was overtaken by a sadness like winter that was very close to hate. He needed God—or something—and needed to do whatever he could, and I think the kids helped some."

"He seems to really love Thimma."

"Oh yes, he does. And the boy hasn't had any glue or booze in days now—this little adventure is doing him good too, I think."

Isha was quiet for a time. "I have a question."

"Ho." Gowda was re-wrapping the rifle into its cover now.

"Why isn't Arun a priest?"

"Oh, he never wanted to be a priest, he just wanted to know if it was possible to get close enough to God to pick a fight. He just liked working with the kids, I think. And wearing the robes helped him convince himself that peace existed, in spite of all he had done."

"What had he done?"

Gowda glared at her, strategizing how to tell this part.

"Did he do something bad?"

"Define bad."

"What was it?"

Gowda sighed heavily; there was no point in refusing her. "One of the boys he taught was badly beaten every day. Arun and the others took notice, of course, and spoke to the boy's parents. The mother was a poor battered thing; the father was a drunk brute. The usual village story."

"And?"

"And, well, speaking to them just made it worse—father pulled the boy out of school and beat the hell out of him just for good measure. The mother was pregnant at the time and every time he got drunk, he'd warn her and everyone else about how it had better be a boy."

"Was it a girl?"

"It was."

"And did the father try to kill her? Did Arun kill him first?"

Ramana Gowda considered her gravely in the firelight. "Thou art a wicked creature," he said, adopting the way of speaking that the characters in *Jungle Book* used. Isha's eyes were sparkling in the light. It was enough of an answer. "Well, Isha, around the time that the boy's mother had that little girl, the father did try to take the baby but had some bad luck. He accidentally fell a few dozen times onto a rock."

The hunter held Isha's eyes, and she grinned back wickedly, savage little thing that she was. He reached for a cigarette, which allowed him to turn his face to the shadow. For a moment he closed his eyes as scenes he'd just as well forget played with perfect clarity: the speeding motorcycle ride after he'd gotten the call, the villagers gathered around the house, the impossible amounts of blood in that room. The man's open skull. Arun drawn against the wall, sitting in blood and broken furniture.

And that was nothing compared to what Arun and Gowda had done together when Anu's killers had been released. They had worked them until their knuckles were raw, enough that they would have most likely died anyway. They had dug the hole together too, and then dumped the three of them inside—the bruised, swollen faces of those bastards lying in a pile. In the flicker of the flame it had been almost impossible to tell where one started and the others began—legs and arms and gashed faces, all swollen and slick with blood like a single tile from the floor of Hell. They should have left it at that and buried them as they were. But Arun poured four litres of gasoline onto them without flinching. The fire and screams burst from the earth high into the night.

It was no wonder that Arun broke in the months that followed—the fits, the crying, the rage, the weeks of sitting sullenly and smoking on the front porch of the estate. All this flashed before Gowda as he lit and puffed. He shook his head, shaking it all away. No, she didn't need that.

"He's a man that believes in peace but will catch fire to defend those he loves. He'll fight an army, that one."

"I like that."

"It can be dangerous. Sometimes it is *we* who have to protect *him*."

Isha nodded and realized something new. "I have another question."

"What?"

"The night those men came to our camp. You were very calm *until* Arun got up. Why?"

"Smart girl. You saw that?"

"Oh yes. You seemed more scared of what *he* would do than of what *they* could do."

"Well put."

"Thank you."

"Yes. I wanted to try and diffuse that little confrontation without leaving bodies behind."

"And you were scared Arun would—?"

"That he would become too... passionate."

Isha played with her lip, thinking.

The hunter spoke. "Arun is the best human I have ever met. But after Anu, he tends to take confrontations too far. He has his demons. Everyone does. It's just that in those situations it is usually best to keep your head cool. You know? He's had enough ugly things happen, but he has a good heart. And that's why we have to protect him. Well, it's your job to protect Kala, and it's Arun's job to protect you, and my job is to protect the lot of you loons! But I'll tell you, I haven't seen him this good in a long time. It's like the old Arun, or the closest I've seen since we lost Anu. It's a good thing he met you."

Isha was silent for a long time. His words had tightened her throat.

Gowda stole a glance at her through the smoke, fearing he had said too much. "You want me to read some Kipling?"

"No," Isha said, "I want to hear more real stories. Tell me some old stories."

"Ah, very well. I'll tell you about the time my grandfather was taken prisoner in the Andaman Islands and escaped to live with the Nicobar tribes."

So went the night.

At dawn, Kala came to where Isha's hammock hung and pushed her head into the girl. Isha moaned and slipped an arm out and around the tiger's neck. Kala waited eagerly, for there was much she had seen and done during the night. When Isha's feet touched ground, the tiger tackled her and pushed her broad forehead into her. Isha fought off the feline embrace, and Kala fell onto the leaves, stretched out, and exhibited the bloody patch on her chest where the hoof had hit.

As Isha gasped and knelt by Kala's side, the tiger tensed, her head snapping up and back. Gowda had been watching from a distance, and once Kala knew it, she grew stern and padded off. Isha waved to Gowda that it was okay and followed her tiger off into the green. She would need to get a leash on Kala and pack that wound with turmeric.

They broke fast on stale Kerala *parota* and a jar of pickle. Arun administered eye drops for Isha, who was still suffering her allergy of the eyes.

They followed an eastward course that day. Hathi's trunk was twitching with excitement. The sweet air of the jungle brought news of fresh jackfruit and a thousand tender shoots and succulent green things. Decaying tree trunks, distant carrion, and something far more intriguing. It was the scent of memories lost—musth and muscle and wise wrinkled eyes. Family. The memories were old— the light at the beginning, his first shaking steps, before he knew

THE GIRL AND THE TIGER · 179
THE GIRL AND THE TIGER · 179

how to use his trunk and before his milk tusks had fallen—and came from something he dared not be sure of just yet.

Thimma swayed atop Hathi as the priest and the hunter came behind. Isha half ran behind Kala and hooted often to stay within earshot of the others. Sometimes Kala would stay close. Other times Isha would trudge on emitting the low staccato chuff of tigers, the language she had learned from Kala. This was her orientation to the unseen tiger.

Walking became difficult, as did maintaining proximity to the group and trying not to get lost amongst the dense leaves and thorns. She found it difficult in the jungle to think of anything outside it. There was such scrambling to be done, such calculating, so much survival that it demanded the attention of all her senses.

"Isha, stay close," Gowda called so that it echoed.

"I am! I'm right here." She stood where the foliage permitted a view.

"Okay. But please!" He shook his head to Arun. "I don't like this. If she gets too far away, we'll never see her again."

"Oh come!"

"I've seen it happen. You don't think you are far, and then! When I was a boy and my father was marching me through the forest near Kutta, I stopped for a leak and he kept walking. *Four days later* they found me. I was starved and beaten up but all right, and that's only because I knew the bush. And if I can get lost, anyone can. Even her."

Arun nodded. "Isha, where is Kala?"

"It's been a few minutes since I saw her."

"But she is close?"

"Yeah."

"You come."

Isha hopped over some rocks and trotted to join the gang.

"Christ, look at you. Eat this." He handed her two *laddus*.

"I don't have time for laddu. Kala is starving. She's miserable."

"Okay then, we need to stop and let me hunt," Gowda said, walking over.

"I don't want hunting." Isha sighed, glancing at the heavy rifle on Gowda's shoulder. She could not imagine such a thing being fired in a place like this. Then again, seeing Kala look so hungry, and feeling the dizzying heat and thick jungle air made Isha feel that even she was growing weary of her principles.

"There's no choice, little bird," the hunter said with hands on his hips.

"He's right," said Arun. "How else is she going to get food?"

Isha sighed, nodded, and walked on.

Afternoon on the next day found Isha and Thimma on Hathi's back. Arun and Gowda were having trouble keeping up with the elephant's grand strides. The large pachyderm could cover meters with a single step, and the vegetation posed no hindrance to his trajectory.

At Arun's orders, Isha spent much of the day on Hathi's back. He said it was to save energy, that she was low. Keeping up with Kala had drained her energy. They resolved to let the tiger follow. Isha didn't mind since in the moist leaves of the forest, leeches seemed to sprout up wherever she set her feet. Atop the elephant, she picked them hurriedly from her legs and stomach.

Once they had sucked on, removing them was difficult, and when she pulled them off, they bled copiously. While burning a blood-full leech on his leg with the glowing end of a cigarette, Arun said that an anticoagulant in their saliva made normal blood flow faster. Isha began searching herself constantly, her hand slapping almost involuntarily to her ankle or thigh. When she found one, she would commit the gruesome act of removal, which left her to hold it there squirming and vomiting blood in her fingers, before she threw it away. She grew to hate them quickly, and for the first time in her life, she was finding her code of peace hard to follow.

At noon, Thimma drove Hathi to a deep stream full of mossy rocks and pools. Isha helped Thimma unload the packs from the elephant's back, and then climbed up to ride as the elephant submerged. Isha and Thimma swam on either side of Hathi beneath the giant ferns, below the green cathedral ceiling shifting high above. The water was clear and bluish black.

Kala came by with wide yellow eyes, drank at the side, and then left. It was hushed and beautiful in the forest. Thimma scrubbed his elephant just for tradition's sake, and because Hathi enjoyed it. Isha joined in. When finished, they lay on his whale's back side by side, looking up into the emerald paradise above, waiting for Arun and Gowda to arrive.

Kala took to exploring the slopes as the elephant and children walked within the stream at the bottom of the valley. The tiger knew she was home, but in this home, there was no food. Not even goats. She wove between the trees. She pushed high onto where the jungle gave way to grassy tops, windswept, where she could see forever—undulating rolling jungle, muscled green landscape heaving mist towards the sky, birds crossing.

When the priest and the hunter caught up to Isha and Thimma, they all ate a lunch of plantains on a rock, and then Isha and Thimma swam to the center of the pool to rest on the elephant's back while Arun and Gowda took stock of their supplies.

The forest was alive, falling leaves, gentle wind rocking the treetops. From far away a great clamor rose. It seemed to race toward them like a sonic wave, the insects in each part of the forest blasting to their loudest for several seconds before the ones earlier trailed off, and the ones beside them ramping up. So the wave of sound traveled with great volume and intensity.

Suddenly Hathi's trunk began to twitch. He lifted it and it curled. He rumbled and his head began moving from side to side, and suddenly his feet pushed below and he rose so fast that the children were rolled off. The rising elephant brought half of the pool with him, waves crashing on the mossy rocks. He stood stark still, facing the distance, listening.

"What is it?" Isha asked, getting to her feet, dripping.

Thimma shook his head: *Don't know.*

The elephant gave an annoyed snort for them to be silent.

Hathi's unseeing eyes were focused on nothing as his ears adjusted for maximum reception. He fit the pads of his feet firmly against the rocks of the stream to listen. When he heard it, he trembled, drew a breath and returned the call with a trumpet blast so loud that Isha and Thimma covered their ears and hit the ground. For some moments of ringing silence, the entire forest seemed to rain from the shockwave of sound that had knocked droplets from the leaves. The elephant stood with ears wide, listening. Isha and Thimma rose, sharing an astonished look.

Then Hathi charged forward.

Thimma leapt to the chase as the elephant hastened ahead.
Isha followed, leaving Arun and Gowda standing confused beside
the pile of packs and gear. Isha and Thimma were running full out
to keep pace with the giant steps as the elephant charged. Ferns
shivered and vines broke as they hurried past. The trees were swaying. The elephant made a sound they had never heard. And from
the dark distance of the jungle, many chirps and roars came. Everything was getting louder, the whole forest in crescendo. Frightened
white egrets leapt from the water and took wing along the hallway
before them as they ran.

The blind elephant tripped on a rock and faltered—his ears
and nose knew the way, but his eyes could not see the details.
Thimma shouted something that only Hathi understood. He slowed
and stuck out his tremendous leg. The boy ran with speed and
stepped up and leapt to clutch the elephant's ear and swung over
his leg. Isha came next and clasped his hand, pulled up by the boy
and pushed by the elephant's assisting trunk.

"*Ho!*" Thimma shouted, and Hathi charged on at full speed.
Kala was running along the side of the stream now, bounding and
slipping through the trees, yellow eyes wide with excitement.

Thimma was constantly shouting to Hathi. He'd never seen the
elephant so excited, so charged, and knew he was not running *from*
something but *to* something. They splashed and crashed and galloped through the Jungle. As they went shuddering on, the boy
deftly patted Hathi on the neck and spoke to him above the roar of
running to signify obstacles. Low branches almost knocked them
off. A fallen rotted log was drawing near. The speed was fantastic.
Isha could feel the rocks shifting beneath the heavy flat feet.

"Hold on!" Thimma yelled as the elephant smashed through a
fallen beam, splintering the wood and tripping and regaining speed.
Hathi's trunk was feeling along the edge of the water and followed
the flow as it rounded a corner. Then suddenly the elephant
stopped.

His trunk rose out before him, nostrils flaring and searching
the air. Isha sat up behind Thimma, and her mouth slowly fell
open.

Before them was a wide elbow of the stream where it became
large and flat at the turn. There, below the limitless canopy on the
opposite side, in the circular amphitheater, separated by a bend of
blue current, were over forty elephants. The great host of giants

stood side-by-side, tusk-to-tusk. They stood waiting, faces of wrinkled concern, trunks held aloft working. They were conversing, chirping, rumbling, watching. Broadbacks, grumblers, broke tusks, matriarchs, trumpeters—all ears flapping.

Above in the myriad branches, birds small and large gathered to watch the great meeting. Butterflies followed one another across the scene, oblivious, trailing in corkscrew flight through the air.

They were the jungle herd. They had been painted and stained, as was their custom, with the red jungle clay—the mark of their tribe. They stood stark against the turquoise of the stream and jungle green.

Hathi was trembling. He took a step forward and then another. Then, he paused and swayed and held out his foot. Isha and Thimma climbed down hurriedly and waded to the stream bank. Hathi crossed the water slowly, sinking up to his shoulder at the deepest point, then rising once again. His steps were tentative, his lashy eyelids fluttering over blind eyes. There was something in his posture, something incredulous, wonderful, and pained all at once.

At the other side of the stream, one old elephant with a long tear in one ear emerged from the herd. The ear billowed like an old weathered flag from her head, torn so that it hung in ribbons.

She rushed forward, and as she did, Hathi broke into a run so that the water erupted into great waves. The water boiled as the two elephants crashed toward each other. Hathi sobbed and the female roared, and when at last their foreheads collided, they wrapped trunks in the tightest of embraces. All the elephants clamored and chattered and flapped and flung their trunks. The old mother caressed her son's great face. The other elephants drew in, their trunks moving tenderly over his face, his fluttering, unseeing eyes.

"Amma," Thimma whispered.

Isha nodded, her mouth ajar.

Isha and Thimma sat, soaked and dripping on the rocks, as the elephants milled and swam and celebrated and learned what they could from their long-lost brother. Hathi looked strange in his naked grayness as the herd of red giants surrounded him. The celebratory congress went on for some time, but gradually grew quiet, and large heads began turning toward the opposite bank.

They began a slow advance across the pool. Isha moved to stand but Thimma held her still. Isha felt herself blinking rapidly. Her heart felt like it was trying to climb out and run away. Ele-

phants had always been soft in her mind, playful, somehow friendly creatures. Meeting Hathi, the mountainous giant made of
animated, wrinkled cement, had changed all of that, but he was still
kind in his hugeness.

What approached her now was a host of the most monstrous
and sinister things she had ever seen. Their orange eyes wrapped in
wrinkles held a severity she had no foundation to receive. From
their heads billowed shredded ears. Hung from their faces were
long, cracked tusks. These were mountains of flesh and bone and
tusk that were aware of her in a startlingly complex way. They had
stories, tragedies, opinions. And now she was the object of their
scrutiny.

Slow-motion steps of tree-sized feet sent the mud and rocks
gushing outward, and fish and frogs scrambled and swam for their
lives. The herd came across the water until they stood above Isha
and Thimma, so that the jungle canopy became eclipsed by flapping ears and wrinkled skin. Isha put her hand to her chest to try
and calm her heart. They came as a host, encircling the two children in wrinkled elbow joints and hanging trunks, until the
elephants stood ear to ear in a circle. All faced inward, three deep,
looking down at the young humans.

Isha was sitting back-to-back with Thimma. The monstrous
faces were godlike above. Thimma put his palms together in prayer
hands and closed his eyes. Isha did the same but still peered upward. Thimma began singing softly. He nudged for Isha to do the
same.

"I don't know the words!" she whispered hoarsely. But he
swore and nudged her, and she began humming whatever came out.
Thimma sang the song that was only sung in his old village. Isha
sang the Sanskrit tune Ajji used to sing her to sleep. And so in
small, scared voices they sang, gazing up the long trunks and tusks
to the stern orange eyes above.

Many trunks hung side by side like a curtain. Some curled and
probed close, domed heads shifting above them, great grunting and
deep vast breaths drawn. One trunk, as thick as her own body,
reached in and gently grasped a lock of Isha's hair. She could hear
the vacuumed air rushing her scent up the curious long tube. The
trunks were great prickly hoses that breathed rivers of hot air onto
them and deposited surprising amounts of mucus. As they breathed

the scents of her, the trunks sucked great quantities in so that Isha clutched her hair to keep it from being sucked up the trunk.

Even in the terror of the moment, Isha's found herself running a ream of internal monologue. *Is this real life? I've never been so scared in my life! Have I?* A blast exhalation came from one trunk with such violent cosmic force that she fell over, holding her ears, and a small scream escaped her lips. The elephants clamored, suddenly nervous.

Thimma helped her to sit up. He began rocking, singing slightly louder now. She could tell from his closed eyes that he was simply praying. He knew from a lifetime around elephants that these creatures could and would kill them if it was so decided by the herd. Isha prayed too, though she realized she didn't know how. She also couldn't close her eyes as Thimma had. She couldn't bear it. So she watched the long noses and orange, beady eyes. She could see them debating what to do, discussing it in their own strange tongue.

Hathi pushed through the border of thick hind sides. The others parted to let him through. He shifted left and right to make more space, and then extended his trunk and caressed his boy's face. Then, holding his trunk above Thimma's head, he dumped a great quantity of water on the boy to the entertainment of the rest of the elephants, who craned and jostled for the chance to see. Hathi's trunk swung back to the water to draw more, and Isha could swear she saw the river lose volume. When the trunk swung back overhead, she closed her eyes tightly. What seemed like an entire bathtub's worth of water came crashing down on her. The herd seemed greatly amused.

Hathi held out his foot, and Thimma, dripping wet, stood. Isha clutched his hand with an urgency that revealed her fear. An ever-so-slight smile crossed Thimma's face as he took her hand. They climbed up onto the elephant's back as the rest of the herd watched and said a great many things to one another that the children could not understand.

The old cow with the flagged ear offered her tail to her son, and Hathi's trunk curled around it. Other elephants were turning now; the group was leaving. Isha became suddenly aware of the vastness of the jungle around them, and the consequences of being left unattended in such a wilderness. Ears flapped and trunks swung. They were already moving. Isha looked back trying to see downstream. Arun and Gowda must be watching, too scared to come close. *They must be*, she thought.

But these hopes were crushed with each lumbering step as the elephant parade went on. She looked backward until her neck hurt, and until the branches and overhanging vines slapped and smacked her and cut her skin. Arun and Gowda were nowhere to be seen. Kala seemed to have vanished. The entire world was a mountain range of broad, moving backs.

Shadow fell over the jungle and high above, in the heavens of the canopy, the latticed branches of ancient trees shone with stars. Isha ducked when Thimma did as low branches raked over Hathi's back. They swayed forward in the gathering gloom, two frail figures nestled on the back of a giant at the center of the herd. Bats and night birds began calling, and the steady crash of pachyderm marching rustled and snapped through the forest.

Isha watched the world around her, half expecting to awake from a fantastic dream. Fearing that her eyes and mind had forsaken her, she kept one hand on Thimma's back and one hand flat on Hathi's shoulder—two pieces of reality made concrete by her touch. They crossed streams and moonlit fields as they moved through the nameless spaces of the great jungle. No, this was not a dream, but it was a separate world from the one Isha knew. A new, strange, dark world, where the conversations of long-nosed giants came in tongues she could not decipher. Where the creaking trees knew centuries, and the permanent forces of wind and energy, tooth and claw, had somehow survived in the primeval shadows, unseen and unknown in the present tense of the modern world. It was the place she had heard of, imagined, dreamed of, even doubted, but never known.

18

THE TRIBE

Kala watched anxiously from some distance away as the elephants spoke in their own tongue and milled about. On the back of one of the herd were two young humans, huddled, cold, and wet in the chilled misty jungle night. Around them, the herd held trunks and rubbed foreheads and said a great many things that she could not understand, and soon the tiger grew frustrated with waiting.

The elephants made their way over the grassy mountaintops and back down into the jungle, down to the depths of the valley. Heavy chains clinked and rushed over the earth. At least two of the elephants present were runaway work elephants that had rejoined he herd. *But from where?* Isha's mind was already calculating days into the future, wondering if Thimma might be able to pilot one of these out to safety. Already feeling starved and dizzy, she watched vines pass. She could catch on to one of them and slide down to the ground, but that would only accomplish getting her off the elephant. Then she'd be lost and alone. Which would be worse. She knew they would have to think of something soon, but Hathi was clearly no longer interested in taking orders, and the herd seemed determined to march into the very heart of the jungle.

All the while the tiger followed, glaring at a distance as the tusked monsters carried away her girl. But the tiger dared not follow when the herd crashed through a wall of vine and thorns into a stream that led through a dense corridor of vegetation. The likelihood of being crushed while inside was too great. Instead, the tiger watched as the elephants filed into the tunnel and vanished. She paced and growled and chuffed to herself in the lonely night as the last of the elephant tails disappeared.

Inside the corridor, halfway down the line of elephants, Isha and Thimma hugged down onto Hathi's back to avoid being scraped off by the vines and branches. The elephants marched, single file, down in the trench of the valley, below the layers of canopy, where they could no longer see the sky. It was nearly an hour before they emerged into the ancient courtyard. The hairs on Isha's neck stood on end when she saw.

Under moonlight bright enough to cast shadows, and beneath stars nearly dense enough to crowd the blackout of the sky, the high broken temple walls stood. Vines and lianas clutched the ancient city, pulling it slowly down, back toward the earth. Banyan trees had grown from the cracks and up the walls like snakes frozen in time. On the walls beneath the ivy, carved tigers, deer, and men were held in static stone agony. Stone elephants marched in endless numbers around the ornate foundation. Above them were maharajas and lovers and saints. The faces of forgotten gods scowled; man and beast alike grimaced in wrath and passion. Scores of monkeys slept huddled in the cracked walls and ledges, their tails and arms hung amongst the ivy like gradually incarnating flesh in the penumbral stone shadows. Ancient pools with cobbled borders held black water where stars and leaves trembled on the surface. Great doorways yawned threateningly, hung with vines pulsing with darkness and ancient secrets.

The elephants lumbered through the courtyard, stepping over giant fallen stones and plucking fruit from thick old jackfruit trees, planted long ago. Abandoned long ago. There were other trees with fruits here too, the elephants knew, that no longer existed anywhere else.

Isha's eyes were wide as Hathi swayed behind his mother, socializing here and there with other elephants, plucking sweet fruit and mashing it between giant corrugated teeth. Her eyes went frequently to the cracked stone stairway that led to the great central doorway, the yawning darkness beneath the vines. The elephants would go to the door and reach inside, as if communicating, touching something in the blackness.

The surreal night seemed endless, and atop the elephant she slept and woke and slept again.

As the night ended, mist settled in the valley, eclipsing the stars. In a blue world of vines and ruined stone, the monkeys woke and began casting stones onto the elephants. With the monkeys waking and millions of bats returning to the temple hollows, the dim morning became chaos. Stones and branches and bat feces filled the air. With a great flapping of ears and swaying of trunks, the herd mobilized and funneled back into the green corridor that lead back along the stream and away from the temple.

Isha clung to Thimma for warmth, clenching her jaw to stop her teeth from rattling. How could the jungle be so cold? It simply didn't make sense. Where was Kala? *Ayyo Deva!* Now it had truly gone too far! She thought of jumping from the elephant, but it was too high up. *It must be twelve feet!* Most times she could not see the ground, so dense was the foliage they marched through. Hours after they had emerged from the green corridor, the sun at last warmed the world and the jungle returned to the chattering, burning heat of the day. There was no sign of Kala.

"What is happening to us?" she asked Thimma miserably. But Thimma said nothing. She tried to count how many mountains they had crossed. Who could tell in so much cold, with so many branches to duck? Who could think amid such insanity?

Questions faded as they went endlessly onward. Over hills and down into valleys. Then up again, to the peaks of forested mountains with golden windswept grasslands. Isha's stomach felt like it was stabbing her insides, begging for food. She felt her eyes lilting and her brain slowing. There was no Arun to cook veggies or provide a laddu or chocolate. Thimma wouldn't talk and the elephants wouldn't stop. Arun and Gowda, those poor men! They would be ragged with worry. Oh, how she missed Arun's fastidious care and Gowda's confident protection. She wondered how it could be possible to miss anyone quite so badly after knowing them for so short a time. She prayed to be reunited with them.

It was on the downward slope near afternoon that Isha awoke with a start, having fallen asleep with cheek pressed on the flat of Thimma's back. He was bouncing a shoulder to wake her.

The herd had emerged from the jungle into a great open field. Yellow grass rippled in the hot breeze as the red herd moved in toward a central pool of water. Isha wiped drool from her mouth, squinting.

"Did you see Kala?"

His head shook in front of her. He was pointing. At first, she couldn't see what he was pointing at. Then he leaned back so she could look down his arm and pointed finger. At the edge of the field, standing in the jungle, were two men. They weren't Arun or Gowda. They were tribals.

Although they were too far away to see their faces, their posture showed their shock. The men watched as the herd moved into the water, unable to believe what their eyes saw.

Thimma began shouting at Hathi and pumping his feet behind the elephant's ears. Hathi groaned and shook his head like a wet dog, his trunk still wrapped around his mother's tail. Thimma shouted louder and beat his open palm on Hathi's head. The elephant paused, his trunk going taut as it held to his mother. He bent and lifted his leg. Thimma swore and struck Hathi on the head, but the elephant shook its head violently.

Thimma scrambled down and then turned to receive Isha who fell into his arms. There were tears in his eyes. No sooner had their feet hit the ground than the other elephants began growing nervous. They had become separate creatures of mysterious agency. Groans came from their throats, ears flared, and tails raised. Something had changed. There was a great shifting of padded feet.

Thimma searched for a large stick and then ran up to Hathi. Through his crying he shouted rapid insults and orders like a little machine gun. His voice was breaking as he raised the stick and slapped it hard across Hathi's hide. And again, harder. Hathi howled at him and showed his rump, moving with his mother into the lake. Thimma whipped him as hard as he could and cursed and spat. Two large cows spread their ears now, trumpeting and raising their tails. They came at Thimma threateningly. Thimma had no choice but to run.

They made their way across the field. Thimma was weeping. Isha felt dizzy. It had been over a day since she had eaten.

At the forest edge, one of the men, a muscular tribal man with curly black-and-silver hair and a heavy mustache, watched them with wonder in his eyes. He was rubbing the thick stubble on his cheeks as they approached. Thimma tried to wipe away his tears. Isha was trying to walk in a straight line, but her mind was slipping. There was a scar on the man's face that ran from his eye up back out of sight into his hair. His eyes were incredibly fierce and full of wonder. The man began asking Thimma excited questions just as Isha fell to the ground, unconscious.

When she woke, she sat up quickly. It was dark, but the air smelled like afternoon, thick with masala and cow dung. She was still for a long time, her mind slowly putting back together what had happened. It felt so good to lie down, to not move, to be safe. She faded out, then woke again later. She stood and went to the door, which was nothing more than a piece of crude cloth hung over the doorway of the house. The floor was earthen.

Thimma was sitting outside. He wobbled his head at her.

"Where are we?" she said in Kannada.

"*Halli. Halli,*" Thimma said.

"Arun? Gowda?"

Thimma shook his head.

"Kala?"

He shook his head.

"Arun! Gowda!" Isha steadied herself against the mud wall of the house.

Thimma made a walking motion with two fingers. "*Hōgu, hōgu*—go, go!"

"We should go?"

He shook his head in frustration. He held out his palm for her to stay.

When he returned, the man with curly black-and-silver hair and mustache was with him and an old woman with a vessel. She sat down and arranged the items around her. She reached down to touch Isha's feet and then her own heart. Then she unrolled a cloth with chapatis. Inside the vessel was sambar. A wrinkled old hand with tattoos across the back passed Isha a plate. She ate like a starved wolf, tearing chapati and soaking it deep into the scalding sambar. It burned her fingers and mouth, but hunger had overridden all other instincts and she could not stop. When she finally finished, she washed her hands, climbed between the rough sheets, and dropped off to sleep.

The next morning Isha woke slowly and rose to one elbow. Arun was sleeping on the floor on the other side of the room. He was splayed out like he'd been shot and fallen dead. Beside him, Gowda's thick stomach rose and fell, more than ever a walrus, save for his feet, which were pointing upward to the ceiling. He was still wearing socks.

Isha rose to find water. She sat on the bench built into the outside of the house like a large single step, dipping a copper cup into the vessel, downing cup after cup of stream water. There were two deer at the edge of the village, and she watched them walk amongst the houses. She had never seen such a thing as wild animals voluntarily approaching humans. Every so often a woman would pass carrying a bucket of water on her head. Each of them sang softly, the bright blue or green or red plastic of the bucket catching the morning rays.

"That's it," Isha said to herself. "I've died and woken up in *The Jungle Book*. This can't be real." She looked over her shoulder and hissed, "Arun!"

There was rustling from inside the hut, a cough, and Arun emerged with a hand shielding the brightness from his eyes. His mouth said her name but no sound came. He hugged her tightly and smiled. She smiled back and rubbed her eyes. He held up a finger—*wait*. He emerged with the little eyedropper bottle and she sat on the *katte* and he brushed her hair softly aside and held her face as he administered the drops.

"Why can't you speak?" she smiled, gently rubbing one eye.

In a very small, very hollow rasp, he tried to answer. He could not. He touched his throat and shook his head.

"You lost your voice?"

He grinned, and put his hands to his mouth, acting out screaming "EEE-SHAAA! EEE-SHAAA!" and she understood.

"I'm so sorry. Hathi just ran. There was nothing we could do..."

Arun nodded and held a finger to his lips. He mouthed, *Thimma*.

"Thimma told you?"

He nodded. Arun held invisible reins, as if on a runaway horse.

Isha smiled, a lopsided smile with her tongue curling out of her teeth. Yes!

He put his arm to his nose like an elephant. She made floppy ears of her hands, bent over, and shook back and forth.

As they acted like elephants, a tribal woman with water balanced on her head nearly tripped watching them.

They laughed together.

A woman somewhere was singing now.

Isha touched her own throat with a questioning wince.

He winked and shook his head. *No, it's okay.*

Her head wobbled.

His fingers moved over his face to make stripes.

Her smile faded at the thought. "No. I haven't seen Kala."

Kala's striped face was long and hollow, her white whiskers spread out white and wild from her snout. The black flecks on her ears moved slowly, pivoting, searching. She had watched as the heavy-footed giants carried Isha and the boy. She had trailed them for some miles and lay angrily in the shadows while they grazed. It had been three days since she had eaten, and her stomach was screaming, but the pain of it paled against the stress of being apart from Isha.

Kala was learning that nothing in the jungle exists without protection. Some lizards vanished as their skin warmed to the sur-rounding moss, while other lizards could extend their ribs into wings and fly from tree to tree where birds raced through the tan-gled canopy. Small snakes carried fangs filled with deadly venom. Bees guarded their honey with the pain of millions. Kala had chased one large rodent that had a thousand sharp quills on its back and tail. She chased a barking deer that vanished into a tunnel of thorns she could not enter. She pawed at fish that were too slippery to snatch. Every creature here was invisible, fast, venomous, or so large she would not dare attack it. The bison regarded her with heavy lidded eyes, their muscle-draped shoulders calm with the promise of horn and hoof that could crush a young tiger.

Kala's stomach hurt. She wished for food. Her hunger was throbbing now and made it hard for her to think clearly. More than ever, the tiger pined for the girl. She wanted terribly for care. She was, after all, still just a large cub and could not understand what had happened. All she knew was hunger. She stalked up through an avalanche and over a pass down into a marsh where a herd of wild bison grazed.

Although the elephants were larger, somehow these were the most terrifying animals she had seen. Each of the monstrous cattle were armed with heavy horns and draped in sheets of muscle. She had chosen a calf and burst out of the grass after it. But her paws sank in the deep, soggy peat. Before she knew what had happened, three adult bison were around her, steaming, rumbling, charging. She tried to run, but the mud sucked at her legs. The largest of them was the first to hit and delivered a blow that sent her spinning.

Winded and terrified, she ran. Eyes wide and ears flat with fear, she had scrambled away as they bore down on her, inches away from being crushed by a hoof or gored by a horn. After the narrow escape, she lay in the shade panting; she slept for a time. When she woke, her ribs were throbbing so that it hurt to breath. The walls of her stomach seemed to press against one another. She stood and then lay back down.

19

There's No Going Home

It was with much shouting and saliva that Thimma spoke to the tribal leaders and mahouts. The tribals were skeptical of the newcomers and had initially been adamant that they were escorted out of the jungle immediately. On top of their general fear of outsiders was the urgent threat of consequences from the Forest Department. Outsiders were not allowed in the Periamangalam. Their supernatural fear, however, superseded all other logic. That Isha and Thimma had come in with the wild herd was so far beyond comprehension that the mahouts and tribal leaders could barely speak of it.

When Thimma told them of the tiger, they had laughed. But their laughter fell away to stunned silence as the village dogs proved his words. Wherever Isha walked, the dogs retreated. Their fur bristled and lips curled in snarls, they would run and shit themselves involuntarily. Her hair and skin and clothes were rich with the scent of a great predator that the dogs had never known, and yet knew in the ancient part of their bones. From Isha to the dogs, and to the dark village eyes, ancient instincts created a shadow of doom around her, so that wherever she walked, bodies retreated in fear.

And so Arun and Isha and Ramana Gowda had listed from a distance as Thimma shouted in a shrill boyish staccato, imploring them, swearing that they had no idea what they were dealing with. After nearly an hour he returned with the news that they were permitted to move camp to the outside of the village, in case of Kala's return. The next morning there would be a meeting of the tribal leaders, and a decision would be made.

Light was beginning to come to the world when Arun found Isha sitting by the fire. He smiled at the sleeping form of Gowda and patted Isha on the head. She watched, rubbing her sleepy eyes as he opened his pack and removed her eye drops. For some silent moments, she leaned back on her pack as he put drops into her eyes. Next, he stowed the drops and withdrew paste and toothbrush. Unscrewing the cap, he motioned for her to take some. She rose on stiffened legs and removed her own brush and squeezed a glob onto the bristles.

They walked into the forest in silence. Near the stream they dipped their brushes in the blue water. For a long time, the only sound was birds calling and the hiss of brushes on teeth. Arun watched her brushing miserably, her eyes unfocused and far away. He longed to see her smile. He held the brush still, bared his teeth, and began shaking his head instead. A frothy smile bloomed on Isha's face. They sat side by side: heads shaking and hands held still, mint and clove lather dripping on their lips. Isha spat and smiled, despite all that troubled her.

Back at camp, Arun washed her clothes and bandaged her wounds (there were many from the branches and brambles that had raked over the elephant backs). Isha could feel sleep beginning to tug at her, but the meeting would be starting soon. Arun watched her as she hung clothes on the line he had tied. It looked as if she had taken the entire world's weight onto herself. He pitied her and prayed that the meeting would go well, prayed the tribals would help them find Kala.

Arun had instructed Isha—as best he could with his voice gone—that this meeting would depend greatly on her performance. He had done it gently and with care so as not to scare her. These were people, he said, who believed in the forest, in myriad animal gods, people who had lost their way. They would be examining Isha to see if she was what they expected her to be—something profound, a girl who could walk with tigers. It was something of an act, he explained to her.

"You need to act the part. They need to see it in your eyes. Your eyes have to be as hard as stone. I've seen you do it, but you must do it in this meeting. You have to talk as if you were sent for this purpose, born for it, and like nothing will stop you. You need to believe in what you have become."

Isha nodded but seemed to withdraw inside herself after Arun's talk. She spent the hour before the meeting listening to Arun's cassette player on headphones. Arun and Gowda took advantage of that time to hold a planning session. They walked along the edge of the village.

The roofs were palm and huts were mud. The pathways were swept earth and there were gardened flowers and fruits everywhere. It was a village constructed from earth and dung by raw human palms. It sat between two streams, one on the east side where Arun and Isha had brushed that morning, and another running north. Arun and Gowda came to the northerly stream where women in colorful robes gathered at the side of a stream. Silver jewelry clattered about their ankles as they sang and beat laundry against rocks at the water's edge. Others, similarly clad in brilliant textile decorated intricately with images of leaves and elephants and trees, lifted full basins of water onto each other's heads. Slender young women walked in a train, each with a basin balancing on their head. Some used a hand to stabilize the rocking water. Others carried vessels in their arms as well as on their heads. The morning sun in the east lit the vessels green and red and blue or yellow.

Ramana Gowda nudged Arun, who wobbled his head slightly, taken with the grace and poise of the feminine contours before them. At the stream stood a woman with uncompromising, piercing black eyes. Save for the tunic at her waist, she was unclothed. She stood as proud and rigid as a tree, her near-black skin tight over her toned muscles and full breasts. Many beaded necklaces hung from her neck across the furrows of her ribs, and above her hand that still clutched a dripping cloth, long cables of sinuous muscle slithered under her tattooed skin. Beside her, the younger water girls saw the men approaching and gathered in, hurrying away as best they could: a whispering urgent procession of jingling bangles and anklets, black almond eyes, fearful, curious glances. The tall woman stood on like a guardian sphinx and made no effort to cover her naked body. She watched the men until they passed.

Soon after Thimma was leading Isha, Arun, and Gowda to the meeting. The village was a pitiful collection of cracked houses among a forest of mostly planted teak. Many men were drunk, many of the women looked battered and tired. Desperation and fear

were thick in the air. When they reached the meeting area, the rest
of the village was already gathered beneath a thatched common
structure with posts but no walls. Bodies at the center were cross-
legged or kneeling. Around the outside, many stood. The space was
hot and tense and full of guarded black eyes, all of which were focused on Isha.

The effect Arun's coaching had had on Isha was exactly what
he had feared. Instead of motivating, it had intimidated her. Now in
the cramped meeting space below the thatched palm roof, her eyes
were downcast, her posture withdrawn. Her few glances up had
identified one woman she found particularly intimidating.

"That's her," Arun said to Gowda, who nodded.

"Who?" Isha asked.

"We saw her earlier, at the stream washing."

"I am Sudha," the woman said. "Matriarch of the Budakattu."

Thimma, through Arun, explained that the village they were in
was only kilometers from the forest fringe. The people here took
jobs in the outside coffee estates. They had regular contact with the
Forest Department rangers and the outside world. They used money. Whereas the Budakattu people were a settlement deep inside
the forest where there was virtually no contact to the outside world.
Sudha's power extended over several hamlets in the Periamangalam range, and though she lived in the Budakattu settlement, she
had come to the forest's edge to settle the matter of the outsiders.

Sudha waited for Thimma to translate with black eyes that
never wavered from Isha's. Sudha spoke:

"Two generations ago there was a girl who, when she was
young, could speak to the animals. She would walk among the wild
elephant herd, she could climb with the monkeys. Some said she
slept nestled in the stripes of warm tigers in the night. Others said
she could shift shape to become a bird. When the girl bled her first,
she came bearing a gift from the forest. It was a peace offering
from the animals to the tribes. It was a single seed. She planted the
tree and took leave of her village, this village, many monsoons
ago."

Isha, Arun, and Gowda listened as Thimma translated from
Kuruba-Kannada. Arun held near to Isha, translating it into a whispered concoction of Kannada and English into her ear.

"She was not seen for decades. The tree grew from a sapling
into a great banyan tree with many rippling vines and muscles and

arms. It spread. Today it is a sacred place in the forest, for each year the bees migrate across the forest to make tremendous hives. That single tree holds as much honey as the entire rest of the forest, and each year the village harvests the honey. And so the gift of the forest creatures, and the wild girl, continues to be a blessing. She is our link to the jungle. Kuḷḷamma, they called her. The *devathe*, the walker, the changer of shape. The last time she was seen, she was five generations aged. That was the year of the blood rain."

Thimma finished translating to Arun and Arun finished translating to Isha.

Isha looked up. *The year of the blood rain.*

They were silent for a time.

Sudha continued. "One week ago, the honey hives were ready for harvest on the tree. Over fifty of them, each as large as a man, hung from the branches of the sacred tree. But they were stolen from us in the night."

Sudha's eyes narrowed and her beauty became terrible.

"It was the Forest Department. They take the honey like they take our timber. They take our forest for themselves to profit from the wood. They sell the honey and give it to their families. They take what is ours for themselves. They will not let us keep cows. Why shouldn't the tribes be in charge of the forest? Let the people *of* the forest protect it. Let us have a say in our own lives. But they will not let it be so."

Isha was still. She could feel every eye in the village moving over her.

"The local politicians in Nalkere have sought to help us. There are plans to build a dam. A dam that would bring us employment, medical access, power over our own lives. We have voted to support it. And for that reason, we cannot risk having any of you here. Our relationship with the Forest Department is tenuous. We hate them. They hate us. So it is. But we know well what misery they can cause us. If we are caught grazing cattle inside the forest, if we are found hunting deer, we will be evicted from our own homes. The home we have always known since the rain first made the rivers."

Arun raised a hand to speak.

Sudha ignored him.

He spoke anyway. "Aren't they your gods? The tiger, the elephant, the trees?"

Thimma translated.

A filthy drunken man who was missing half a leg leaned in and shouted something that Thimma seemed ashamed to repeat. Arun nudged him. Thimma translated: "The gods are gone from this forest. We killed them long ago."

Sudha's face was black stone with obsidian eyes; her purple lips were twisted with passion around broad white teeth as she spoke.

"It is true that in the days of our ancestors, the people and the animals were one. We were all forest people. But now we are trapped in our own land. Now the government calls us uncivilized. Primitive. And when we protest these names, when we fight for our own land, they brand us Naxalites if we do not follow their every wish.

"And while no one can see into the shadows, while we are chained by rules, they do what they like. They harvest teak, they steal our cows. They build new roads. They are starving us out. And then what? They choose some places, build for foreigners, plant fruit trees and spread salt along the pathways so the deer come—so that the tourists can see the creatures of the forest. So they can call it a tiger reserve and make *crores* of rupees? In this way they even use the tiger against us. Tribal people are forced out of tiger reserves."

The air was getting hotter. Isha struggled to control herself. Emotion boiled in her, pushing against the weight of all those eyes, constricting her throat. She drew a deep breath, gathering the courage to speak.

"The tiger belongs in the forest too, and you have no right—"

Sudha's voice came down on her like a hammer before Thimma's translation was complete. "Do you want to speak to me of rights? Ask your friend Thimma how his village fared at the hands of the government. Ask any of our farmers how much of crops are taken by the elephant's trunk, how many lives have been crushed beneath the elephant's feet. Ask Seena of our village where his foot went, and how it felt when the tiger bit it off. Ask the children and mothers who died during childbirth because we are forced to live as animals here with no access to medical treatment. How many villages have been forced to move from forests that are suddenly 'tiger reserves'? *We* have no rights. *We* have nowhere else to go! Do not speak to me of rights."

Isha felt herself buckle beneath the ferocity of Sudha's gaze. Sudha's eyes had been forged in hardship Isha could not imagine, and the woman's gaze held the girl like a vice. It was a gaze wrought from a life of loss, full of abject desperation and ferocious will to survive. To this woman, Isha was just a child, a spoiled rich child of the world that had ruined so much. To these people she was a city person, one of the throbbing millions who stole their timber, their water, and cut their forest back.

Suddenly she thought of home, of the gadgets and cell phones and roads. Somehow in the vast, modern world, this tiny Jungle Book village had endured. Along the way, these people had lost almost everything. She was the enemy. How could she look them in the eyes? How? Even Isha, *Isha Iron Eyes* as Appa always said, stood no chance against the lifetimes of suffering that was etched in the eyes of these people.

She sat beneath Sudha's glare and focused desperately on disappearing. No, here iron eyes were no good. These people had eyes made of something much harder. She realized how long it had been since she had even thought of it all, of *them* all, back home. A wave of weariness and sorrow washed over her.

With Isha defeated, Sudha turned to address the rest of the forest folk. What followed was chaotic squabble. Ramana Gowda tried to speak and they silenced him. He, they said, was an estate owner, an enemy like the rest who would just as soon cut down the forest to earn his riches. Arun tried to speak but still couldn't, and anyway they called him a foreigner and a missionary. He was too weak of throat to explain that he was neither. His face reddened with the accumulated disgust for names he had been called many times before.

The tribal council's decision was clear: the outsiders would leave the forest at dawn. Thimma, they said, would not be permitted to leave. He would accompany the village's lead mahout, Killahuntha, into the jungle and attempt to bring in the runaway elephants.

An hour before dusk, Isha was sulking at camp. Arun and Gowda had gone to walk and smoke, despite Arun's throat. They needed time to discuss the next move, if there was one. They were standing beside the village water basin when a Forest Department vehicle pulled out of the jungle and parked between the huts. Three officers emerged from the car. Arun and Gowda watched as they surveyed the scene. They wore brown official uniforms and black belts; each carried a baton. One had a rifle over one shoulder.

Gowda swore so that only Arun could hear.

"What happens next?" Arun asked quietly.

Gowda sighed heavily. One of the officers began walking toward them. Arun stood beside Gowda. The officer did not offer his hand. He looked in either direction, pushed his mustache down from the sides, and spoke.

"You are the ones with the…" He hesitated before saying what sounded ridiculous. "With the tiger. Yes?" His eyes were direct and strangely candid. Neither Arun nor Gowda moved. The man continued, "The CCF is coming in the morning. The girl's parents are with him. They are in Nalkere now."

The officer drew a breath and nodded as if he had done something he had deliberated greatly about doing. He turned curtly and walked back toward the jeep.

Arun sat down as if he were ninety years old. Gowda, rubbing his coarse, gray-spiked face, turned so they faced each other. For a long moment, they were silent. Gowda watched Arun carefully as the information moved through him, and the implications manifested on his face. Arun drew a deep breath and shook his head.

"You knew this would happen eventually," Gowda said in a gentle rasp.

Arun's hand was over his mouth. His eyes were wide. The hand followed the hollow contours of his cheeks and down. He shook his head. "Not yet though…" The words were almost silent. He shook his head as if he could disagree and deny the outcome. "Not yet! It's not over." He looked up at Gowda. "What do we do?"

Ramana Gowda gave a long pause. He was keeping the part of him that felt panic deep inside the barrel of his chest, far behind the theater of his gray eyes. Suddenly Arun looked remarkably like the lost fifteen-year-old boy that Gowda remembered. He looked a lot like Wolfgang, but young and handsome. Gowda couldn't remember Wolfgang ever looking so young. The hunter felt a surge of love for him. It was accompanied by a hollow dread in his stomach where the memory of Arun's depression lived. He was steady and calm, like some legendary thespian. What Arun needed now was calm.

"What do you think is the right thing to do?"

Arun made a disgusted face and held up his hands. "Well, why'd he let us know? He is giving us time to run."

Gowda shook the question off. There was no time to contemplate the strange machinations of a forest officer's brain. "That's not important right now. What is the right thing to do? I want to hear you tell me. Think about all the things that could have happened to her by now, that somehow—thank God—didn't. She should have been crushed or starved or…" He gathered himself for a moment. "This is not a game they are playing here—there are lives at stake. These people have fucking nothing and they'll fight like hell to protect it. And the Forest Department is full of wolves. They won't like a little girl coming in…" Gowda cast about for gentler words but could not find them. "Think of Anu, Arun."

Arun looked up with a fighting rage in his eyes at the mention of Anu, but it cooled on the gray sternness of Gowda's gaze. Gowda locked his gray eyes on the boy. Arun glanced down, back up, and then away again.

"Look, if you want to go chase after that tiger and give her a deer each week, I'm happy to do it. But think about what the *right* thing is to do. For *her* safety. For her poor parents, whoever they are. Think about what you do next. Okay?"

Arun's head was shaking. His eyes were already a thousand miles away.

That night they sat around the fire on the outskirts of the village. Isha's arms were crossed tight. Her face was a storm of anger and defeat. She knew she had let everyone down, and it was eating her inside. Ramana Gowda had run out of cigarettes and cigars and was monologuing and pacing like an angry buffalo. Thimma was nowhere to be seen. Isha scowled into the fire as Gowda's rant ran on.

"They're jackasses. Absolute drunken, useless scum. That's why they have nowhere left to live. Every time they get paid, they drink it away. Every time a rich politician dreams up a new dam or road, these people believe it will help them. They actually believe it! Little do they know they are signing their own deaths. It is brilliant, I suppose, to make them think they'll get anything out of it. What are jobs to these people? Ha! Give them a dream, some cheap booze, and let them die off! Smart men, these politicians. And the tribals can't see it. But what does a dam do? Flood the forest! What do roads do? Let in the outside!

"They deserve what they get, I tell you. People that stupid shouldn't have anywhere to live. You know how many of them I employ on the estate? Do you know how many I've sent to school with my own money? And what do they do? They drink it all away—they don't want to be happy, I tell you!" Gowda gritted his teeth, swatting away a flying ember.

"So it's done then?" Isha said weakly.

Arun's hood was up. He said nothing.

Isha glared at him. "C'mon! You are the one who is supposed to be able to make the wrong decision. How do we get out of this?"

Arun held his throat as he spoke in a voice that was still faint. "I told you already the only thing we can do is fight. We have to go out now and find Kala, move back into the forest, make a run for it. That or we need to kill time until we can convince them to have another meeting. Except this time, you need to speak up and not just sit there like a scared little girl."

Isha's mouth fell open. She felt as if he had slapped her face. "*I* need to speak up this time? You hardly said anything."

"What I say doesn't count. You are the one with the tiger."

Isha shook her head, blinking like someone who had walked face first into spider webs. How could he expect her to have spoken in a meeting like *that*?

"What did you expect me to say? They don't even believe us that there *is* a tiger. And right now, there *isn't* a tiger."

"She'll come out eventually. You know that. And you are the only one she'll go near. When people see that, they'll be in awe of you. Which means you are the only one who can speak with any authority. You are the one who can save us from looking like grown fools—you're the only one who can bring this home."

"Why is it *me*?" Isha's eyes were watering against the flickering light.

"Why is it you? This is your show. It's what you did. It's all to do with what you believe in."

"I never said that!"

"It doesn't matter what you said."

"Yes it does. I didn't want all this. I just wanted to take her home. They were going to—"

"Yes, they were going to throw her in the zoo, kill her, and you decided it was wrong—you knew it was wrong. *You* took action. And now it's on *you*. It's not like a book or something—this is India. It's complicated."

Isha was reeling. Arun was being a jerk, an ass—no, worse than an ass. How could he have expected her to stand up to so many angry faces? To the scowl and hard stare of Sudha? That woman was terrifying. Isha looked about as if the words could be found on the ground around her.

"I am here to take care of Kala, not to talk to tribals and the Forest Department or to go to meetings. That's not my job."

"You know that my father started the sanctuary?"

"Yes, you told me."

"Yes. Well, he cared about each flower, each bee, each little bird and snake and leopard. He loved being out there, studying it all, walking in the early morning. That's what he *loved*. Just the way you care for Kala and every small thing in nature. But do you know what he had to do? He spent half his time going to village meetings, talking to politicians, writing letters, papers, begging farmers to keep their cows off his land, and being active in the community. He *hated* all of it."

"But that was your father. He was a man—I mean, an adult. I'm... a kid. I'm a teenager. I just wanted them to not hurt Kala. I didn't sign up to be some kind of protector of everything. I'm not some hero in a book. I'm a kid with parents, and... and friends and I'm scared and I'm tired. Okay?"

Gowda was quiet now, watching them. His eyes moved between them as they volleyed.

"There were mothers at that meeting today the same age as you. But you think I should treat you like a kid?"

"Well, no, but—"

"That's exactly it!" Arun turned and threw back his hood so she could see his face in the firelight. "Then I won't. I never have, and that's why we are here. You did sign up. Most people wouldn't alter their stride to save a bird with a broken wing. They are too concerned in their own mundane lives, or their own fears. You are the person who would save the wounded bird, only you stole a tiger. No one else would have done that. *You* did it and now *you* have to bring it home.

"My father loved the animals but hated the politics. The politics were what kept him up at night, what ran him ragged, what stressed him to no end. But that is what he had to do *so that* he could protect the things he loved. If you want to do things that no one else has done, you have to be willing to do things that no one else will dare to do. Look, what I'm saying is that tomorrow morning you are going to have to make a decision..."

Gowda grunted. His eyes were a firm warning, boring into Arun's to go no further. By unspoken agreement, they were not telling Isha what they knew.

Isha coiled into herself, drew her knees up and wrapped her arms around them. She kept her eyes on the floor. So much of her longed for her own bed and to never see a leech again, to wake up in the morning at home, to Amma making *dosa*...

Arun spoke in a soft, patronizing voice. "Isha, it's good. You did it. Kala is in the jungle, and that's what you always wanted. Sure, she can't hunt yet. Sure, the tribals want her gone and will probably help the Forest Department find her so they can send her to the Mysore Zoo. But you did your part. From here on the adults will be in charge, ya?"

Isha's eyes were narrow and moist, her right eye nearly closed. He was being deliberately nasty now. She drew a shuddering breath. "So what do you want me to do?"

"Let's call another meeting, tomorrow, let's go find Kala and tell them—"

"I'm tired." Isha's voice went trembling up an octave, dangerously close to breaking. "You don't know what it was like out there, with the elephants. We had no idea if we'd ever come back. They could have crushed us at any moment. You don't know what it was like every night alone before we met you. I'm tired. I'm so tired. And we are here. Why can't it just work?" She put a hand over her eyes.

"Well then, that's it. The tiger is in the jungle. Time to go home. What the fuck else do you want?"

Isha looked at him, stunned. He had never spoken so violently to her.

Arun felt a flush of regret wash over him but scowled at Gowda's reproachful stare. "What?"

Isha kept her eyes on the fire, her eyebrows jammed down and together. It was the end and she knew it, but it didn't feel like the end. It felt horrible. She had never said goodbye to Kala. How could she ever know if Kala was okay, or what would become of her? She felt so angry that she could cry. It came in waves. Emotion flooded through her so powerfully that she wished there was something to make it stop.

"Arun?"

"What?"

"Can I have your music player?"

"No. Go clean up. Go take a bath or something. You smell like an elephant."

Isha's eyes narrowed. "A bath? Since when do you care? No!"

"I said, go!"

"*No*, it's cold out. And what are you, my ajji now?"

"Just get out of my face, or no music and no chakli."

"You still have chakli?"

"Yes, I have chakli and music, but you smell like elephants. Now go!"

"Hallo! *Elli chakli? Thorsu bega!* Give it here!" She held out a demanding hand. "Why are you being like this?"

"Like what?"

"Why are you being such a… *chutiya!*"

Gowda's eyes went to the ground, and suddenly the silence was blaring.

Arun rose slowly and stalked off. Isha turned to watch him go, instantly regretful of using the worst most vulgar word she knew.

She pivoted to face the fire again, brimming with rage and regret. She wished there was something heroic they could do. Some way to change the decision. But everything felt so hard and cold and real. She could think of no alternative. And on top of it all, she had said a terrible word that she had not meant to say. She put her head in her hands and sat quietly.

When Arun returned, he walked with purpose until he was behind Isha, turned, and dumped a full bottle of cold stream water over her head. As the water glugged out of the bottle, she shrieked and leapt to her feet to face him. She stood there, dripping and wide-eyed with rage, and for a moment he met her with equal animosity.

As she held his eyes with rage, she felt it bubble up into the corners of her eyes and lips. She tried to push it down, but Arun had already seen it. They broke together, peeling into absurd laughter.

Isha went and toweled off and changed her clothes but would not bathe.

When she rejoined the fire, Arun shook his head. "Here, have the damn chaklis." He threw them for her to catch.

She caught the pack, tore it open, and began contentedly feasting on the green spirals within.

Arun glared at her but made sure she could see his smile. As they sat by the fire, he pretended to read, though really he was reproaching himself for his own lack of control. *You were truly furious there, for a moment.* It dawned on him there and then just how invested he had become. He was no longer the supervisor. Perhaps a week ago he had been guiding a strange child home, ensuring that she was not hurt along the way. It had been *her* adventure. He had had distance. He was able to treat her as a kid, a student, like his orphans. But the adventure had become more. It had become his own, *their* own. Thimma and Hathi were back in the jungle. Ramana Gowda was back to life after years of rotting boredom on that plantation. *And you*, he thought. *Just look at you.*

Arun sat reflecting and Isha, nestled at his shoulder, lay with knees drawn to her chest, humming faintly to the music playing into her ears. It was *Ghost Towns*, her favorite song for the hundredth time. The fire was popping in the cool jungle dark. He listened to her voice and held Ramana Gowda's gaze across the flames. It would all be over in the morning. Her eyes were a thousand miles into the fire as she sang.

20

PARTING

There was a time when the whole family had been on vacation that Anya had swum across a rushing river. Isha had begged Amma and Appa to let her try, but they said she was too small, too frail. At the time she had been only eleven, and far more slight of frame. She had jumped in anyway—and was instantly pulled by the dark, muddy current. Even under the water, she had heard her mother's voice shouting the muffled watery sound of her name.

"Ishaaaa!"

She had risen to the surface and began swimming, full of frantic excitement and worry of consequence. On that day she swam with all her strength across the flow, kicking against the blackness below.

Isha rose from the dream like emerging from the dark water. Again she heard her mother's voice, watery and distant, calling out to her. Only this time she emerged to find she was lying on the ground beside a cold fire. The leaves above her hung still. A yawn rushed into her, filling her lungs with cool, earthy jungle morning. She rubbed her eyes and rolled onto her back. Maybe it had been a dream. It was daylight already and the forest was cool and still, the sky matte gray.

Then she heard her name again. Just like every fawn or cub, she knew it even without hearing it properly, before it had reached the surface of her consciousness—as if there was some invisible current that uniquely bound mother to young. She sat up.

"I want you to listen to me very carefully," came a deep voice she did not know.

Isha sprung to her feet like an animal, fingers poised on the ground, ready to run. Her heart was pounding. The tall man was sitting on the log opposite the dead fire. His long legs stretched out before him as he sat, hands clasped together. He was wearing the brown khaki of a Forest Department ranger and had a thick gray mustache that ran like a heavy line of authority across his wrinkled face.

"Who are you? Where's Arun?" she asked, breathless.

The man unclasped his hands. "Listen carefully." His eyes were stern and held Isha's with a hostile intensity. "Several things are about to happen." Isha recoiled, still on all fours like a hunted animal, panting. The man nodded as if she had confirmed something he had suspected. "I don't know what mental illness afflicts you. I don't know why you ran away from home or what you think you are doing. But what you need to know is that I have protected this place since the time of Veerappan. At the boundary of this forest are ten-foot-deep trenches, rebar spikes coming out of the ground, electrical fences. At the edge of this forest is the front line, the battle edge between two worlds, and it is my job to protect it. Are you understanding my words?" Isha nodded and swallowed hard. "No one is allowed in this forest. No one. Not mentally ill young women. Not semi-psychotic murderer priests. And certainly not bastard poaching coffee plantation owners. You have no concept of the fragility of this place, or the implications of what you have done."

He leaned over his knees and stood slowly. Isha let one knee fall to the ground. "What is going to happen next is you are going to follow me to the center of the village. You are not going to argue; you are not going to struggle. There will be no talk of tigers. You have no idea of the trouble you have already caused. I am talking to you civilly now only because your parents seem like respectable people, and I pity them to have a daughter like you who would put them through what you have put them through. Then again, who knows what you've been told by those two unhinged friends you've found—a wanted murderer and a known poacher. Well done. Either way, I need this to end quietly. There will be no discussion. There will be no resistance. It will not be ugly. This ends now."

For a long moment Isha held the ranger's eyes. *What does he know about my parents? Has something bad happened?* Her entire

world felt like it was spinning down some drain. Suddenly guilt
and doubt covered and crushed her like python coils. She felt sick
with dread and regret; she felt caught and cornered and miserable.
What he had said about Arun and Gowda had created something in
her stomach like the brown spoiled patch of a putrid apple.

"Am I really crazy?" she asked, tears gathering in her eyes.
The ranger shook his head as if he were watching something tragic
unfold.

"I don't know," he said, rising with a sigh. "But it's over now.
It's time to go."

His long tree fingers clasped over her wrist, taking her prisoner. They walked to the edge of the village where a second Forest
Department jeep had arrived, and the tribals were already standing
there with blank expressions, watching like there was nothing else
in the world for them to do. Isha saw Arun and Gowda talking animatedly with a fat forest officer, and beside him were Amma and
Appa.

She stood for a moment beside the ranger, disguised by stillness, held by the incongruous sight of her mother and father in
their clean western clothing, standing between the cracked, burned-
out huts with the savage jungle canopy above. She thought of a
filthy water buffalo in an immaculate library, knocking over chairs
and chewing the books. They didn't belong here.

Her mother, eyes red, looked over the surroundings with slight
horror. "Isha!" her mother called out. Amma wore a face that
wrung Isha's insides, squeezing her organs like rags until the guilt
bubbled out her tear ducts. She began to run, and a few hurtling
moments later fell into her mother's arms. Amma said her name
again and again, and Isha cried violently against her chest. For a
long time they rocked and sobbed and made animal noises against
each other.

"Let me see you!" Amma said, sniffing and holding Isha back
at arm's length. "Oh my! Your hair! Look at it, Isha! It's a wreck.
When did you brush it last?"

Isha laugh-cried and pulled herself back to Amma's chest
where she could let the rest of the crying out freely. Where she
could hide from further scrutiny. Amma smelled like their house in
Bangalore, like homemade tea, like warmth and home and everything wonderful. With her eyes closed, wrapped in those arms, all
the weeks of worry came out of her the way water chugs out of an

overturned bottle, halting and messy with release. It was like breathing again, like coming up from years below ground to see the sun itself.

"Where's Anya?" Isha said, still pressed tight.

"At home—she had school. We've been searching for you for *weeks*."

Isha smiled. *School*. What a wonderfully mundane concept. She was passed to Appa, who smelled of car leather, and his stubble hurt when he kissed her head. She hugged him tightly, and he rocked her back and forth in arms so much stronger than Amma's were. For a time, the three of them became an inward facing island as they hugged and cried and traded small sounds. Isha thought of Hathi and the herd when they had been reunited. *Isha, where have you been? Oh! We were so worried, so worried.* Isha could only smile and cry and bask in the sight and touch of them.

Gradually, the clutching and crying ebbed, and she became aware of something very similar to dread growing in her. As the first wave of emotion passed, her mother found the constitution for secondary observation: "Isha, really though, your hair has leaves in it. You really couldn't brush or wash it? Ayooo! And look at your feet! They are black and that callus is…" Amma was overwhelmed to speechlessness as she fussed over Isha. "These clothes are torn to threads!"

Behind her, against the Forest Department trucks, Arun and Gowda were watching, and Isha suddenly felt a mortified flush run over her. "And why are you rubbing your eyes so much, come here." Amma grabbed Isha's face and held it back. "You have to stop rubbing, you'll start a rash. We need to get drops. We'll go to a medical store."

Arun heard this and came forward some moments later looking like a boy returning mangoes he plucked from some aunty's garden. He was squinting, ready to be scolded. Gowda came behind him, his large hands searching for some purpose, his faced screwed up into a ridiculous attempt at respectability. They looked like two lunatics, standing there. Isha could suddenly see them through her parents' eyes: weathered ruffians with wild whiskers and hard eyes. Ruffians who had harbored their runaway daughter. *Murderer, poacher*. Isha prayed that Amma wouldn't shout at them.

Isha took the eye drops from Arun and uttered an almost inaudible thank you. Arun nodded, his face twisted as though something he loved greatly had died. There was silence for a time when Amma and Appa regarded the hunter and the priest with uncertain expectation. No one knew quite what to do.

"Amma, Appa, this is Arun and Ramana Gowda. They, um…"

Words failed her with dizzying abruptness and suddenly she was left plummeting mortified off a vast precipice. The glowing peaks she had felt and wished to say vanished in the air above her as she crashed down into the muddy truth that nothing she could articulate would ever do any fraction of justice to all that had passed. Suddenly it was all ending. Over the miles and dark nights, the adventures and small victories that forge friendship, the connective tissue that had grown as quiet as ivy—all stung as it was pulled apart, a new part of herself now torn away. Sweet sadness tightened her throat.

"They kept me safe," she said with a half smile and something like a shrug, and then winced as she heard herself—a beautiful thing slaughtered by inadequate words.

Amma and Appa smiled politely and they all shook hands.

"Hi Aunty, sir," Arun said, like a boy. Appa winced as his hand was enclosed in Gowda's.

In the distance, two Forest Department men were watching. The tall ranger's eyes never left Isha. Another officer was making an effort to catch Appa's eyes. When he looked at them, Isha saw the forest officer wobble his head sternly, hurrying them on in a way that indicated there had been a prior discussion establishing that they would not waste a single moment in leaving.

Amma was craning her neck and expectantly looking past the huts and trees.

"So? Where is this *tiger*?"

Gowda sat beside Arun on the clay stoop of a hut as Isha's mother ushered her through the process of leaving. There was a constant scolding chatter from the mother that made Arun look like a dog that had been tied and left out in the rain. Gowda put a hand on the young man's shoulder as they listened to the sounds of Isha's mother rifling through clothing and gear.

"Isha, why haven't you folded these clothes? Where did you get them? Don't you know better than to wear such filthy things? Don't you clean anything? Leave that!" Her rapid questions and commands rendered so much of the girl's effort to nothing. It was all deconstructed and questioned and ruined. "Ugh! Stop rubbing your eyes! Come here! Sit down." Soon Isha was lying back. As the drops were administered Arun sat neglected, his head resting on his hand. The charge of her care was no longer his.

There were awkward goodbyes. Isha was distant and her eyes were unfocused as she was ushered into the jeep. Two of the Forest Department boys climbed in and the engine started and soon the old metal jeep was belching black smoke and shuddering away down the trail.

Just like that, she was gone.

Gowda sighed and lit a beedie cigarette that he had bummed off one of the tribals. He flicked the match and filled his lungs with smoke and then offered it to Arun, who shrugged it away. Gowda smoked, and for a long time the two were silent. Each was delaying the inevitable conversation of what would happen next. Gowda knew full well that he had come mostly for the purpose of protecting Wolfgang's son. Arun had come for the sole purpose of protecting Isha, who had, of course, been completely committed to Kala. Now the girl and the tiger were gone.

What are we doing here now? And where the hell is Thimma? Gowda's eyebrows raised as he realized the boy had missed the terrible goodbyes. Lucky kid. The hunter put a thick hand on Arun's back. He spent some time looking up at the trees, the sky. The hunter searched for something reassuring to say. He sighed.

"Come on then, Baloo, you know it couldn't last much longer…"

Arun gave him a reproachful glare.

Gowda put up a hand of surrender.

They sat for more time in silence with their thoughts. The leaves wavered lazily on the trees beneath a repugnant white sky. Everything felt deathly silent. Somewhere off in the forest a deer barked. Crow pheasants called and insects droned on. Neither of them noticed as the tribals began gathering in the spaces between the huts. By the time Ramana Gowda looked up, most of the village was watching. Dark bodies with wide, anticipating eyes were everywhere. He nudged Arun, who returned from some far-off daydream with a start. He looked left and then right. They were completely surrounded. *Oh shit.*

Forest Department officers rushed in from either side and through the doorway behind, shouting a cascade of furious Kannada commands. Rifles were aimed from their shoulders as they ran. The tribals joined the din, shouting and drawing in behind the officers.

Ramana Gowda sprang to his feet and was struck on the back of the head by the butt of a rifle. His legs crumbled beneath him. Arun rose too, only to be tackled to the ground. They lay side by side with arms covering their heads as kicks and blows fell, and they were engulfed in the sudden crowd.

21

THE STAND

At the hotel in Nalkere, Amma washed Isha's hair, cleaned her nails, scrubbed her feet. Amma seemed to think callus was something to be eradicated, not celebrated. They spent the evening making calls to relatives and friends—"We found her!" Amma thanked many people, and for a few of the most important ones handed the phone to Isha who gave halfhearted thank yous and supplied answers to their questions as each one showered her with reassurances that everything was going to be fine. Amma, Appa, and everyone else seemed to keep doing that—telling her that everything was going to be *fine*—like she was a lunatic returning from some mental episode.

Isha was loath to speak to anyone over the phone but willingly accepted the chance to speak to Ajji. She spent some time elaborating answers for her grandmother. Mostly that she was indeed okay and emphasizing that she had *just now* had a bath, actually. Somehow, after everything, this was still at the top of Ajji's list of concerns. Ajji also had a thousand other questions, and Isha had to beg her to understand that she was just too tired but would tell her everything once they were back home in Bangalore.

Speaking to Anya was a blessing. When Isha heard her sister's voice, she had to close her eyes and breathe to let the twisting in her throat pass. Anya didn't say much, knowing through some beautiful sisterly telepathy that anything of substance would have to wait until later, when they were home, together and alone.

Isha slept early and all through the night beside her mother. Appa slept in the opposite bed. In the morning they got into the car for the long drive back to Bangalore. It would take all day. By now, the dreadful feeling of regret she had felt yesterday had hardened into a stone in her stomach. Isha looked at the immaculate car seats. There were glossy magazines on the floor. Appa's business hands-free headset was lying behind the steering wheel where the speedometer glowed. In the jungle, you can't hear someone you can't see. In this world, you could.

Amma was on her cell the whole morning, making plans, arrangements, giving directions to the maids back at home for her imminent return. She was indeed the sun, the center of a cluttered and chaotic motherly universe rotating with children and aunties, social dates and school papers, Bharatanatyam dance lessons, cycles of baths and meals and meetings and details.

As Isha sat there waiting for them to finish talking to the Forest officials, she stared at the back of the seat and thought of Kala. The tiger's hot breath—the loving urgent press of the tiger's head against her ribs at night. The soft fur and the smell of the jungle. All she could smell now was pungent shampoo. She tried not to think of how scared and starving Kala must be. She physically held her stomach, trying to push down the thing that rose inside of her, that begged her to run out of the car and back to the jungle.

Even her own clean skin seemed to miss the dirt and grime—the realness of wild life. She thought of the herd and how they had been painted in mud, and how naked Hathi had looked clean. She felt naked now. It had all been scrubbed away in the bath, a world erased. Now she was in the real world, hard and modern. Arun and Gowda and Thimma and Hathi—the jungle and all the wild adventure seemed little more than a memory. She felt like someone who runs out onto the railway station just as the train pulls away. They were still out there, without her.

Soon she'd be home. She'd be home and there would be school and surely doctors to assess her mental health. All the people she had worried about, who she knew had been so worried for her, all knew she was safe now, and suddenly it seemed like nothing at all had changed. It was shocking and surreal to find the world so unaffected after traveling so far, of foot and of spirit. After so much agonizing worry. It was all still there. No one had died in her absence. No one had gone insane.

Turning in her seat, she looked out the back window. Appa was finishing an urgent business call (they were all urgent). Amma was talking animatedly to the Forest Department men and thanking them.

When Amma came to the car, she grasped Isha in a powerful hug, and for a time they cried.

"Oh, my baby, my girl."

Isha struggled in her mother's arms like some wild creature unaccustomed to touch. They drew apart and Isha covered her eyes with her hands, drawing trembling breaths.

"What is it, Isha? What is it?" There were tears in Amma's eyes as her fingers stroked her daughter's hair.

Isha was nearly gasping, eyes hidden beneath her hands as she spoke. "Ma, I need to go back to the forest, I just..."

Amma's comforting hand grew still. *Oh God it's happening again.*

She turned out the window and called to Appa, "Santosh, let's go! We need to go now!"

They pulled away down the countryside road that was busy with cows pulling carts, lorries, motorcycles, and herds of goats. This was India. She was back in the world she had known. She closed her eyes, but all she could see were Kala's desperate, vital eyes. Isha sat up feeling like her insides were going to explode.

After a half hour of driving, they stopped for tender coconuts. Amma was horrified by how skinny Isha had become. She got out of the car to talk to the man as he expertly cut open the tender green coconut. "Ganji," she said, requesting a coconut with thick, nutritious flesh. Amma called Appa over because the man didn't have small enough change. Appa turned and said he'd be right back, smiled, and left the car.

Isha felt her heart racing. Her ears were ringing in the silent car. *This is it.* She knew it with certainty. Everything had come to this moment. Either she left now or she would never return. Tears welled in her eyes and her breaths began to shudder. Two minds fought viciously for agency and she closed her eyes and put a hand onto the seat to steady herself as something powerful built and surged in her.

The ringing grew louder, her shuddering unbearable. Her lower lip pulled down from the force of the storm within, tears slipped out the corners of her eyes. At that moment she resented, almost hated herself for not being as courageous as the characters she had loved. From the lonely cave days with Kala, to the mountain and the jungle—none of it had been easy. But greater than the thorns and leeches and cuts was the centripetal force that kept her incessantly orbiting between polarized emotions. How could a single mind permit her to be sailing on courageous exhilaration and, only moments later, dash her across the barnacled rocks of crippling guilt and self doubt? No wound or hunger or thirst had once come close rivaling the cold pain of uncertainty. Her bitterness came from the realization that even after rallying so much courage, that it had been there for her waiting, sharper than a tiger's claw, colder than the nights. And so she had obliged her doubts, acquiesced to the stern mandate of the Forest Department, of familial duty. She had followed her doubt and given it all up. The dream was over. Yet still the wild voice within her sang:

Run to the wind, to the leaves and the sky.

When Amma opened the door holding two coconuts with pink straws, she held the door open with her knee and handed one to Isha, who took it. Amma sat beside her and Isha curled forward, crying. She felt the car lower as Appa sat, and the *chunk* of the front door closing. Amma's arms were around her as the motor started. Isha wept with her face pressed against the big green coconut as the car pulled away.

Arun was laying on the cool earthen floor of a mud hut. Outside the sun was well into the sky, but inside the hut it was nearly dark. He rolled over and could see Gowda sleeping. His face was resting on the dirt, and with each snore the sand would rush towards his nose, and then scurry away. Blood stained his white whiskers. Arun rolled over again with some effort—having your hands tied behind your back didn't make anything easy. There were cigarettes in his robes, but getting to them was the issue. For some time he contorted on the floor, reaching, straining, and swearing.

As Arun writhed on the floor, Gowda woke and sneezed several times. Like a furious old walrus, he growled and threw his legs up into the air and then down to hurl himself upright. His hands were also tied. With his palms on the floor he was able to scoot towards the wall, where he leaned against the cool clay and sighed. Arun was still twisting on the ground working on the cigarette problem. The box of Gold Flakes was out his pocket now, and he was attempting to open it with his teeth. Gowda watched for a time as Arun struggled.

"That wasn't such a bad beating," Gowda said, tonguing his lip where it was swollen.

Arun grunted through gritted teeth, and then shook his head like a dog to remove the cellophane packaging on the box.

"Where'd you get those?"

"Forgot I had them."

Gowda nodded. "You *do* know if you just pull around you can use your hands to do all that?"

Arun paused. No, he hadn't thought of that. He rolled over and pedaled his legs so that he rotated and his hands found the box. Now he easily removed the cellophane and removed two cigarettes. He began maneuvering back around to retrieve them with his mouth. Gowda watched in the dim light.

"What I can't figure out though," Gowda said as Arun writhed on the floor, "is how did they know? They could not have found out and come *that* fast. He had her *parents* with him. If it was just the FD we could have fought it, we could have run, but bringing parents into it… That lanky beige bastard knew what he was doing. Something doesn't make sense."

Arun didn't need to explain that it didn't matter now. They were caught. Chinnappa and the other rangers were out in the forest with tribals, spread out and searching for the tiger. They had tranquilizer guns ready. Surely by nightfall they would have Kala. Once they did, Chinnappa had explained, Arun and Gowda would both be taken back to the Forest Department station where police department goons would be waiting to charge them with all kinds of poaching and trespassing and God knew what else.

When Arun finally managed to get a cigarette between his lips and sit up, Gowda had a similar struggle producing matches and had to bend over with Arun's face to his rear to light it. At long last they sat side-by-side, hands behind their backs, smoking in the dark and squinting as the smoke stung their eyes.

"Well it was a good old adventure for a time there, no?"

Arun said nothing.

It was nearly noon when Thimma pushed the wooden door open. His face was full of shock and distress. Before Thimma could speak, Arun demanded to know where he had been, and Thimma explained that he had tried to go and find Kala. He had not been successful. The two men caught him up on Isha leaving, and the rest he already knew from talking to the villagers. Thimma hurried them through the account, certain that whatever they might say, he had more urgent news to give. He came and knelt between the hunter and the priest and lay what looked like a newspaper on the ground. None of them could see well enough in the darkness, so Thimma found the matches.

The match clicked and fizzed and orange light filled the room, making them squint. On the ground between them was a copy of *The Hindu* dated three days earlier. In the lower left of the front page the caption read: "Bangalore Techies Meet Legendary Tiger Devathe on Coffee Road." Below the bold letters was a slightly blurred image of Isha and Kala in mid stride, looking straight at the camera with wild eyes.

Arun spat the cigarette from his mouth and Gowda swore. Thimma looked at one and then the other in the eyes and could see the implications rushing through them both. He nodded. They knew now. With his message delivered, Thimma stood and ran for the door.

Hours passed in the dim room. It was evening when a gunshot sounded in the distance. The sound sent Gowda to his feet and Arun followed. At the door Gowda shouted and kneed the wood. A fat Forest Guard opened the door. Gowda charged out first, the Forest Guard's hand against his chest. There was no stopping him. Out in the gray afternoon light, the entire village was draining west. Another shot sounded. There were shouts in the distance where the big field was. Gowda demanded to be told what was happening.

"You get back inside, *bai saab*!" The guard was young and frantic. He was half guarding the men and half looking over his own shoulder to where the commotion was sounding.

A strange and desperate roar sounded that resonated through everything between the earth and heavy gray clouds.

Arun, Gowda, and the forest officer ran together toward the big field. Women were rushing from their houses, dresses swaying. The jingling of anklets, the panting of breath, people calling to one another—everything was moving towards the action. At the periphery of the field, everyone had gathered. Sudha was there at the front, as tall and stern as ever, with her sari wrapped about her arms. She was staring out across the field. Far in the distance, at the opposite side where the jungle rose out of the grass, tiny Forest Department men were marching—they had guns aimed at the sky. They were calling out to each other, walking in formation towards the center of the field.

"What are they doing?" Arun asked.

"They have her surrounded. She's in the grass out there somewhere." Gowda swore quietly.

Another roar sounded, and this time it was clear that Gowda had been right. Kala was out there in the grass. There were several uniformed men visible now, they were crouched and hesitant as they advanced toward the center of the field. Kala was surrounded.

When she charged one of them the man fired his gun in the air and fell over. The tiger vanished back into the grass as screams went up from the officers. At the edge of the field, Arun, Gowda and the rest of the village watched in grim silence. Kala's roar came like a miserable howl that echoed with stunning force through the air. Arun closed his eyes, his head shaking in despair. The villagers were whispering now.

When Kala roared again, Arun charged forward. *What are you doing? You bastards!* Behind him, hands grasped the lashing on his wrists. He flung himself forward and was forced down. He struggled to his feet, swearing viciously at the uniformed men who held him. Another shot rang out and Kala howled in terror or pain, they did not know which.

No one noticed the sound of the motorcycle tearing into the empty village and dropping to its side. The sound of hurried young steps. The crowd couldn't tear their eyes away from the hunt before them. Somewhere behind them, slender fingers dipped into mud and moved over skin. Out over the field the sun broke below the heavy clouds and suddenly the gray world was brilliant with orange light. Villagers were shielding their eyes from the blazing west and moved easily as Thimma wove and pushed through the crowd. He was shouting and cursing, one arm forward moving people, the other arm behind him clutching Isha's hand. When they broke to the front of the crowd Thimma flung her forward and she ran at full speed, the chappals flying off her feet.

She sped across the grass in the golden light, screaming, *"Kala!"*

Arun stopped struggling to watch her cross the field with disbelieving eyes. Gowda bellowed, his voice full of dread, "Isha, no!"

Out in the field, Isha hurtled passed a uniformed man with a gun who shouted something she could not understand. She kept running, eyes searching as she called for her tiger. Kala shrieked and a moment later the tiger impacted Isha mid-leap and the two went down. Tumbling to a halt, Isha threw her arms around the frantic tiger. For a moment they embraced and Isha grabbed Kala's ears and held her cheek against the broad face of the tiger. Kala was full of tenderness and urgent love. She was crying and panting hot air all over Isha.

They stood together, and as the tiger looked out to the field, the tenderness dropped from her like a mask. Her black jowls peeled back to reveal long teeth, her ears pressed flat against her skull. A deep rumble sounded from her throat. Isha held Kala's collar as a young uniformed Forest Department officer appeared nearby. He stopped in his tracks and blessed himself, his eyes bulging. He'd never seen a tiger.

Chinnappa the ranger came up beside the young officer. He had seen a tiger before, but not like this. His gray mustache betrayed a quivering lip; his eyes were wide and blinking. Isha had streaked her face and arms with muddy stripes, and her hair was full of red earth. She held an urgent, open palmed hand toward them: *Stay*! Her other hand was on Kala's neck.

"We have to get control of the tiger," the ranger said softly, almost to himself, an automatic phrase that slipped out long after its relevancy had passed.

Isha stood bent and panting, eyes wild as she roared, "If not here then WHERE ELSE CAN SHE LIVE?"

Her voice hit such a shrill register that the sound trembled and cracked and it rattled their eardrums. Every man in the field froze.

224 · PAUL ROSOLIE

For the first time in his career, Chinnappa stood speechless. He nodded and stepped back.

At the fringe of the field, Arun and Gowda exchanged a look of wild awe. The two Forest Department guards that held them were craning, squinting, shifting where they stood. The larger one blessed himself. Many of the villagers held prayer hands to their foreheads. Somewhere a priest began singing. Sudha's stern eyes moved from the girl and the tiger to the people of her own community. They were standing on houses and up in trees with faces were contorted with fear and wonder and disbelief. Birds were chattering in the trees and the brilliant rays illuminated the flying notes and wisps of the forest air.

Sudha studied the world around her, recording it, savoring it, acutely aware that this moment, this fleeting inconceivable instant in reality would become part of the legends passed from parents to children and on to unborn generations.

22

NIGHT OF STRIPES AND FIRE

What spread across the green vine ranges in the months that followed Isha's stand beside the tiger traveled over the ground like a flood. Leaves were shaken from trees. Stones were transported. It traveled on the elephant roads out across the Nilgiris, down the Kerala backwaters, and up the Malabar coast on fishing boats. Bangalore techies sent text messages of the image to one another in cold office buildings. Rickshaw drivers from Chennai to Mumbai sipped chai on the corners and shouted and swore over it. Pigeons made their nests with the newspaper. Street vendors sold samosas in it, and later when it was discarded at the roadsides, cows chewed it.

Inside the jungle, elders leaned over glowing campfires to tell of the girl with striped skin who spoke to tigers. No comet or coincidence could have charged the earth with a more humming electrical wonder—it was not a centuries' old myth, or an event that ended—it was *happening*. She was out there *now*.

The secret that Arun and Gowda traded in conversation across rising embers at night was the fascinating dissonance in perception between myth and humanity. To a growing number of people, Isha had become a figure of mythic significance, as if she had sprung from the pages of the *Bhagavad Gita* in Krishna's own chariot. To them her journey was an archetypal odyssey, a mythic structure in dazzling modern valence.

The power of it magnified exponentially when considering that those millions marveled merely at the visible manifestation—a girl and a tiger—but were blind to its meaning. Like desert nomads, fallen to their knees in awe at the discovery of some massive old statue, wholly ignorant that it is merely the pinnacle of a vast, ancient city below the sand.

Within the confines of their small inter-species tribe, however, the view was different but no less spectacular. Gowda related their role to that of stagehands at the show of some great magician. They were hauling the ropes on the curtains, fully aware of how the illusion was accomplished, and with what equipment. They produced the show and yet were still mystified by its effect, awed to contemplation by the sobering dedication it required.

On the one hand, she was often still childish and continued to grow cross and sullen between meals until prompted to eat, just as she would mercilessly grind her eyes out unless Arun stopped her and applied the drops. At times she was unquestionably, almost pitifully, human. She wavered constantly between determination and self doubt, and had relinquished her role as hero and had returned instantly to being a child at the arrival of her parents.

But she had also returned. The fact was that no matter how terribly she struggled or how many times she faltered, she continued forward. Forward on a path no one else would dare step. It was this, they mutually admitted and agreed, that only increased the complexity of the question. Was she awakened to something that the dreaming billions could not see? Or was she simply the product of fortunate mutation, born with a tiger-sized heart between her slender ribs?

Late that same night, the night that came after the day Isha had stood mud-striped beside Kala in the field, Sudha came to them. The forest officers were sleeping in their jeeps, fully expecting a meeting the next morning that would never come. The mahout Killahuntha stood beside Sudha in the light of flaming torches held by younger men. Flames danced in his black eyes as he uttered words in Adivasi to Thimma, who in turn spoke to the priest and the hunter. With a single breath of hushed syllables, Arun and Gowda were instructed to gather their gear. A freshly cut bamboo cage was presented and Isha coaxed the starving Kala inside with strips of deer meat. The cage was closed and tied by young men who worked like church clergy, frightened to silence, as if executing some ancient sacred ritual.

Deep in the bosom of night, the procession fled the village on the slow strides of great limbs. Their exodus made a course into the depths of the jungle. Two elephants carried the tiger's cage, which

hung between them on great ropes made of palm fiber. The young
tiger paced uneasily, moaning softly as the foreign cage swayed.
Isha spoke reassuringly to her from atop one elephant, while Arun,
Gowda and Thimma walked amid the torchbearers. The men went
quietly through the jungle night, their steps barely audible beneath
the heavy throb of insects and frogs. Sudha walked in front, her
shawl wrapped about her shoulders and head, her black skin
eclipsed into the night so that her clothing seemed inhabited by
some ghost with sparkling eyes.

Isha rocked drowsily on giant steps, her legs spread over the
neck of the pachyderm. Great, dry, fleshy ears flapped against her
knees. Behind her a mahout sang softly as they went, speaking at
times to his elephant. The weak yellow beam of Arun's flashlight
bobbed amid the orange torch flames. At times the glint of metal
came from Gowda's shouldered rifle. Fireflies played in the abyssal darkness, shining and vanishing like magic in the night.
Branches and tangled vines passed overhead, a complex ceiling
that rose far above, allowing only glimpses of the starry heavens.

Hours of silent travel brought them deeper. Isha drifted in and
out of sleep. Only once they stopped, and Arun passed up to her a
blanket, which she wrapped around her shoulders to shield her
from the cold. In the darkness of sleep, centuries seemed to slide by
like black tectonic sheets, layers of some ocean of the mind. When
she woke there were lights in the dark distance.

The procession emerged from the jungle trail into a clearing
where a fire burned. Around the fire were a host of dark faces, dis-
cernable only by reflection of light in their shining eyes. Figures
wrapped in cloth like Bedouins, leaning on staffs, crouching in the
billowing shadows of the flame.

Sudha held up a hand to still the procession, and the mahouts
stalled the great elephants, which slowed gradually like ocean lin-
ers coming to port. The ropes were lowered so that the cage that
held the tiger came to earth. The host of dark figures drew a cau-
tious step in. Gowda caught Arun's eye in the flickering light.
Together they shared a stunned transitory moment of undisguised
reverent awe.

Sudha once again spoke some words to Thimma, who translated to Arun. He came to the flank of the pachyderm and reached up
for Isha. The mahout uttered a soft command and the elephant's leg
rose. Isha came down into Arun's arms—her back against his left

arm, legs draped over his right with her arm over his shoulders. As he carried her around the front of the elephant, the dark host of new faces watched and craned. He felt the blanket and bones and little else as he set her gently onto her feet beside Kala's cage.

Holding the blanket tightly around her, she knelt beside the cage and put her nose against the tiger's. Kala curled with longing and stress and love. The host of dark faces leaned in, whispers were exchanged. There she stood, holding her own arms, beside the tiger in the bamboo cage, framed by the vast godlike cliffs of the elephants. Their trunks hung to the ground before their great pillar legs. Between the bars of bamboo, firelight glowed lantern yellow in the eyes of the tiger like some caged demon or angel that had been carried by giants into this hallowed limit of the wild. The host of cloaked men and women uttered strange songs, palms were placed together in prayer. The jungle chorus boomed on as the fire snapped and rushed upward, sending embers into the night.

In this way Isha and Kala reached the zenith of their wild journey. The Budakattu was the deepest and most remote of any village in the Periamangalam complex. Unlike the other tribal settlements of the region, it had never been re-settled or molested by the outside world.

The village of the Budakattu was a collection of mushroom-like mud and dung huts. The roofs were grass and bamboo and filled with unseen nesting birds. On high branches along the boundary of the ancient settlement, machans stood, watch posts manned by night to guard against elephant raids. Many of the gourds and pumpkins they ate were grown in the small gardens in the center of the haadi. There, life was woven intimately with the earth. In the day, women carried fallen firewood from the jungle or carried water and washed in the stream. Men did not work for other men, but for each other, chopping, gathering, collecting. Some of the men still climbed high trees to harvest honey. They walked streams for fish. Women wove cloth directly from the fibers of the forest. There was no pavement to cover the earth. It was the world as it had once been.

That morning, Isha and the others were fed and cared for as esteemed guests. Isha relied on Thimma to explain that she did not eat meat or even fish, a concept that no one in this particular village had ever heard of. They accepted this as just another celestial eccentricity and graciously provided her with yams and rice and fruits, many of which she had never heard of or tasted. All of it was delicious and strange.

After they ate, women came and led them into a hut where they painted stripes on Isha's face and bands around her legs and arms. She changed from the filthy rags she had been wearing to a vivid cerulean kurta that Arun had until now kept hidden in his pack. Bought but never worn, it fit her perfectly. White and yellow temple tree flowers were placed into her hair.

As she was prepared, Arun, Gowda, and Thimma watched from nearby. It was as if their journey had been attempting to take off and had at last taken wing on the currents of some old magic.

It was during this preparatory time, while she was painted by the women and eye-dropped by Arun, that she filled them in on how she had been brought back just in time to save Kala from the rangers the previous day. She had been crying against her coconut when Thimma's knuckles had hit the car window at nearly seventy kilometers per hour. Thimma drove the motorcycle with one hand and with the other pressed *The Hindu* against the window of the car. Amma had screamed so loud that Appa swerved and almost hit a cow.

Isha's mouth had fallen open at the site of her and Kala on the front page of the newspaper.

Minutes later, parked on the side of the road, she suddenly understood what she for so long had not. At long last, certainty rushed out of her heart and into her eyes and fingertips as she held the paper. Somehow she had found the words to tell Amma and Appa that this was something that she had to do. Holding the paper in her hands, the picture of Kala on the front, she wiped her eyes.

"Amma'ppa, it's real. You can see it now. I'm not disturbed; I'm not in danger. I found a tiger. A real one. This is her, her name is Kala. I left Ajji and Ajja's because there was no other choice, or no other choice I had at the time.

"The Forest Department doesn't care what my grandparents say, or what my parents say. You can't stop them. Some people don't care if a girl cries, or a tiger dies. They have rules. I did what I had to and we survived. Arun and Gowda are good men, no matter what anyone says. They have kept me safe."

Isha was shocked at the evenness of her voice, the clarity of her own eyes. It was exhilarating new dimension. "You can treat me like a child and make me go home. But there are *mothers* in that village younger than I am. And I am telling you honestly that I will not survive if that tiger dies. This is something special. Something that I have to do and alone. The more attention from outside, the worse it will be."

Amma looked stunned. Appa's eyes were glassy with emotion, almost pride, which Isha bookmarked in her mind for later consideration.

"I have to go back. If I don't I'll regret it the rest of my life. That tiger needs me. I'll write you once a week. Send me some clothes. I'll figure it out with Arun. Please don't worry. If you love me, you have to let me do this."

Some back and forth had followed. Unfinished sentences from Amma that started with "but you can't just" and ended in much blinking and quivering of lips. Appa had let her go with his eyes. Somehow he understood. Ultimately, at Thimma's urgent ushering, Isha shrugged her shoulders.

"I'm sorry. I promise I'll write. I have to go."

Thimma had piloted the motorcycle through traffic to Nalkere as if he were trying to break the sound barrier. Then for three bumpy, jolting hours, past the forest gate and through the jungle, to reach the village.

How my bum hurt after that long ride! As she narrated the story to the others, it all felt like a distant dream: Amma and Appa, the hotel, the doubt and worry she had felt. Her eyes and mind were now calm, her hope luminous, as if she had shed the skin of doubt and emerged into a new and wondrous reality.

"So you just left them there on the side of the road?" Arun asked.

"I had no choice but to make the wrong decision." Isha grinned back.

For the rest of the morning, Isha sat on a palm platter with flowers at her feet like some devathe. Strung mango leaves adorned the air around her. Men and women came to touch her feet and say things that she could not understand. She nodded and smiled to them, permitting them to worship her. Isha's Stand, as Gowda came to coin it, was already legend. That dozens had seen it made it truth.

"Thou art truly of the jungle," Gowda said, nodding with a strange smile.

For hours she held her post before Sudha's hut as tribals from communities near and far came to pay their respects, to see the incarnation of Kullamma, the Huliamma. They called her Ishamma and traveled by foot or with oxen to see her. They brought flowers and spices before her. Children reached out to touch her, and sunscorched men and gap-toothed old women tried to touch her feet. For the children Isha would remain still, and when their timid hands were almost at her skin, she would strike out and tag them. They would run and smile, and she would smile back, wobbling her striped face. Mothers came to her with gifts of spices and food. They would touch their own lips and then her feet, smiling proud, as if she were their own daughter—as if they were slightly surprised by her humanity and kindness to smile. But after hours of this, Isha's eyes began to wilt and Arun stepped in. He led her by the hand to the hut they had been given. Isha fed Kala and fell onto the bamboo mat bed and pulled a thin blanket into a cocoon.

After the morning exaltation, Gowda and Arun were sitting on the front porch of the hut that would be their own, tearing chapati and dipping it greedily into dahl.

Gowda shoveled the hot food into his mouth, head shaking. "Budakattu actually exists. No one would believe it."

"No one sane, that's for sure."

"Isha is sleeping?"

"Out cold."

"I'm going to be soon too, just as soon as I eat every bit of food these people have."

"This is good stuff."

"Yeah! It is! Let them keep thinking she's magic if they'll feed us like this."

Arun grinned. "Ishamma."

"Ishamma." Gowda nodded.

"Do you think they'll come for us? The Forest Department?"

Gowda considered. "Out here, no. I don't think they will. I think this is it. We need to get the tiger hunting and on her own—weaned off Ishamma—before she *eats* Ishamma."

"I agree." Arun's eyes were dazed and wilting with weariness. The previous day had comprised of such polarized swings from tragedy to triumph that he craved unconsciousness to rest his haggard nerves. Now that Kala had returned and the stress was lifted, they all felt exhausted. Arun was tilting as his eyes fluttered shut

when the hunter clapped a meaty left hand on his shoulder. Gowda
went to the trough where a girl was waiting to pour water over his
food hand. He washed his hands and then cupped them to drink. He
let the water fall over his face and down his chest and rubbed his
face roughly. He belched and thanked everyone present and stumbled off to sleep.

It was a blue morning when Arun shook Isha awake. "Let's go."

So began months of tiger training. Isha, Arun, and Kala would
cover miles a day through a world of towering trees and tangled
vines. The black-faced langur monkeys would leap down to low
branches to watch them pass. Giant, muscled guar blew smoke
from giant nostrils as they wallowed in mud, amazement in their
glassy eyes. Kala regarded them with an electric wonder, the yellow of her eyes burning between stripes and white whiskers.

The clan of the tiger was permitted to erect a camp in the jungle on the outskirts of the Budakattu settlement. The strikingly
generous villagers also provided them meat, food, and blankets for
the cold nights. At feeding times, Isha would throw Kala a chicken
and then scurry away as the tiger tore it apart. Arun was always
nearby, grimacing, laughing. Isha's eyes stayed closed, hands over
her ears to drown out the screaming and tearing.

Gowda made a weekly tradition of hunting. He and Arun
would leave in the morning with several tribal men. Isha would
hear the concussive blast of the Winchester no matter how far off
they were when it fired. Most often they returned with boar or a
small deer. The tribal men were greatly impressed with the sound
of the thunderous rifle and argued over who would get the privilege
of joining the hunt to see it at work. The hunter took great pride in
their childlike awe of his weapon and in his ability to reliably bring
in food for the growing Kala. They would stride into camp like heroes who had somehow regained everything life had taken from
them. Gowda with the gun slung over his shoulder, Arun in slacks
and filthy shirt, with a deer over his neck, holding the legs to his
chest. Both were sweat-soaked and filthy, their tanned faces grinning, and a train of small dark men in their wake.

Anything they hunted was left in the agreed-upon feeding area before Kala was brought in. Once she saw it, the tiger would bear down on the carcass with her massive front limbs and guard it fiercely. Her claws emerged from pink sheaths to sink deep into whatever flesh she was given. With ears flat against her skull and long canines bared, she threatened to eviscerate anyone who came close.

With Arun standing by, and Gowda a little farther off with the rifle loaded and ready, Isha began the unpleasant ceremony of parting the tiger from her kill at each feeding. As months passed and Kala's size increased, so the danger she posed had increased exponentially. In spite of that danger they all agreed it was necessary that she remain submissive to Isha. So Isha would move in, a six-foot pole held in both hands, calmly reassuring the tiger. She'd drive the pole into Kala's mouth, prod her nose and eyes, compress her throat. The tiger's response was savage: snarling, swatting, ears back and tongue curled, her claws opening deep gashes in the carcass she possessed. At first, no matter how hard Isha pushed with that pole, or how shrilly she shouted, the tiger would charge, swat, and scare her away.

Some days they would trail herds of deer, allowing Kala to light out after them. She had all the stealth of a wounded buffalo. At full speed she barreled at them, the frantic deer becoming a river of spotted, tawny panic. The tiger at full speed was a sight to see, her muscles shimmering—a phantom in the dappled sunlight and shadow. Beneath shade of ancient trees, in the blur of speed, the furnace glow of her coat vanished as the primal calligraphy of stripes bled into the deep shadows. All her explosive power never landed her a single victory. She would return, panting and frustrated, to Isha who would nuzzle her and reassure the now monstrous tiger.

When they weren't training Kala, Arun began teaching Isha plants and trees. They spent hours walking the trails and hopping over rocks in streams. The depth of his knowledge of the protean life forms that are the jungle spellbound Isha. He showed her how to cut vines to get clean water, how to know when elephants were close. They would stand side by side practicing "deer ears"—hands cupped behind their ears so that their palms, like the large ears of a deer, would funnel and amplify the sound.

The first time he showed her, Isha's mouth fell open with wonder at a whole new sensory power. Suddenly the chirping frogs in distant swamps were audible. She could hear a stick crack below the step of an unseen elephant. The smile spread across her face, her tongue peeking out by her right canine, as the symphony of the jungle flooded in.

After two months, the callus on Isha's feet began to thicken into thick brown soles that no thorn could penetrate. Gowda was tracking enough boars that he'd begun losing the gut he'd collected loafing about his plantation. Arun's eyes held light and he smiled often. He was different than he had been. Thimma had sparked friendships with some of the mahout men and was busy training elephants. There was talk of launching an expedition to reclaim the runaways that Isha and Thimma had seen with the herd the night the elephants had taken them.

Kala seemed to grow larger each week. Isha continued to push the tiger off of each food item at feedings. She learned that the way to get kills from Kala was a ready substitute. Just after Kala had tackled the carcass, she would walk in with calm. Arun and Gowda were always close by, gun loaded. Isha pressed Kala's throat and poked her until she got the tiger to roll over onto her back. Howls and moans of frustration came from the infuriated tiger at having her meal disturbed. Then Isha would present cubes of meat from her palm that Kala could have. Giant teeth as long as a man's finger parted, the black jowls pulled back and the pink tongue pulled the meat in. As Kala worked on the treat meat, as Isha came to call it, she would carefully tie the carcass with rope to the nearest tree. Then she would lead Kala away so that Arun could remove it. Later, when Kala had calmed and was submissive, she allowed the tiger to have her meal in peace.

During these months, Isha wrote detailed and reassuring weekly letters to her parents, grandparents, and sister. These were delivered on foot by tribal men who passed them on to others who mailed them in Nalkere. In each letter she reiterated her love for them and her thankfulness for their patience, support. For Amma and Appa she included lists of items she needed. New kurtas, new hair ties, chappals, homemade chakli.

Though she wrote devotedly, she would not allow them to visit, not even to Nalkere. At home Amma had contacted veterinarians, reporters, and enlisted armies of support with which they could fight from the outside. But all of it Isha refused sternly, dragging deep underlines in the parts of her letters forbidding them to help or visit in any way. She could not articulate the fear she held that if she saw them, she might somehow fall back, deflate, or lose balance. That reporters and so much outside influence might burst the bubble, wake her from the dream. Perhaps the time would come, she consoled her mother, but it was not yet.

The result was that Amma sent packages to Nalkere that would be collected on the monthly trips Arun and Gowda made. Resupply forays into the outside world allowed them to keep up with Isha's food (chakli, laddus, and piles of salt), Gowda's cigarettes, plantation reports, and news from the "real world." The same week that they had been accepted in Budakattu, Ramana Gowda had asked his most trusted worker Narayan Swami, to deliver the old Pajero jeep.

Isha kept notes of Kala's progress on borrowed pages from Arun's journal and spent hours sketching or writing letters to home and listening to his cassette player. He read her some of the many books they had packed, an important departure from the demanding reality of tiger training in deep jungle. At times when she was not training the tiger or reading, Isha forged friendships with the villagers while playing games with the village children. Their smiles were disarming and genuine, their laughter pure. For the first time she found herself in a world that made sense and was glowing with adventure.

One afternoon in their second month, Isha ran along the stream as Kala chased a herd of deer. Arun was sprinting behind. Kala would extend out, her front paws catching the earth and pulling it under her, and then spring forward on her hind legs to fly out again. Each bound was monstrous—her eyes wide as for the first time ever her claws clasped around the body of an old doe. They hit the ground together, tumbled, but the doe rose and sped off leaving Kala to lick the blood from her massive empty paws.

"She almost did it!" Isha whispered in proud awe.

"And we know it can be done," Arun said.

During this time Isha often wondered if the jungle had acted like a filter through which her worry and hesitation had not been able to pass. In the hallowed shadows and vast halls of the jungle, there was something that whispered to her. She no longer doubted her decisions or worried about her family back home. Her thoughts became fixed on the matters at hand: the maintenance of her clothing, her tiger's diet, health, and progress; Arun's endless lessons.

"You have to watch and listen and feel," he said, "which way the birds fly, how they hold themselves. They compose the melody, the song of a forest that dictates the tempo of a given moment. They'll tell you how fast you can walk, and whether or not you should be still. You must learn the sound of their contented innocent chatter and how it changes to deathly ominous silence at the shadow of a raptor. The mad scolding of a passing snake. When a predator walks through a forest it ripples through the air in birdsong. The deer will begin to stress trot and call."

"Watch where the elephants work. They are the gardeners of the forest; they are the ones who made it." That's what Arun would say, for it is what Wolfgang had told him as a boy. And Isha could see that it was true. Each day the trees drank the light of the sun and each night would breathe vapor into the moonlit air that would later become the clouds that wept the rivers down onto the earth. The flow of water and meeting rivers would eventually flow out of the jungle and become the arteries of India. The connections that she watched and touched and tasted during these months had a profound effect on her mind, even entering her dreams as her immersion in the jungle world deepened.

There was a fish that swam up a dark stream. She could not tell if she was the fish, but she could feel the cold on her scales. The water was frigid and clear. At the edge of the stream, the fish scales became snake skin, winding through the jungle. Far above, stern trees rose in fantastic size. It was a pleasure to turn and push through the leaves, to glide effortlessly and unseen.

The snake came to the base of a crumbling stone staircase. This was the ancient city the elephants had gone to. Suddenly her coils would not gather; she could not control them. She had not learned this form. Then suddenly there was a langur. This she was watching. This body she could manage. She watched her black hands as they walked up the steps. This body was not suited for walking upright. At the top of the stairs was a tiger. Not like Kala—much larger and as terrifying as it was beautiful. At the side of the tiger was an ancient woman with clouded blue eyes and a face of infinitely wrinkled skin, singing in a language no one knew.

Isha woke.

The world was still blue and thick with mist when she left the village. She searched for Kala along the stream, and out on the field where the chital herd was sleeping amidst the blanket of azure that lay on the grasses. For a time she skirted the field, the dew clinging to her clothes and soaking her through.

Then she saw a man in the mist of a field. Surrounding him were a host of cobras standing before him like worshiping statues. This time she was not dreaming. The thick bodies of the cobras, as thick as an arm, were curled like chakli. Their tall necks were straight, two feet off the ground with hoods spread. The man's gaze never left them, like a sorcerer commanding objects to float with his mind. At once terrified and powerful, he held them, palms up, fingers stretched—a plea for inaction. The seven snakes wavered in hypnotic adoration, transfixed. When his eyes met hers, even across the distance, through the mist, the cobras wilted and slipped like eels into the grass. He stood, at once furious and relieved. His chest filled and fell while he watched her. Then he walked off.

She hopscotched through the deep elephant tracks where the herd had been grazing a day prior. Out in the fields, she watched where bison wallowed. Further on, out of sight, the elephant herd was chirping and crashing through bamboo. Isha trailed her fingers over the moist grass. *Who was the man with the snakes in the mist?* she wondered. There were many things she could not yet understand. The deer that came to the village fringe each night for safety. The bowl of rice that Sudha left beside the mud oven behind her hut for the forest gods. The tribals seemed to hear songs, small notes, tongues that others could not. Perhaps it was passed down or maybe it was genetic. Perhaps it could be learned. She wanted badly to learn.

Later, in another part of the forest, she climbed into the low branches of a tree to watch a young spotted chital doe give birth to a fawn. It fell onto the ground and tiny hooves ruptured the glistening placental sack. The doe was alert, ears swiveling, as she bent down to lick and coax her fawn to its feet. Isha was still watching when a pack of yellow wolves approached and the mother sped away, leaving the fawn in the grass to hide.

From the low branch, Isha's heart raced. The doe made it only two bounds before she was surrounded and brought down in a flurry of tails and teeth. No, the wolves would not climb a tree. But Isha was terrified all the same. A moment ago the deer had been a living, breathing, thinking thing. It was beautiful, proud—a mother. Now it was a wreckage of dismembered parts and blood.

As the wolves pulled and tore at the carcass of the mother, gradually painted redder, the fawn sat quiet. Its head was down, its eyes shut. Its ribs rose and fell rapidly. And she realized that the fawn knew. Isha could neither bear to watch nor look away.

Then one of the wolves raised its head, blood dripping from its jowls. Its ears pointed toward the fawn as its nose worked.

Isha prayed inwardly. She closed her own eyes and tried to enter the hidden deer. *Don't move. Not a muscle. The only chance you have is to stay still, so still.* She was certain she couldn't bear the tension, the dreadful worry that the wolves would discover the fawn and it too would be torn apart. For the hour the wolves continued their feast, the fawn remained hiding. It was afternoon by the time the dogs departed the kill to find water. Isha climbed out of the tree and took the fawn up in her arms and ran back as fast as she could.

At the village, Ramana Gowda was passionately lecturing on the perils of the dam proposed by the infamous JCB Vijayan. He was sweating as he spoke, citing example after example of other communities that had bought into the false promises of men like Vijayan.

"Every time a new dam or road proposal is brought up in a forest area," he said with a stern finger, "it means a few men are going to get very rich at the expense of everyone else. That's it. You people don't get it, and neither do the people outside the forest. I don't know why."

The conversation had evidently sparked as a result of a newspaper, now several days old, which Arun was reading aloud from. It was a precious bit of information that Gowda had brought from the outside world. The hunter and several tribal men stood listening. Isha came up behind him. The article was by someone named Suprabha Seshan. Arun had been translating for the men of the village, but they had already become lost in debate. Gowda was breathing out smoke, elbow on his knee. He turned and saw Isha with the fawn in her arms.

Arun saw her and looked confused, but continued to read: "It is said that you may not kill a cow, but you may dam a river. It is said that the goddess resides in the temple, and no longer in the living river. It is said that men did not trap the goddess indoors, that she came willingly... It is henceforth decreed that mothers can be dammed, diverted, polluted and emptied, and powered down to power up their sons in big cities crunching into the wee hours of the morning on their cybermachines—"

Gowda held up a finger, met Isha's eye. "She's talking about the dam they are planning to build, which, by the way would flood everything in this forest. Listen."

"Our homes were in the proposed area of submergence. We'd have to move with our friends and families, our dogs and cows, and forsake our home gardens and fields, the plants we had planted, the birds, butterflies, frogs, snakes, and other beings of this valley, and this tiny headwater of a stream we'd nurtured... The project was shelved, momentarily at least. The church was active in this case, luckily. And very few of us were Adivasis... Sister, I'll never forget the feeling of impending displacement, of grief mixed savagely with rage at the thought of being forced to leave my home for the sake of someone else's electricity."

Gowda nodded as he read.

"Rest assured, on this tiny strand of irrefutable sanity, my sister, when the dams come down (by earthquakes, decay, hubris, or our own decommissioning actions), when our beloved rivers flow unfettered once more, there will be fresh drinking water, fish, and fertile soil for children, the land, the trees and the animals, for all our descendant generations, and perhaps even for you and me... You cannot dam a river and have it free."

Arun came to Isha and stroked the fawn. He did not ask from where it had come. Instead he told her the things she needed to know. Tension in the frontier was growing. Next month elections would be held. Tribal panchayats across the jungle range were second-guessing the dam that JCB Vijayan was pushing if he came to power—partly because of Kala and the resurgence of a strange feeling of magic in the forest, and partly because of this woman writer and the thousands of others who were savvy to what the dam would mean. He handed Isha the paper and pointed where she should read.

The Tribal Rehabilitation Commission had also been con-
vinced that Vazhachal is just 500 metres downstream of the
proposed dam site. It concluded that the construction of the dam
will have a social, economic and ecological effect on their habitat,
which must be "suitably addressed." Isha skipped to a line Gowda
had heavily underlined. *It is said that the opposition by primitive*
tribal groups stands in the way of the needs of the civilized people
and of progress, hence they are to be damned.

That night they ate a dinner of *aloo bonda* and hot mutton curry.
Isha did not have the courage to disrespect Sudha and carefully
picked around the mutton. She checked for Kala, but the tiger was
ranging in unknown spaces. Isha let her be and slept alone outside
Sudha's house. In the night, the deer came into the village, and the
soft songs sang from beneath the thatching.

Isha could not know that across the hills and in various villages in the night, beside fires and across dark rooms, whispers of
tigers and forest and dams and plans were trading. They called it
legend, they called it farce, they wondered if it was true in the villages and opulent government halls. The story of the girl and the
tiger and the dam and the gods, the river and the elephants, was
about to be written.

23
THE DEER AND THE TIGER

Kala lay beside Isha with her shoulder blades like knives, hind legs set to spring. There were forty chital deer. The stags' long antlers bobbed as they grazed and chewed. The does moved on long, slender legs, and fawns chased one another. Isha tried not to think of the tall forest ranger. Damn him to hell. What did he know? She could teach Kala to hunt, if she could prove it, maybe he would let them stay.

"Be still, girl, still."

The tiger's eyes were pits of hunger.

Isha closed her eyes and listened to the birds. She drew a surrendering breath to melt into the landscape. Slowly, she crept forward one elbow at a time. Then one knee, then the other. Kala inched forward to match her. Isha's heart was pounding and the tension made her want to pee. She drew deep breaths for calm, and kept a staying hand on Kala's left leg. *Just another few moments, a few feet closer*. The tiger's breath was a deep drawing sound as she sucked at the scent-rich air, her stomach yearning for meat. Around them the grass stood tall, bending gently in the breeze, full of various insects and pollen.

The langurs above were lazing on branches, grooming, and chewing on fruit. Isha prayed they would remain oblivious. She was willing them to distraction.

Then suddenly the birds began to chatter, the langurs reacted, and in moments registered the tiger. Instantly the alarm was raised, and the entire visible canopy became a riot. Monkeys leapt and shrieked, and leaves and fruit fell to the ground. The deer received the alarm and shrieked out their own warning calls. With a crash and bound and great hurrying, the entire herd was gone.

Kala ran for the deer like a giant puppy chasing a squirrel. She was devoted, but Isha realized that there was still an element of play in the tiger. Isha was uncertain, but she felt like the tiger was more interested in the monkeys than the deer, and it worried her.

The next morning their approach took nearly two hours, and when they were within range, it was hot and still. Kala's breath was shuddering with hunger. That morning she had searched all over Isha for signs of mutton cubes or wild boar. Isha had deliberately given her nothing. Now in the grass, Isha had to work to get the tiger to lock on the deer. Her nerves were ragged from knowing that time was running out. She had dreamed of an hourglass, and of school tests, of time and consequence and stress. For the first time in a long time, she had a dull headache behind her eyes.

Once again, the monkeys saw, told the deer, and the chance was gone.

During this time, Isha joined Arun and Gowda to Nalkere only once: for her birthday on October fifth. Arun's promise of ice cream had overpowered her worry for Kala, and they traveled from Budakattu back to Giri Haadi, where Kala was tied to a large temple tree by a *pooja* stone with a heavy rope. Thimma was instructed on penalty of death to keep safe guard of Kala until they returned in the evening. So the boy sat at the edge of the clearing beneath a vaulted green canopy as the tiger paced on her rope among the ancient stone idols.

The way out had been great fun—Arun had let Isha work the shift as he drove Ramana Gowda's Pajero. Isha found it exciting to see the outside world. Even the small town of Nalkere had a bustle and throb that was startling after so much time in the peace of the forest. Motorcycles, buses, and cows created a hectic, swirling river of traffic. Colorful families crammed onto scooters. Isha had felt harried by the commotion and worried that something would happen to Kala. In the end, she only allowed them thirty minutes to buy supplies, eat ice cream, and collect the post before returning.

It was two months later that Thimma, Arun, and Gowda returned from a similar journey with a letter from home and news from Nalkere that stressed her greatly. The election was just weeks away. Her mother was pressing harder to be permitted to help. By all accounts, their time had been spent and was drawing to a close. Thimma said that the mahouts suspected that a Forest Department intervention was at hand. This news settled between Isha's eyebrows and she became sullen with stress. Despite coming close numerous times, Kala had yet to bring home a successful hunt.

Isha was loitering about the village when a mosquito landed on her knee. She shooed it away without harm. She dragged a stick across the ground. Later, she found a pack of Arun's matches. Sliding the box open, she took a match and struck it. The flame caught and she watched it turn the wood black until it burned her finger.

The teachers tried to take away her books. Even though her marks were good, even though she tried not to break any rules, they could not tolerate that one comfort. They could not let it go. And now these men, these government men of the Forest Department. They would not allow the tiger to live in the jungle. *A tiger!*

She struck another match and watched it burn.

Her hand idly went behind her knee and found the moist bulge of a leech. Isha recoiled. She turned her leg and groaned. It was as big as her thumb and leaking blood. She pulled at it but found the glut and texture revolting. She paused and for a moment sat nodding her head to a beat that wasn't there. There was something growing in her.

She lit a match and turned her leg, pausing for a contemplative moment. Slowly, she held the match to the fat, terrible body. As the moisture retreated before the flame, the thing crackled and curled. The giant leech vomited blood and fell to the ground dying. Then Isha held the match to the body until it curled, crackled, and was still. She had ended the suffering, ended the problem. All with one match.

She was still staring wildly at the ground where the leech lay when the fawn she had rescued from the wolves woke from slumber and came from Sudha's hut. It walked drowsily toward Isha, who for a time pet it and spoke softly into its large ears. She stroked its soft forehead. The wide, black, wet nose, the pink tongue working. The glassy, innocent black eyes. She kissed it.

The ears tickled as they moved and swept radar fashion back and forth. *Deer ears.* How could it be that the only way for some things to survive was to kill such innocent, beautiful creatures? She thought of the first time she had given a goat to Kala and how they had snuggled. The tiger had not learned yet what she was. It seemed so long ago. Now there was no more time. There were no more matches.

Isha stood. She lifted the deer in her arms and began walking. Sudha came to a doorway and Isha met her eyes meaningfully. Sudha looked stunned, sad, as if somehow she knew.

Inside the forest the deer sniffed the air as they went. At the pooja stone clearing, Isha whistled for Kala and soon the tiger came. She placed the fawn on the ground and the tiger lunged in to inspect her new playmate. She pushed the deer over with great paws, like a giant kitten with a sparrow, then fell onto her back, licking, nuzzling. Isha drew a deep breath of remorseful certainty. She tied Kala to the tree with the rope and buckle collar and returned to the village with a storm in her eyes.

"Arun, I need your knife."

He rose as she took it herself. He followed her through the forest but did not speak. It was only when they came to the pooja stone clearing that he understood the dark determination in her eyes. The tiger and the fawn slept beside one another in the green verdant clearing. The tiger's arm was across the fawn. Dappled light fell on stripes and white spots. Isha stood watching them, Arun a safe distance away.

"It's a pity, isn't it?" she said.

She turned to hold his gaze as if it were the last time she would see him. Then in silent, barefoot steps, knife at her side, she went to where they lay. One of Kala's eyes opened; the fawn shivered away a fly. Neither knew any fear. Isha placed the knife on the ground and unclipped Kala's collar. The leather creaked and the buckle clacked metallic and fell.

Then she lifted the knife and knelt beside the fawn. She lifted the long head, and the fawn's eyes opened. She whispered to it, comforted it. She kissed it and rubbed the large ears. She drew one more breath, and then took the knife and placed it under the neck so that she could feel the windpipe flex. The fawn was drowsily content, at ultimate peace with the world. Isha's left hand grasped its muzzle as the knife hand prepared to draw.

As the small deer flailed and kicked, Isha held it, but there were tears in her eyes. She was shaking as Arun came in, and Kala leapt up and away. He leaned over and put his hands over hers. Without a moment's hesitation he drew the knife up and away, opening the deer's throat. Isha stood up and back, gasping. For the first time in her life, there was blood on her hands.

Kala dove onto the fawn. Her eyes became dangerous and as her teeth sank into the fawn's soft flesh. The bloodlust filled her, and she turned on the girl and growled, guarding *her* kill, *her* deer. Isha stood where she was long after Kala had dragged the fawn out of the clearing. There was blood dripping from the knifepoint onto the leaves.

"I thought you don't believe in killing," Arun said.

"There isn't any time left for what I believe in."

Kala devoured the fawn over the course of hours. She ate its legs first, and its organs, then she cracked through its ribs. The bones were soft, and she crushed them easily. Only a portion of spine, the pelvis, and the very dome of the cranium were left when she had finished. She lay panting for an hour and felt full, but soon the satisfaction began to ebb. The fawn had only whetted the tiger's appetite. Suddenly she was eager to return to the fields.

Kala trotted past where Arun had left Isha sitting alone in the forest. She did it intentionally so that the girl would see. The tiger was about to demonstrate something important. Together they went, the girl and the tiger, for nearly an hour. Kala's eyes were wide, her feet light, her ears perked. Isha followed barefoot and sullen.

They found the deer at the edge of a large clearing. The tiger had learned what the girl had not and felt the air. It was blowing from the east. She moved downwind so that her scent would not be caught. Isha followed quietly, dropping low as they stalked in. The tiger was no longer a student. Isha kept her hand on Kala to tell her to stay, but the tiger pulled away. She would do this alone. She stalked off into the grass, eyes locked and lusting over the many deer. High above in the trees the langurs were alert, on the ready. They had not forgotten the tiger they had seen. But after a half hour of slowly drawing near, not one of them had noticed.

Isha's breath was trembling. There was no sign of the tiger. The deer grazed and langurs preened and groomed one another above. All seemed peaceful. Kala gave no warning but materialized out of the grass and charged into the clearing with fantastic speed. The monkeys were screaming, and the deer ran for their lives as the tiger sped across the jungle floor like a blurred orange missile. She ran behind a doe that zigzagged and sped away over a bush. The fawns had all vanished almost magically into the green. Stags flew through the air like a torrent of white-flecked golden comets. For a moment Kala was behind one of them, a race on open ground. The tiger's powerful body lunged and coiled and lunged again, the ground racing below. But the deer was always one step ahead.

Then a thrashing in the lantana sounded, and Kala's face snapped around to where a single unlucky stag had gotten his antlers stuck. The tangled mass of thorns and leaves thrashed as the young buck struggled.

Kala was on him in an instant. She roared as she came down on the deer. Her powerful shoulders rippled with lean muscle as her arms spread and then closed. Her claws tore into flesh, and she and the stag tumbled down onto the ground where with her great yellow teeth, the tiger clamped the neck. For a time the stag kicked, but in just moments the animal, which was already hyperventilating, grew dizzy and disoriented. Kala's fangs sunk deeper. Warm blood flooded into the tiger's teeth and over her tongue. The stag was still. Kala had won.

Isha's eyes were red as she walked off to get the pole, leaving Kala to lick the warm body of the dear.

24

A LIGHT IN THE FOREST

With each passing week, Isha continued to train Kala more urgently. She spent entire days in parts of the forest unknown to others, with creatures few could accurately name. There was an effortless courage to her, only feasible to one unaware she is mortal. She became an animal herself when playing with that tiger, pawing and snarling with her striped sibling. She rubbed Kala's ears, bit her nose, rolled in the leaves with the monstrous thing—now many times larger than she was.

By now Sudha had witnessed enough of Isha's *zid* determination that she permitted something approaching friendship to form. They would spend time cutting vegetables side by side. Theirs was a friendship of mute gestures and smiles. Other times Isha played slap-hand games with tribal girls or scuffled with the boys while Sudha cleaned rice or mended cloth.

When darkness fell and the droning song of the forest was sung, candles glowed from the machans and the fireflies lit the village, blinking in the darkness as the deer gathered. She would reach out to them, walking—almost dancing—through the jungle twilight, arms outstretched, singing softly. Smiles met her wherever she walked. That such a mythical being could live among them with such pleasure, as well as possess such vibrant humanity, was a startling and disarming revelation to them.

To Isha, this was not the violent, brutal place she had been promised. These people were not dangerous heathens or primitive ingrates. They were vital, authentic, and more real in many ways than the people she had known in what now felt like an earlier life.

Each morning Sudha's husband Siddajja placed a small bowl of rice behind their hut. They said it was for the gods, an offering to keep the insects away from their home. Together they observed, as the days passed, that it was the ants that carried away the grains. When Arun asked if it was not just the insects themselves, and not some god, that carried away the offering, Sudha smiled. "The gods are all around us and smaller than you think."

Isha remembered an argument Arun and Gowda had had on the trail. Arun had told the story of an atheist man lost in a snowy wilderness. Half frozen and certain to die, he had prayed to God to save him. On a cold night when there were no more matches for fire and he could not find a way out, death was all but certain.

It was then that local hunters, inexplicably out deep in the wild, found him and gave him food and warmth. The atheist would tell that God never showed, angels never came; this was human madness, according to Arun. Gowda disagreed, and they argued on, the priest and hunter, an ongoing dialog for times of rain and waiting.

Isha followed these closely but never spoke, for she savored the act of listening. Sunlight and trophic cascades, energy and reincarnation. Their words were psalms that echoed within her, which she carried beneath ancient trees and through stream beds. Possibilities she craved like food, to be considered and chewed, eventually becoming part of her. There were days that theology sounded mad and science sane. And there were days when the latter was dry and unseeing of the magnificent whole. In the jungle, science and religion are not so easily divided.

Isha was alone at camp the evening when Hathi appeared. She was lying on a blanket in the open. Her hair was in a ponytail and the heel of one hand fit into her cheek, her ankles crossed in the air. The new glasses that had come with the latest care package from the outside world meant she could read for hours at a stretch. She was deep inside the story when the silent mass of the elephant in the leaves startled her to her feet. She stood and went to him cautiously, speaking tender words. He seemed hesitant in a threatening elephant way. But the sound of her voice seemed to soften the now wild elephant. He stretched out his trunk and drew the scent in off her hands and hair. When she moved closer, he opened his mouth.

She told him that she had no bananas or jaggery to give him, and he seemed to understand. He shifted in frustration and took a sweeping step into camp.

"Hey stop, no?" she said, her voice raising an octave as she shuffled to keep between the elephant and the items he was inspecting with his trunk. Hathi turned to her and opened his mouth again. She put a hand on his cheek and begged him to understand that she had nothing to give. He threw her back a step with a flick of his head and moved threateningly towards a tent. This he threw over with a turn of his trunk. Inside, items clattered and fell. Isha tried to hold him back, but her entire body was no match for even the tip of his trunk. With a tremendous flat foot against Gowda's prized rifle, the blind elephant threw his trunk over his head and opened his mouth. Isha hurried to lift the heavy gun and stow it behind a tree, worried that he seemed to know which possessions were of the most value.

In time the elephant advanced to the most valuable human item of all, Gowda's jeep. Beside the jeep, Hathi pressed his large head against the coach. Each time she begged him to stop, he opened his mouth. *I'll stop if you give.* Each time she provided no treat, the elephant seemed to say, *Very well, then I'm forced to proceed.* The jeep was lifting off its suspension, creaking and groaning. If she didn't find something soon, he would surely topple it.

She lit a torch and ran down the path to where the men were sitting amongst the tribals telling stories. Moments later they all returned at a run, and Hathi grew nervous in the glare of their lights. He voiced an echoing chirp and shuffled backward. Thimma came in first and whacked him hard on the face with a switch. Gowda went for his gun to be certain it had not been harmed. Arun unlocked the jeep door and produced several bananas. Hathi rushed in with mouth agape as a timid Arun trembled and placed them one at a time inside the gaping jaws.

Once he had received what he wanted, Hathi lumbered off into the dark jungle, vanishing just as quickly as he had come.

Hathi's visits became a bi-weekly tradition in the weeks that followed. Sometimes, when the fire was stoked, they would lift a log and chase him away before he could cause chaos. Twice, Arun used a mug full of cold water to quell the slow extortion. He'd throw the water on the elephant's face, shouting until Hathi retreated. When Isha was alone, she learned that the easiest thing was to simply give him whatever sweet fruit she could find. She enjoyed the elephant's visits.

She found it fascinating that an elephant could negotiate with such shrewd intelligence. He used his supreme power to get exactly what he wanted. To deny him was to risk grave consequences to whatever property might be around. In time, she became certain that he did in fact know which items were most valuable to their owner. But there were other things the elephants knew. Isha would eventually realize, first as theory and later as a certainty, that elephants, both wild and captive, viewed humans as two different species: men and women. The men who beat them and shouted at them, they associated with fear and aggression. But women, including Isha, inspired a gentler reaction from the giants. When she was alone in the forest, the herds would permit her to creep closer than they would ever allow a man to come.

It was not just the elephants who were clever. A pair of crows who scoured the village for scraps made sport out of robbing Gowda's cigarettes. They did not eat them. For the crows it was purely a game. They *enjoyed* snatching them from him on the wing. They *enjoyed* the hunter's shout and chase.

In a similar but far more sinister game, Kala had developed the habit of stalking Arun. There were times when she would vanish in the foliage and crouch low, her shoulders emerging above her spine. With wide, wild eyes, she would come in silently behind him. Sometimes the rustle of grass or the hysterical birds would give her away. Other times, Arun would feel the hairs stand on his neck and spin around to see the tiger behind him. He would clap his hands and shout at her—he knew better than to show fear to a tiger—but the pale color of his face and his trembling hands betrayed the shock he had felt.

Slowly, Isha came to realize that the animals knew far more than even she had ever thought they could.

As Isha learned and grew into life in the forest, Arun watched her and marveled. She seemed dangerously liberated, devoted, and focused. With October's passing she turned sixteen, but her age and authority had increased disproportionately to the passage of time. At times her dedication was so fierce that her eyes became like the tiger's, gravely focused to a frightening degree. There was both a lightness and certainty to her that Arun found mystifying.

As she developed, her magnetism continued to increase. Like a newly formed star, with sudden gravity all things were drawn to her. Not just in the ordinary social sense but extending across the lines of species. The tiger had come to her, a dangerous and precious thing for which she had done what no one else dared imagine. The *chance* had come to her. He and Thimma had come to her. How many others would be drawn in? Just two months ago, Ramana Gowda was over the hill, an ember of his old self. And look! He was stoked to crackling life, stomping about the jungle, rifle on his shoulder, like the good old days.

With each additional object added to her orbit, her mesmeric inertia increased. Some camera flashes her silhouette, her fleeting signature against the sun, and the papers print it. It travels on bicycles across the Malabar south to newsstands, chai shops. Into the eyes and minds of the countryside. Incredulous elders wonder, children dream. Muslims and Sikhs and Hindus, everyone from Dalits to Brahmins—all are captivated by the image on the page: the swift-footed girl beside the trotting tiger. And so like a sudden storm, the landscape pulses as she travels past, quenching to life so much that had died, a monsoon disguised as a girl. People will remember the year of the tiger girl the way people remember passing comets or hundred-year floods.

The sun was gone, and she climbed up the tree into a machan. There she called for Arun, and he went to her. Arun's eyes scanned the canopy. Beside him, Isha was alert, her eyes drinking in the world. For a long time they were silent. A firefly lit her face in the soft gloom. She smiled as the soft yellow light fell on eyes sparkling with wonder.

"What was it that you shed when you came to the jungle?" Arun asked in the purple twilight. She looked at him for the briefest moment. "There was a darkness in you when I met you. I thought it could have been weariness; you certainly had had an adventure. But now I know it was something else. It is something you had when I met you, but do not have now, something you left outside the forest."

"I think I've always had it. Everyone in the cities, they zoom about, the news, but no one can *see*."

"What do you mean?"

"I used to have birds. They would come to the window during class. I left them seeds and crumbs at the windowsill so that they would come and keep me company all those long, boring hours. There were three in particular that used to come. Perfect, beautiful little things. They were my friends. The teacher hated how I would look only at them, he hated it. And he hated me. And so one day he invited me into his office and locked the door."

Arun felt the hair on his neck rising.

"The birds were lined on his desk. He had had the local boys kill them."

"I'm sorry."

"But that wasn't all. He made me sit there, in his office, and read this story. He had printed it just for me. It was about a man who travels all over the world with a microphone making recordings of nature. He's been doing it for decades. And what he found is that the world is growing quiet. We can't hear it because of the car motors, horns, sirens, music—but outside the silence is spreading as the animals vanish.

"It said there that we've killed off half the animals in the world in the last fifty years. That there are now more farm animals than wild ones. It said that we are on track, across the world, to lose far more in the next half century. This teacher, he knew what I loved and he had the birds lying dead before me as I read about how the entire world was dying. He said it was us who were doing it to them, the animals. He said *I* was doing it to them."

Epiphany lifted Arun's brow. For all these months he had wondered and toiled over the mystery of from what seed her convictions had stemmed. For no matter how many mosquitoes assaulted her, she never struck even one. Leeches broke her skin by the score but could not penetrate her resolve. She maintained her refusal for violence to every living thing with a dedication that inspired wonder. And though they joked and prodded her, they worshipped her certainty. *What is it you think you are protecting? They are millions.*

It had only gradually become visible in the dimness of their understanding, like a sunbeam illuminating the once invisible multitude of particles suspended in the air of a room. *What could possess one so young to risk so much, to suffer so much discomfort and peril?* Now it was clear. She had accepted invitation to astonishment that is ours for the taking upon entering this world. Only hers had not atrophied with age. Instead, she followed an invisible bearing and offered no description of her vision to the blind around her. She could hear all the heartbeats. The culpability of her entire species had taken up residence within her, poisoning every conversation, each ordinary pleasure, with the uncertainty of the guilt.

The death of rivers, the slaughter of the mockingbirds, the violent silence like a hurricane of nothing.

"Once I knew these things, what hope was there to enjoy anything? Being told that you are part of a species that has reproduced like a virus until the world is dying robs you of all human dignity. And I was expected to go to school, to sit in a desk and fill out papers as if everything was fine. No one realized it was a funeral."

Her breathing was growing heavy. "And do you know the worst part? I knew I couldn't tell anyone. What would they think of me? Most of the people in the city have only ever swum in a swimming pool. The rivers are too filthy. These people who have never climbed a mountain or had to walk anywhere that had not been paved or cleared for them. They know nothing about the *real* world.

"But then I thought I am crazy for thinking these things, what if I'm ill? And Amma and Appa were upset because I was doing poorly at school and at being a stupid little girl, while..." Her eyes had glassed over, but she shook it off. She wiped them and looked toward the great trees above.

"Isha," Arun said gently, "I know you've seen an ambulance in the street. We all have. But this is India and no one moves. No one clears the road because they won't give up the chance to get home faster, to get ahead. Even though there could be someone dying inside. This is the country we live in, the world we live in. We only know what we see, feel, and experience ourselves. And that is why there are protests and movements that span decades waged by lower castes, minorities, and even women to try and convince others that they are worthy of respect and consideration. If we can't hear the other humans in our midst, whose words we can easily interpret, what hope is there for us to understand what animals are saying?"

"They want to live, have their babies, feel love, find food. And they need enough space to do those things. Just like us. It's that simple."

Arun watched her as he spoke. "*Pain and suffering are inevitable for a deep heart.* That's what Dostoevsky said."

"Who is Dostoevsky?"

"A writer you'll love when you are older." Arun smiled.

For some time they were silent.

"How can I ever go back... after all of this?" Isha said, shaking her head.

Arun half smiled.

"Are they really going to make us leave, and take Kala away?"

"I don't know," Arun admitted.

They talked for a while about the possible outcomes. Arun reminded her that Kala could be killed by a guar or a poacher at any moment. He also spent some time reassuring her, reminding her of the universe's strange way of working things out. He imagined Kala surviving to have cubs, the village cooperating, the Forest Department ultimately agreeing. Surely Isha would have to go back to the world, back to school, at some point. But in the summers, what if they came, the whole crew, to monitor Kala, spend time in the forest, and continue on learning in the jungle? Isha swelled as he spoke, full of hope.

"We can't have come this far for nothing."

"Even if we succeed, what will it change?"

"More than you know."

"Sudha says I was chosen for this. That it is my destiny, that it will all be okay."

Arun thought for some time.

"I don't know if you were *chosen* so much as that you *chose*, and that might be even more extraordinary. You became chosen by the volition of your own decision. You have come far, Isha. We all have. Don't let doubt in now."

The black lattice of canopy against the cobalt night sky shimmered with hard white stars. Within the leaves and dark places of the forest, fireflies came like fallen stars, burning softly down to earth. The night birds sang and far off, the voices of elephants could be heard amid the droning darkness.

"Look at it all. Just look at it! Everything is alive in this place!"

"It certainly is."

As Kala began to rack up kills, they began ranging farther. Isha would vanish for days with her tiger, so that the others could only wonder where she was or if she was safe. The jungle sent its roots up through the soles of her bare feet and deep inside of her. She began attuning, sharpening in some indefinable way. Arun knew it because she was interpreting notes he could not hear, seeing things invisible to others: a curled viper among the moss, a mantis in the leaves, the places butterflies slept. Her sense and acuity became prodigious.

Her time was increasingly spent out in the jungle, away from the others of her kind where she saw things they would never see. She would tell stories of what Hathi was doing, how he stayed so close to his mother. She had been with the herds in the secret places they went at night.

They adopted the habits of each other in those jungle days. Or rather, the girl adopted the habits of the tiger—rising before dawn and launching vast explorations tracking, scenting, observing the sambar, the guar, the chital. Each in her own way was watching, listening with wide ears and eyes to the whisper of the forest. The ripple of rock and water, the softness of moss, brail: brief epithets to a vast matrix indecipherable to mortal blindness.

In the hot Indian afternoon, they both would laze and sprawl into extravagant naps, the girl and the tiger. They played as animals together, chuffing and nuzzling, pawing at each other and rolling on the ground. Two cubs nearly grown. But twilight was their golden hour when they would run, and the savoring pulse to their adventures seemed to hone and unfurl when the enchanting call dragged in them like a tide, pulling them deeper.

In the forest she often moved in the trees. Arun or Thimma would climb with her, all in fun, but they could only pause and look at one another at the times when she continued, navigating her way upward through the vines, pulling herself over thick limbs, climbing to places they could not see. Or when, some nights, she and Kala would stalk out after the deer and find some stream that they would follow.

What howling adventures had she run in the night? Arun noticed, the others noticed. The tribals noticed. She would return from these nights in the morning, wild haired, red eyed, and filthy. She seemed to be willing to push further, but it was not courage or competition that drove her. Had it been, they could have recognized it, understood it. She seemed transfixed by the things they could not see, some truth between the trees.

For months their lives had taken place in a time capsule insulated by leaves. But soon it would be time to discuss the future. Arun was hopeful that if the Forest Department could see Kala's self-sufficient hunting, they would permit her to be radio collared, monitored, and free. He confided this to Gowda, who listened with a cynical scowl. The hunter was convinced the greatest battle was still ahead, that although in any other country something so wondrous would be hailed as a miracle, India would have its way with the tiger Kala yet. There would be too many permits, thick webs of politics and influence, shark-like scientists waiting to swoop in and bite off their own piece of credit. None of that, however, was what truly worried the hunter.

Gowda had been watching his young friend over the months with equal parts wonder and concern. Prior to this tiger madness, Arun's fall into darkness had been grave. The last time Gowda had seen him, before they had showed up at the plantation, had been the night of a tragic rain.

Arun had knocked on the pantry door after twelve in the night. Gowda had flung the door open to see him drenched and weeping, the rain tears running off his chin. "You've been a good friend, really," Arun had said. His face was trembling and twisted. He was suffering. He turned and vanished into the curtain of rainy darkness beyond the back porch light.

Gowda had been left for an agonized moment with the sinister finality of his words. Then the hunter had run blind into the rain. He tackled the boy in the driving darkness, and together they had hit the ground where the rain fell so hard that millions of muddy tears splashed up from the earth. In the weeks that followed, Gowda held him prisoner at the plantation, but there was nothing in the boy's eyes. He woke but never rose. He slept but never rested. He lay in bed or on the veranda smoking with sullen, empty eyes. He had lost his tether to the world.

Ramana Gowda had watched Arun grow. He had seen every chapter. From the start, Arun's intelligence was unquestionable, his curiosity insatiable. Wolfgang used to say that if reincarnation were real, Arun was an old soul. He was so captivated by wonder for animals, moments, people, and the larger questions of existence that the happenings of mundane life escaped him. Life was observed through some window, a step apart—an undefined observer inhabiting the body of a human, perpetually overwhelmed by the contours of creation.

Sometimes he would walk into a room and seem surprised to be there at all. Perhaps it was this distance that had drawn him so deeply into books, as if he were hoping to flip a page that would answer the question that everyone else he had ever met already knew and had never needed to ask.

What was certain is that he found his connection to the world through nature. Encountering a new insect, flower, or snake could spark weeks of enchantment for the boy. He had a wonder that was infectious and exhilarating to witness. He would return to Gowda and his father breathless and full of brimming excitement at the treasures he had found while running the estates and the sanctuary. But of all the things that had delighted him, Gowda had never seen him love anything quite the way he loved her.

The contrast was astounding; the cracked clay of the dry riverbed in summer, strewn with dead fish and devoid of hope, suddenly surging with the rich monsoon flood. The dying thing that lay fading away on Gowda's veranda was now rushing through the jungle, thrumming with engaged focus. In her he had found fierce purpose that somehow roared louder than all the demons.

There was no load he would not carry, no concept he would not explain. At camp he spent hours teaching her the birds and seeds of the forest. They would trade feathers and bones, arguing over origin, miraculous with wonder. When she grew weary and sullen he would find some way to make her laugh, but also knew when what all she needed was music and quiet. He would sit beside her by the fire mending clothes or writing, silent but close. He would read to her for hours, and if she fell asleep on his shoulder he would often remain motionless long after his legs began to tingle and scream.

When the weather in her head was particularly bad, he would set her free in the forest with his cassette player and headphones. With storms in her eyes, she would make him swear to keep watch on the trail so no one would see, stalk off, drop her guard, and dance to Hindi songs until the batteries failed. Losing herself in music and movement was the only way to burn off clouds in her mind, and often she would return renewed and breathless, ready to purge whatever had burdened her. In those times that the high mood took her and she carried on incessantly about this and that without breath or pause, he was barely able to hide his delight. He seemed to wilt in her absence and draw energy from her light. His enjoyment of her was so great that it did the heart well to watch. She was sunlight to him, and around her he seemed to nearly over-flow with life.

Gowda could only shake his head in wonder, unsure still of what futures the boy's heart swam in. If he himself knew. She was a creature on the cusp of finished beauty, and he could only guess to what degree the inevitable had seeped into his cognition. *Who can blame him?* The hunter watched them running together through the jungle. *Soon she'll be grown*, he thought with a narrowed eye, certain that even now he could lay his ear to the boy's chest and hear her name in the syllables it spoke.

"You know it will be over soon, don't you?" Gowda told Arun one night by the fire. "One way or another this has to end. And *she*'ll go home." Arun had looked dazed. All the wind left his sails.

Gowda put his large hands on the boy's shoulders. "I know." Arun's mouth had not been able to form words and the hunter's stern gaze never faltered. He had been able to divine the younger man's heart and told him, "It's okay to keep a small fire burning. I've survived half my life by dreaming the little dreams that only I believe. Just be certain that you never let it catch, spread, and burn you down. I don't want to see you fall back. Do you understand?"

As Isha continued to train her tiger, a part of her must have known, as everyone else did, that their time together was winding down. An eclipse once again reveals the moon. Kala had heard the call and was growing quickly. Although the tiger seemed to always return, she was increasingly seduced by the pull of the forest and spent longer and longer periods away.

When Kala didn't return for two days, Isha stayed around the village at first, and then began striking out searching. With each unsuccessful foray, she became increasingly distant. She slept often and when she woke, spoke to no one. Arun watched her helplessly, wondering if he should talk to her, explain that this could be the manifestation of all she had ever wanted, and that perhaps Kala had become truly wild.

At dusk on the third day of Kala's absence, the tiger roared from the distant hillside everyone knew. Isha ran off down the trail. Arun stood up and ran down the path after her.

Isha met Kala at a run, and together they leaped away. Isha raced over rocks, bounding, dancing, tapping her way over the moss, spinning at times when the balance required it. Then they hit the forest and dodged between the trees at speed. Leaves slapped her shoulders and she ducked branches and bounded over others. As they burst out into the field, the deer fled like a spotted river.

To see it in slow motion, her bare feet fell to shatter dry leaves. Slender legs exchanged in long stride, hair wild, as she smiled with blazing eyes over her shoulder. Her hands were flat as she cut through the world at full speed. At her heels, the tiger's thick paws came down and spread on the earth, sending striped shockwaves up the glowing flesh that shivered in waves over heavy bone and sinew. The golden eyes intent, the banded tail out-stretched as the back legs sprang and the front paws folded into the long leap.

For a sparkling moment, the deer, the tiger, the birds, and the girl were all suspended in flight through glowing air rich with illu-minated dragonflies, pollen and leaves, swirling in the wind. Isha spread her arms, flying on unbroken wings at top speed through the world. They went together, their hearts pumping at capacity the transitory ecstasy of their braided youth.

25

CHINNAPPA

"Time is short and so I will begin. Let us first discuss the incident that occurred yesterday morning," Chinnappa said.

Isha and Arun sat sheepishly before a grand desk with a golden plaque that said "KT Chinnappa, Chief Conservator of Forests." Sitting behind his desk in the Forest Department head office, the man loomed over them, the height of most standing men. His eyes were discerning, searching, hawk-like.

The photos on the walls illustrated his many decades on the Forest Department. One frame showed the tall ranger walking his beat with a rifle. Another showed him frozen mid-gesture, passionately explaining something to some important politician in a Forest Department jeep. There was one photo where he had blue surgical gloves on and appeared to be investigating a tiger that had been hit by a car, rifle slung over his back (he was much younger in that photo). Framed articles from newspapers and magazines hailed his name as "the protector of the Indian wild," the "Sentinel of South India's Forests," and "the Man who Speaks to Elephants."

But to Isha, what was even more impressive than the captured memories or human accolades was what he had taken from the forest. There was a pair of six-foot elephant tusks in the corner behind his desk. A tiger skull of frightening size sat atop a cabinet. Isha watched the frames and bones as he spoke, preferring to see the summary of the man rather than the man himself, who was too tall and intimidating to look directly at.

When he met her eyes, Isha maintained a stony expression. This man who had enlisted her parents to banish her from the forest, this man who had told her she was mentally unhinged. This man who had called her a child. No, she could not look away, and instead held his gaze with defiant cool. *I'm still here, you see?*

For a long moment, the staring match endured. Then, with great difficulty, Chinnappa looked down to arrange the papers before him. "Yes, I would have to be a fool to allow what I have allowed. A fool."

Isha maintained an implacable glare.

"Then there is the issue of my ranger, Ravi. Ravi has been here for two decades. He is a forest guard and not a Bollywood actor, and so I know that the look on his face is true. Ravi, will you join us."

Ravi walked through the door behind them, a fifty-year-old man in a brown Forest Department uniform that swelled at the belly. He wore an agonized expression, thick black mustache, and a cast on his right arm.

"Show them your face, Ravi."

Ravi hesitated, then held an open palm below his chin in presentation. "It is here only, sir: my face."

"Thank you, Ravi. Please sit"

Ravi did as he was told. Everyone seemed to do as they were told in the presence of KM Chinnappa. Isha and Arun had only been in his presence for five minutes but had the distinct impression that to disobey this man was a grave risk. And so they both did what they were told and remained sitting side by side before his desk in the sparse Forest Department office. Isha had the distinct feeling she was at the principal's. They both knew exactly why they were being summoned. A cool breeze blew through the metal bars, along with the chain-clink of a tusker working with a team of men to haul logs onto a rusted lorry parked among the trees.

"Ravi," said the head ranger Chinnappa gently, "tell these two what you saw yesterday."

"Sir, I was on my beat, deep in the forest, going to deliver the message you asked me to tell." He hesitated.

"Tell them Ravi."

"Sir, they know it! She was there." Ravi waved an irate finger at Isha.

"Just tell us Ravi, please."

"Well, I look up into the sunny cloudless sky, wondering why I hear earth trembling thunder. Then a tiger appears from nowhere. From simply nowhere, sir. Bounding towards me, and Lord Krishna, I was certain my life was finished. I was a thousand percent certain this was my lastest moment. And so I screamed and turned to run, and the tiger peeled off. She aborted the predation, and I went tumbling down the rocks."

"And then what happened, Ravi?"

"Then this girl—this *junglee* woman—comes and asks me, 'Uncle, are you okay?' To which I said '*No*, I am not okay, my arm is broken!' and to which she says she is very sorry for the scare, the tiger didn't mean harm, and she will get help." Ravi's head continued to wobble furiously, his eyes wide, blinking as rapidly as moth wings.

Chinnappa held his long hands up on either side of his face. "Ravi was tasked with the simple mission of telling you all that I was requesting a meeting. The result is not surprising. I was foolish to assume anything normal can be asked at a time like this. I ask myself why there is a little city girl living in my forest with a stolen tiger. A city girl and her mentally ill, fake-priest murderer-friend. Oh! And let us not forget Ramana fucking Gowda! The last time I saw him he was nineteen and killing every leopard in the region! I promised him what I'd do if I ever saw him again. And these three lunatics traveling with a tribal boy drug addict and a blind elephant."

He shook his great head. "This is because of what I have allowed. I have been watching the chital and the sambar, you know. The deer are acting differently. They are staying to the clearings and only using the forest for travel. They are staying out in the grass where they can see on all sides, or in the open teak groves. Do you know how long it has been since I have seen this behavior? Either it is so dry that everyone has lost their mind, including the deer, or... your tiger is beginning to hunt."

Isha's eyes wavered before the ranger's harsh gaze.

"If you have lived with the tiger for this long, then you know as well as anyone that it is not your pet." His eyebrows went up. "Am I correct in this assumption?"

Isha nodded.

"I've done my research. I know about the mother, and the other cub, and about the dog fight. This was all in the report filed by the FD in your grandparents' village. The papers said the tiger attacked you. But I made phone calls, spoke to your Ajja actually, and heard a different story. You were rescued by the tigress from the dogs?"

Isha nodded.

"Then you found the cub."

Isha nodded.

"And let me ask you this, did you ever sleep in the grove, in the time leading up to the mother's death?"

Isha hesitated. *How could he know*? She nodded that she had.

"This is my theory: you spent so much time there that your scent was part of this animal's first learning. That the tigress and her cubs knew your smell. You know these cats operate on smell to a degree we cannot fathom. It's how they communicate in the forest. I believe that the scent of where you slept, where you urinated, and all of that were part of the tiger's youngest memories. And that after the mother died, you still smelled like its mother. It must have been in your hair, your clothes, what have you. This is my theory, that this tiger imprinted on you in some olfactory way. There is no other explanation."

Isha stared dumbly past the ranger, her own mind spinning with realization.

For a long time he watched her.

"*Achha*." He rose slowly, extending upward so that Isha wondered when he would stop. Then he went over to a glass cabinet and removed an object wrapped in blue silk. He returned to the table and placed the object on his desk, then sat. Then he slowly unwrapped it, playing the spherical object in his hand as the other unwound the blue wrapping. The hollow eyes and yellow teeth of a rusted human skull sat in his hand. His eyes never wavered from Isha's, noting the briefest of shudders when she saw it. With care he rotated the skull to show the cranium, where four long gashes had been cut from the top to the spinal junction. He placed the skull on the desk.

"The jungle is not just a place; it is a state of mind. By now you have seen the elephant trenches dug at the boundary of the forest. You've seen the electric fences. All of this my men maintain. And do you know why? Because each time an elephant raids a farmer's crops, each time a tiger kills a cow, the threat to the forest increases. The more the outside world wants it burned. And so we stand guard. Still the elephants escape. Do you know why? Because they are not meant to be held captive. The elephants have been marching across India since before men arrived, before all this Hindu–Muslim shit, before all of us. They know their old maps, and nothing will stop them. They know the water holes, you see, they can smell where their ancestors have been, and they too want to go, continue the tradition, walk the invisible roads.

"But beyond those trenches and fences and spikes is India. Modern India. The farmers that have lands near the forest are poor already; they cannot afford to lose their crops and livelihoods to these animals. One elephant can destroy a plantation—imagine what a herd does. They eat truckloads of food, trample crops, and the farmers hate them for it. They throw fire at them, shoot them, rig explosives, electric wires, whatever they can find. And the elephants fight back. They know their rights. Last month a man was chasing elephants off his land and one of them decided he'd had enough. The elephant walked right over him. I have the poor bugger's skull in a bag, and it is nothing more than chips and teeth."

Isha winced.

"This is what comes in the paper. The 'elephant conflict,' the 'tiger conflict' is what they write. And the fat people in the cities think these are the problem. They cut down the elephant's forest or build roads and mines through them. Then they worship Ganesha, ha! They hit them with trains, they cut off their tusks, they use them to beg on the roadsides, whip them in circuses... And yet these daft bastards worship Ganesha. And do you know what they do on the elephant god's holiday? They make obscene idols and dump cardboard and cement and styrofoam and chemical paint into the water. It is madness, pure madness. They desecrate and destroy elephants while worshiping the image of Ganesha. Where else but India could such a thing be possible?"

Isha opened her mouth to speak, but the ranger held up a hand.

"There is this preposterous idea that we are separate from nature. We clearly struggle to truly fathom the things around us, the very forces from which we were granted life. Ancient people wanted control, they wanted power. I think this evolved into wanting to be separate from nature. That view worked its way into our religion, science, and our deepest self-image.

"But the truth, like a river eddy, runs opposite to the current. Where else but in India? The rivers are so dirty the goats will not drink them. What will India do if the people do not have rivers? Steinbeck said that 'all war is a symptom of man's failure as a thinking animal.' Then what, I ask you, is man's destruction of his own reality? In Kerala there are fishing communities where you can no longer find fish in the sea. The forest is cut so small that the animals cannot hide, let alone survive. Of course the elephants must raid our crops. And where in the modern world does the tiger fit?"

"I just want her to live and be free."

"Your tiger is in the jungle and the jungle is no longer united. The tribals and the animals are no longer allies, but enemies. And the entire outside world just wants money. You think I am against you, but I am actually your greatest ally. If that tiger stays, someone will kill it. Maybe with a snare, maybe with poison. One way or another, it will happen. I am certain of it.

"The tribals are your friends now, but months ago they were supporting the plans for the dam. Now they are not. They are fickle and confused, easily manipulated. Vijayan's election is upon us, and he has made promises to men that care nothing for flowers and butterflies and trees. Vijayan has worked tribal villages to access resources before; how else do you think he became so rich? He'll persuade them, con them, employ them, distract them, and gradually force them out of the forest. He'll give them just enough rope to hang themselves. And without the tribals, well, then he can truly exploit the timber, sell the ivory, dam the rivers. If he is successful, the next forty generations in his family will profit from what he sucks out of Periamangalam."

Isha stood from her chair. "I'm sorry, sir, but I don't need your help to despair. What I care about is my tiger, and that is all. Once she is able to hunt, I can go home and see my family. I have been away for many months now and I want that very badly."

Chinnappa snorted. "You want to go home, do you? Are you under the illusion that this ends at any point? Do you think this is like the stories you read in your little girl books? No. This is real life. The struggle never ends. Even if that tiger learns to hunt, where will she find a mate to reproduce? Who will stop the tribals from poisoning her and selling her skin and sending courier packages with her powdered bones up north toward China?

"And let me remind you that no tiger has ever been reintroduced into the wild. No one on any continent in any century has succeeded at it. Only a mother tiger can teach her cubs, and once that connection is broken, it is hopeless. A captive tiger is nothing more than a mirage, the illusion of a tiger. Its only value can be for producing more captive tigers—striped ghosts for us to gawk at. Your tiger is on human life support. In the wild she will die. That is a certainty. All of this is a sham. This is all for the appeasement of your ego or your sympathy. And are you both truly so foolish to believe that how much you care will change the futility of your actions?"

He had been practically shouting and the room was startlingly silent when he stopped. He regarded Isha from behind his spectacles. From where she sat, he looked like a statue; she could not see his eyes. He thumbed his gray mustache where it curled over his lips.

"I know you have been through a great deal. I can see it in your eyes. And what you have done required terrific audacity and strength. But this is the end. The Forest Department was created for a reason, and it has rules. Per those rules, you are not allowed in the jungle—neither is Arun or Gowda. We are obligated to take control of this situation. We need to tranquilize and collar the tiger, and we will hold her until we can find a suitable place for her to live."

Isha's arms were folded, her eyes dark.

Arun lifted a hand. "If I may, sir..."

Chinnappa held up a hand for silence. "Let me be perfectly clear. You have no qualifications. None whatsoever. The only reason I am not arresting you is because this girl needs a ride back into the forest to collect her things. Entry into a protected zone, which the Periamangalam is, is restricted and I have already shown you unfathomable, absurd levels of compassion. But this ends now. I cannot allow you to continue."

"Isha, leave the room," Arun said.

"I'm not leaving." Her eyes were storms. Suddenly she was back in school.

"Isha."

"No. He has no right. It's a tiger, on earth, and this is the jungle. He has no right. It's nature. It's the world, you can't just tell people what to do. She deserves to be free." She pointed a finger at the regal ranger. "You have no goddamn right!"

"*Isha!*" Arun's face was flushing red.

She growled and marched briskly outside to stand below the window so that she could hear them continue. In the distance, the uniformed men were shouting orders as the elephant lifted a large teak beam into the truck.

Once they were alone, Arun came up to the ranger's face. "You can't treat her like that. This girl has been through hell for that tiger, and she—"

Arun was full of passion, but the ranger's rage was bigger; he was bigger.

"Shut up. I've spent the last forty years guarding this forest. Do you know why there is still a herd of elephants left in that jungle? Because I have been *fighting* for them. I've lost more than you can know, and I can tell you this: What I am doing *is best*. Listen closely. What do you think the papers have been doing? What do you think a man like JCB Vijayan will do when he wins this election? Do you think he has not heard that the tribals are thinking of revoking the proposed dam? Do you think the people will allow his fancy hydro-dam projects to go through if it is a *tiger* sanctuary? Or do you think he would wipe them both out just as easy as he clears villages? The life of one tiger is not worth every other animal in the forest and the tribal village."

The ranger's face was inches above Arun's. "Make no mistake," he glared fiercely down at Arun, "Vijayan will win the election and the moment he does he'll come for you all. This is the jungle where beasts and men make no truce for the young. Is the life of an animal worth more than a human being's? I'd like you to think about that, in the time you have left. Now get out of my office."

"Humans aren't going extinct, but tigers are almost gone," Arun said gravely.

Chinnappa held his long arm out, finger pointing to the door. Low threats were coming from Arun. Isha was in the doorway now. Chinnappa advanced and Arun backpedaled with hands up. He was growing louder, and together they moved across the room for two steps until Arun boiled over.

He shoved the ranger back a step. The ranger swung and hit Arun squarely in the temple. The ranger's left came next, and Arun ducked under it easily and delivered a hard uppercut that sent the older man back. Together they hit the floor, kicking and rolling.

"Your robes fool no one."

"Your uniform means nothing."

Hands clasped clothing as they grunted and rolled. Ravi was up and excitedly shouting. Men from the yard were running in.

"Everyone!"

Isha stood with the tremendous tiger skull in her arms. Arun and Chinnappa froze to look up, the priest's hand still smeared across the ranger's face. She lifted the heavy skull higher. The ranger shouted with beseeching urgency for the precious skull just before she cast it down. It came apart on the floor, the heavy bone parting, teeth chattering and rolling across the hard floor.

"If you two are done trading fashion insults, I have to get back to the forest." Isha was trembling.

The two men parted and rose.

"My uniform does mean something," Chinnappa said, feeling his lip with a finger and then checking for blood. "What it means is that there is a system, a vast, complex web of laws and rules, a collective fantasy called *India*. Because of this there are men and vehicles to enforce my word. You are a broken man—it is sad for someone so young. You feed some children and think you are a saint? You willingly help a little girl run away from home with nature's greatest weapon and think you are virtuous? You are thieves: brigands with delusions of grandeur. The tiger is dead. It was dead when its mother died. You are only prolonging the inevitable."

"Kala needs me," Isha said quietly.

"You are delusional," Chinnappa sneered.

"But without me—"

"She'll starve? Is that it?" He was shouting now, blood coming from his lower lip. A section of his gray mustache had gone pink. "Then nature will have taken its course. You are not from here—you have no say in what happens here."

He grew quiet now. He shook his head wearily. "It will take me some time to assemble the necessary experts, and honestly, before Vijayan's parade we are stretched thin. You have until the parade—that's a little over a month away. The very day after, you will lead my men to the tiger and your priest and hunter will be arrested. The tiger will be tranquilized, and the Forest Department will decide what happens next."

Isha frowned, unable to interpret the dissonance between what he was saying and why he was granting them another month when he could remove them tomorrow if he pleased. She wondered at his decree and thought of how Ajja had seemed just before she had run away with Kala. Was the ranger allowing them time to make Kala wild? Could it be done in so little time? She leaned in and spoke deliberately.

"Chinnappa Sir. You say I am not from here, but I am. I know the creatures of this forest—I am one of them. And one day you will mistake my voice for theirs. This place is a part of me and I am a part of it. I have seen and learned things that even you could not know. The rivers of this forest run through my veins."

Chinnappa's left eye twitched almost imperceptibly. The truth he guarded was that since the day in the field when she'd stood beside the tiger, he hadn't slept through a single night. That moment had replayed in his mind almost incessantly, causing him to spend midnight hours pacing in the darkness. It had loosed a brick in the foundation of his authority, exposing a portion of the initial material of his resolve. It was a rusted but unalloyed love of the wild, and the remembrance of a time when the Law of the Jungle was his only constitution. It was something he had kept hidden beneath his uniform as a younger man—buried by the crushingly complex responsibilities of decades spent holding back the hungry millions from eating up the rest of the forest, navigating the corrupt government brass, and maintaining his hard, razor-eyed exterior—until he had all but forgotten it existed.

What Chinnappa was now grappling with was a reaction within himself—one that required deep contemplation about where his allegiances would ultimately lie. For to regard it directly brought him back to his younger self and to a sense of duty that cut against the strict rules that he himself toiled so ardently to enforce. It was madness, and he knew that with a single breath of syllables he could dispatch men and end it for good.

No matter the threats he spat or how much conflicted rage trembled through him, the gavel of his decree ultimately remained poised. He could not bring himself to give the command. Not at a time like this, when the very thing that he had set out to protect so long ago—and that was on the brink of vanishing forever—was somehow manifesting itself one last time.

Isha read all of this and more in his eyes. As she did, her own eyes narrowed, incredulous that so much could be communicated in silence. Her posture altered with uncertainty, and on some animal level he knew she understood.

There were several uniformed scowling men in the room now. They could make no sense of her words and only watched as she bent down to pluck a large canine from the floor. Arun pointed a threatening finger at Chinnappa and the old ranger glared at Arun with hatred in his eyes.

Arun didn't wear a helmet on the ride back and leaned indulgently into the many turns. They retraced the route they had done in the morning, which took them up and around the southern side of the jungle border, out into the luxuriant coffee hills of Coorg. At a roadside stall they bought coffee. They sipped together overlooking the verdant hills. Arun's eye was swelling shut now, and Isha complimented him on his wicked uppercut. He told her he couldn't believe her shattering the skull. They exchanged a brief smile, but it wasn't funny. They both knew that the worst of their fears were coming to fruition: the people knew and were gathering. The tribals, the Forest Department, the outside world. They would come for Kala, one way or another. Arun finished his cigarette against the gray sky, robes billowing against the unfathomably green hills. Isha's hair swirled black about her eyes.

"You said it was important to make friends with Chinnappa. What do we do now?"

"That could have gone better, I agree."

She climbed onto the bike behind him and held back her foot as he kicked it to life. The rolling hills were layered with cultivated bushes, perfect green save for the places where flecks of orange or purple or blue showed: women with woven baskets harvesting the leaves by hand in the hot sun. But as they leaned into turns, rushing beside precipitous valleys, it was all cool and brisk on the bike. Isha held Arun's shoulders as they went.

After an hour she grew tired and sat with her face pressed into Arun's back, watching the world go by. The wind rushing through her hair, other scattered forces whirled inside her. Out in the distance, smoke rose from jungle where someone was burning cropland. Kilometers to the north the river broke away from the jungle boundary like a timid brown snake. She thought of the ferns and the clouds at the mountain pass and wondered how far the river must slither through the vast, unseen forest. She wondered at what point it turned from clear to brown.

Later, while riding over another valley, there was a small town below. It was too far off to see individual people, but she knew it all the same: butchers, merchants, rickshaws, street cows. Somehow the wind carried the sound of honking horns up the mountain. Beyond the settlement were fields, large fields of rice and ragi, tea and corn. From far away the city seemed like an inward facing hive of small creatures, antennae interlaced, toiling, trading, and steadily swarming.

That evening after a long and bumpy ride in the dark, they reached the village by 8 p.m. Moments after they arrived, while Arun's bike was still ticking and cooling, whistles went up in the forest and the watchmen in the trees began calling.

Killahuntha's elephant Chinmaye and the two recaptured escapees came jangling in down the trail. Thimma sat behind Killahuntha, emaciated and filthy. The boy exhaled beedie smoke from atop the elephant as he watched the villagers cheer and gather. He tried to look as fierce as he could so that they would not see as warm pride filled his chest and reddened his face. He had gone out into the wild with the most famous and accomplished mahout in the region and returned victorious.

The mahouts tied the elephants at the village fringe, and Thimma was taken down, stripped, and wrapped in a heavy blanket and placed by the fire. He spent the rest of the evening lying in a hammock, sipping tea. The proud and fierce Killahuntha recounted the tale, while nearly everyone in the village crowded in to hear. He said that he had never seen anything like it. He and Thimma had gone up close to the herd, and the bulls had chased them with ears spread and trunks raised, threatening to kill them. The scarred mahout leaned over the fire with fierce, unashamed eyes as he admitted that there seemed no choice but to turn back. But it was the boy, he explained, who had had the courage to go in. Only the boy was *allowed* in by the elephants.

The big, hard, hairy men stood five deep listening to the tale of how Hathi had refused to part with his mother. Killahuntha explained how the elephants had charged Thimma and how he had been brave. Isha caught Thimma's eye and called him Toomai and smiled. Thimma looked like he would cry if he weren't so tired: for sadness at saying farewell to his companion, with pride for having earned the respect of the hardest mahout in the land.

And then he smiled, and for the first time since she had met him, Thimma was grinning ear to ear, with glassy, red eyes: he was happy. Isha shared smiles with Arun and Ramana Gowda. Her eyes moved to Sudha, who sat in the flickering shadow against the cracked wall of her house, her own child nursing at one breast, a young wolf nursing on the other. Isha grinned in the firelight, and Sudha could no longer restrain from grinning back.

26

LAST DAYS

There are many adventures that took place in these Wild Jungle Days that cannot be accounted for here. The day monkeys stole Isha's chappals and she and Kala went roaring after them as they taunted from the trees. Or when Isha returned from one of her jungle forays to report that she had in fact seen an ancient woman with blue-clouded eyes, half grown into the vines of an old ruin. Sudha emphatically warned Isha that this was an exploit she must not pursue, that there were forces in the jungle capable of binding a soul so deeply that it could never leave. That Kullamma too had once been a young, very real girl. These, and many others, are stories for another time.

In the days after the meeting with Chinnappa, time began draining rapidly. Isha spent long hours with Kala in these last days, savoring what she knew would end soon. They would lie together in the golden grass, Isha with her back against the panting stripes of the now immense tiger. The tiger's size had increased so that at close quarters, any rational person in possession of basic self-preservation found the dimensions of her skull disturbing. Her paws had matured into heavy mittens of claw and bone. Her wrists and forearms were far thicker than Isha's legs. The body was a shockingly long tube of stripes that gathered in thickness and density around her haunches.

For long hours Isha would lie reading, her slight form sprawled between the paws and stripes. Since the cerulean blue kurta was useless for camouflage, she never wore it when they were hunting, but always did when they were lounging. So the blue cloth and brown skin would lay stark across the black and white and orange of the tiger in golden fields, in the pulsing green light of the forest. Kala would sleep or doze, yawning at times so that her mouth would open fully, her saber teeth flashing at the finish.

When they wrestled, the tiger knew the great care she needed not to injure her friend; a massive hound at play with a kitten. She would grasp Isha between dinner plate–sized paws, and throw her down. As the tiger rolled over to expose her white stomach, Isha would scramble over the roll. Nearly eclipsed between the great limbs, Isha would push her face into the white throat, grasp the black ears, and whisper her urgent, wild love to the tiger. The birds and monkeys watched from only the highest branches, a look of shared horror on their faces.

Thimma became a hero following his exploits with Killahuntha and the recapture of the escaped elephants. He was also credited in part for leading Isha and the others to the village, which now had begun to work in his favor. By now, in haadis across the land, the whisper that something special was happening had blown life into the flickering thought that perhaps they would overturn the decision to allow the dam. Thimma added to this by viciously stating his position. Now people listened to him. His actions had earned him agency and status. Furthermore, many in the village knew the story of Thimma's family, of his village, and what he had suffered. He had experience. They looked to him for guidance as they held repeated meetings regarding JCB Vijayan's dam project.

The mahouts began making trips to Nalkere with their respective elephants and returned with the news that Vijayan remained adamant that Thimma join the parade, Hathi or no Hathi. They agreed unanimously that it would be easier, and most likely safer, for Thimma to simply oblige the politician's request.

This confused Thimma and caused him great turmoil. To put the boy at ease, Gowda and Arun went with him into town in Gowda's Pajero. In Nalkere they drove to the central town office, where they were told they could find Vijayan out in the elephant yards working with the mahouts.

Instead, they found the infamous politician down a long blue hallway and through a heavy teak door. There were several other important looking men in the office as they entered. A stuffed leopard sat snarling beside the entrance to the room.

After introductions, Gowda got right to the point. "This boy here got wind that you were thinking of having his elephant, Hathi, come in behind Ramachandran in the parade."

"Ah yes. Mr. Ramana Gowda. I have heard your name."

"I've heard yours. The thing is, the elephant Hathi has rejoined the herd."

"Before we jump in, let us get to know each other. You are an accomplished hunter. Do you like the leopard by the door?"

"Like it?" Gowda shot a look to Arun.

"I bagged him myself near Mysore."

"Doesn't take much strength to pull a trigger."

"But you are a hunter, are you not?"

"A hunter. A mariner. An estate owner. Yes. But my contests are always fair."

"Well then, you'll appreciate that I shot this one from three hundred meters."

"Let me tell you the secret about hunting."

"Please."

"Whatever rifle you used was made of wood and metal, and maybe plastic and glass if it had a scope. Those materials were mined, and the craft and technique of that mining is the result of thousands of years of human learning. Then there are the explosive properties. That metal work, the wood shape, the perfect ballistics, glass, etcetera, is the result of how many discoveries across how many cultures over how many years?

"Did you mine the metal? Cut the tree? Did you forge it? Did your own alchemy create those rounds? No. And so the question is, if you didn't have the supernatural sum of ten thousand men in your hands, would you still be able to exert any influence over that creature's life with the flick of your finger? Could you bring down a deer with your own speed and cunning? Could you drive a spear through a bear's heart without being torn apart?"

"That is a fascinating point."

"Yes it is, my dear Vagina Sir."

"Excuse me?" Vijayan's face flushed red and he coughed smoke.

"Vijayan. Vijayan Sir!" Gowda theatrically shook his head at having mis-spoke. "But yes, a rifle is a magical thing. And that is leaving out the point that such a weapon allows you to attack your target without any skin in the game. You have no physical risk from three hundred meters."

Vijayan shifted in his chair.

"My old grandmother could pull a trigger. Sure. So could a toddler. And let me guess, that leopard in the doorway: you took him at night with a spotlight and a dog as bait?"

Vijayan was glaring now.

"Yes, spotlighting. So you blinded him with the headlights of a car, a car you were safe within. Some daring hunt, sir, some daring hunt indeed."

"And what about a tiger?"

"Well, there you go."

"Yes, that is the issue isn't it?"

"Have you ever seen a tiger?"

"Of course! I've been to Ranthambore."

"Ah. So you've seen it from what, a jeep? With fifty other tourists about? Were there martinis in your hands?"

"No, we were on elephant back, private safari. It is the way the maharajas did it."

"Ah, private tour. Elephant back. Yes. So you were ten feet in the air."

"Why is it important where I was?"

"Because on foot, a tiger will never let a man see her. On elephant back is different. If you were on your feet, in the wild, and even glimpsed a tiger, it would be something. I can tell you that not a man alive, on any continent, has a chance against a tiger. Not without a rifle. And that's why every beast in that jungle knows what naked cowards we really are. You see, it is all about perspective. Inside a car's cabin you don't feel like you are speeding, but the ground will tear you apart. On an elephant with a gun you *feel* safe. But make no mistake. They are striped gods."

Vijayan flashed a grin he hadn't used in years. "This is true. Perhaps we should move on. Thank you all for coming to see me today." Vijayan fumbled for a cigarette. He held the flame to it and stoked it madly, his cheeks sinking in, his eyes bulging. When he exhaled, his lip curled and his eyes rolled up involuntarily. He was a man who blinked frequently, who struggled to find the right way of holding himself. His eyes were searching as he waved away the smoke, scanning the room. "You have not brought the tiger devathe?"

"*Tiger devathe?*" Gowda leaned in as if he was hard of hearing.

"The tiger girl."

"The what?"

"The tiger-amma-girl. Can you hear me?"

"Yes, I can hear you," the hunter growled. "I just wasn't sure if *you* could hear you. You are referring to Isha."

"Yes, the girl with whom the tiger is friends."

"It's not quite so magical," Arun said massaging his forehead as if it might crack.

"Oh really? I was led to believe she rescued a tiger cub and ran away from home to raise it. I was led to believe that she survived an attack by thirty dogs and a mother tiger and lived to tell the tale. I heard that you three helped her cross over the back of the Periamangalam spine and into the jungle where she has personally been teaching the thing to hunt. I've also heard that it's almost fully grown and she's the only one it will let close. That the tribals have seen them together, the girl and the tiger, and are mystified. They are saying it is a most auspicious and momentous thing to happen in modern times. That is what I think. Are you saying I am misinformed?"

He was looking back and forth between Arun and Gowda, ignoring Thimma. He pushed the newspaper forward. There on paper was Isha beside Kala. The photo the boys from Bangalore had taken on the road. His finger tapped the paper obnoxiously.

"The reason I ask is because this Periamangalam, this forest, is not suited for tigers. It is not a tiger reserve, you see? The tribal people have become accustomed to living without tigers being present, and soon they will be developing, modernizing. To help them do this there are some important projects—dams, roads—in place to help these people live better lives. Progress is happening in this little corner of the world. Tiger presence could hurt all that. You must understand, I have to protect my people. That is my job."

"You are a servant of the people," Arun offered.

"Yes, yes I am," Vijayan tried.

"And building a dam to clog that river and kill the fish, that will help your people?"

Vijayan was having trouble keeping the polite smile on his face. "Yes, I believe that economic opportunity, security, these are things the Adivasis want."

"Oh really? How do you know what Adivasis want? You are not our leader." Thimma's voice was shrill.

Arun put a quieting hand on Thimma's arm. The boy pulled away.

JCB Vijayan glared at him and reached for a new cigarette, which he lit.

"We'll return to the issue at hand. I saw what this young boy did last year in the elephant yard. And many of my mahouts remember too. It seems that only with this Hathi holding his tail will Ramachandran behave."

"If you had half a brain, you'd leave that old bastard out of the parade." Gowda said.

"No, no, no. You see, we must have the greatest of the elephants in this parade. He is a very powerful image. One of might and strength."

"Yes. I understand," Gowda said in a perfectly respectful way. "The thing is, he is the most dangerous thing since the plague, and putting him in with a thousand people is ludicrous. The other thing is what we came here to tell you: the boy would like to decline your offer."

Vijayan exhaled grotesquely and began twirling his eyebrow between his fingers. "Oh? And why would a young mahout refuse an honor like this one? After all, I am asking him to come to the greatest event of the year, where many important people will be watching. I am asking him to demonstrate his skill as a mahout, which is a proud tradition, I must say."

Thimma's eyes were savage as he sat slumped in the chair. He wanted nothing more than to leap across the desk and claw out the eyes of JCB Vijayan. He remembered the posters, the propaganda in the streets. He remembered when Vijayan had come to his haadi, back in the old days when the light in the world was warm, when his family was intact. It was Vijayan who had asked them to trust him. He who promised them a better life, that they must support his projects for the jobs. And in the end, they had been uprooted and left to die on that hillside. They were simple, honest people who could never imagine the evil they would endure. He thought of his mother's body lying in the field.

"Why would I help the man who killed my family?"

Vijayan straightened now, and sweat bloomed onto Ramana Gowda's neck.

"Do you think that we don't know how you work—one hand with food and the other with blade? That you lure people in so that you can destroy them? My entire village was destroyed after you promised us a better life. You made them trust you, and then you took away their lives."

"Let me tell you something, boy—"

"No, let me tell you." Thimma's finger was aimed now; he was nearly shouting. "The Adivasi people know what you are doing. They know who you are and what you want. And I know. Because I've seen what you do, and I won't let it happen again. So fuck your parade, and your office, and your dam."

Two men came now and took Thimma by the arms. Gowda and Arun sprang to their feet, fists ready. But Vijayan held up a hand for peace.

"Release the boy," he told his men in Malayalam. "*Achha, achha.* You make a good point. India is a complicated reality. That is a certainty we can all agree on. But we will have to see. Why don't you take some time to think about my offer? Let us see if you can't at least come help the mahouts prepare, no? We would be honored to have you. And we need great mahouts if we are going to keep that Ramachandran in line. It is a matter of safety, for the people."

The politician's cordiality dissipated Thimma's rage into confusion. The boy wobbled his head.

"Well, thank you all very much for coming to speak with me then. I am glad your Huliamma or Ishamma is doing well. Thimma, I hope to see you the day of the parade, okay? Hopefully your Hathi can join, it would greatly help us keep things safe."

Thimma was silent as they were shown out.

They found themselves in the dusty brightness of the elephant yard.

Arun was squinting and took a cigarette off of Gowda. "So do you like my leopard?" he said, cigarette bouncing.

Gowda grunted and lit his own. "Very much, Mr. Vagina."

Arun laughed. Thimma looked confused and was still trembling. Arun tapped his shoulder. "Hey, who is this Ramachandran chap? Can we see him?"

Thimma led the way through the dusty yard. The sun was staggeringly hot.

At the tusker's cage, Gowda and Arun both stepped back.

"Son of a bitch! Rama…Rama!" Gowda took another backstep.

Arun looked around the rest of the yard, the way he did when something he saw made no sense. The elephant was soberingly large, to the extent that many who saw him were forced to wonder if he were not the product of some syndrome that caused unreasonable and indeterminate growth. His high back above the shoulders was a mountainous hump of muscle from which his thick spine ran down into his rump. Atop his head, a pair of heavy bulbs emerged from his freakishly large skull. Long tusks turned toward them below burning orange eyes that were filled with hatred and pain. Thimma showed them how brave he was and went closer.

Ramachandran stuck out his long trunk towards the mahout boy. The elephant remembered the boy. The nostrils drew in the scent of tiger and of Hathi, the herd. The herd! Ramachandran drank the scents the boy brought from the jungle. This was Hathi's boy, a good boy.

The great old tusker reached out quickly and grabbed the boy's shirt. It tore, and the boy leapt back. They smelled of fear, and the elephant enjoyed that. This piece of fabric he brought into the timber cage and breathed deeply from it news from the forest. The tiger, the herd, the girl. It was all there in the rag of cloth. The feeling rose in the old elephant that the time was near.

Back inside the office, JCB Vijayan had dismissed the other dignitaries and no longer needed to control his expression. He scowled and pulled at his Gold Flake cigarette. He crushed beetle nut and tobacco and lime and rolled it into a leaf, which he shoved into his mouth. As the flavor seeped out, gently masticated on his molars, he searched his Rolodex for a number he had not seen in quite some time. When he found what he sought, he dialed the number. He announced himself and requested to speak to Kamu Shikari.

That evening, hours later, he was alone in his office when the phone rang.

"Kamu, *hegidira*? How are you? *Accha!* Good, good! There is an urgent matter, something I must discuss. Two years back, you had asked me for permission, you wanted to run a beat, and I promised you that if the time ever came, you would have it. Well, have you been reading the papers? Good, yes, we've all seen it.

"What's that? Yes, it is true. True indeed. I need it to be made untrue. Listen: I need you to assemble a team. You'll only have one day, but you'll have free reign and can run it your way. Every cop and forest ranger in the region will be in Nalkere for the parade; the forest will be unguarded. But there are some criteria I need met. If you could, assemble your men and come to Nalkere on the twenty-second, the day before the parade. We can talk payment then, but I promise you, you won't be unpleased with what I am offering."

There was chatter on the other line.

"No, it's a female, nearly grown, from what I can tell. Oh, and Kamu, do you remember when we cleared out that haadi, what was it called?"

More chatter.

"Yes, Kolengere. That was it. The one with the blind elephant. Let's get some of the same men." More chatter. "No. I don't care. That is up to you. Like I said, that is all up to you. Bring whatever arms you have. We can supply a few rifles as well."

The following day Thimma, Arun, and Gowda had returned to the village. Isha led them west from the village, out past the banyan tree and pooja stone. Kala was busy devouring a kill, and while the tiger was busy, Isha wanted to show the others one of her favorite places in the forest.

They discussed hunting methods as they went. Arun said that Kala's strategy of running stags into lantana bushes was a good start, but she'd need to develop other techniques. Hamstringing seemed like the next logical step in her learning. That was when a tiger slashed the back hamstring open so the deer fell.

Gowda pointed out that at least one tigress in Ranthambore chased her prey into water where it was easier to overwhelm. They all agreed that Kala might utilize this if she could see it working. They also all agreed that without the example of more experienced tigers, Kala might never graduate to taking on full-grown bison and clamping their throats until they fell. But that didn't mean she wouldn't survive.

Isha was convinced of this already and was far more preoccu-pied with the threat of human intervention. She proposed a plan that involved coaxing the Ranger Chinnappa out into the jungle and forcing him to watch the tiger in action. This, she was convinced, would persuade him to come over to their side and support the re-wilding of Kala. Arun and Gowda were less certain than she, but after their meeting with Vijayan, agreed that they needed the help of the Forest Department and potentially some big cat experts, of which Amma had already compiled a list. Isha practically danced over the jungle floor at the hopeful tone of the conversation.

Isha led them to the edge of a beautiful stream. The sun was brilliant, and the forest sang with fresh chatter and the quick flitting of birds. Reticulated sunlight sprang from the surface of the water so that the jungle pulsed with light.

At dawn that morning, Isha had managed to coax Hathi from the herd. The blind elephant simply could not resist the lumps of jaggery she offered. His willingness to rejoin the human world at intervals at the beckon of Isha's feminine voice was something she demonstrated with pride before the others.

Thimma grumbled at her suggestions that he do less whacking and more talking to the elephant, but he could not conceal his smile at the elephant's return. The promise of bananas and a good scrub was enough to keep Hathi with the human gang while his mother grazed half a kilometer away. Thimma was so happy that his throat tightened. He swore out loud and would raise his stick to the elephant to hide any sign of emotion, but Isha's accusing eyes made him hold his blows.

The stream she led them to fed into a pond where Hathi submerged up to the ears in the deep green pool, as content as could be exploring the moss and rocks with his trunk. A red dragonfly played in the thick black hairs on Hathi's head. On his neck and back Thimma was working hard with the scrub brush to clean off the red earth stain Hathi had taken on. Hathi knew, and Thimma knew, that the red earth stain would be replaced that very evening, but they both enjoyed the old tradition.

Isha chased butterflies around the edge for a time and then swam out to the elephant's back to sun bathe. She had recently eaten and was in a fine mood. She spoke incessantly, partly to herself and partly to Thimma, who was not only not listening, but also, of course, couldn't understand. She was reciting a long stream of consciousness of this and that.

"Nagesh Sir once took away a fig I was eating, and he told me I couldn't eat fruit during lessons. I told him that a fig is not actually a fruit, technically I mean, it's actually an inward facing flower—but all of the boys in the class, *boy childs* I tell you, they all said I was a freak, and I told them that I…"

Gowda groaned from the near shore, removed the gun from his lap and placed it butt to the ground against a tree. "Oh devare! But does it ever stop talking? I feel like I'm in some warped dream!"

"This goes on in my head, imagine what I feel!" Isha said earnestly as she pried at a toenail. Then, looking up, "Arun, come in, yah!" Isha pushed off of the elephant and swam frog-style toward the edge.

"Oh, not just yet." Arun smiled. He was puffing a cigarette and watching the birds. He had come to greatly enjoy Isha's run-on gibberish-talk moods.

Isha swam to the side and climbed out. She caught Gowda watching her.

"Do you swim, Uncle?"

"Certainly, like an iron tortoise!"

"Well why won't you at least come to where you can stand?"

The hunter grinned. "Thou art very persistent, little bird. I don't have my swimming costume, otherwise I would."

Isha glared at him, unable to form a rebuttal. She simply could not picture the heavy hunter wet, not with all of his belts and leather and heavy boots. He would certainly sink. Instead she returned her attention to Arun. He was at peace, leaning there beside Gowda, one arm behind his head, blowing long plumes of smoke into the still jungle air.

Isha left and returned moments later with a butterfly on her finger. Gowda gave her a quizzical look and she shot him a wicked grin: *Watch this.* Then she went into character.

"Arun, look at this! Oh, look! Come see!" Isha knelt with the butterfly at the edge of the pool as if over some great treasure. Arun rose and came to her side.

"Beautiful. Look at that proboscis going!" he said, as the butterfly lapped happily at her finger. "He's eating your salty sweat."

"Isn't it?" Isha stood slowly, butterfly on her finger. "Hold out your finger, see if it will come to you." Arun obliged. In a flash Isha, clutched his finger and turned it at an angle to which fingers do not bend. The butterfly fled away and out of view. Isha hurled Arun into the water, robes and all, and jumped in after. Arun emerged sputtering and shocked.

"I'll kill you!" he said, swimming toward Isha to dunk her under. Hathi's ears flapped with excitement, and Thimma was standing barefoot on his elephant, cheering. Ramana Gowda was laughing so hard that he could barely breath.

"Look at Uncle!" Isha said, pointing. They all turned to watch him go. The hunter was red faced, tears streaming down his face. Long cascades of ferocious laughter made him hold his sides.

"Oh fuck off!" Arun yelled, splashing toward the hunter. Gowda waved it away, wiping his eyes. For a moment it looked like he might be through the worst of it.

"Your face!" he roared and was overcome once again with a fit that shook him so that he doubled over, eyes tearing.

"I think you killed him." Thimma grinned.

Gowda tried again and again to speak but simply could not manage. Tiny Isha's cunning to throw a grown man, and the shock of it on Arun's face, was more than he could bear. He was fitfully undone and finally had to walk off into the jungle to cough and clutch and compose himself.

So they spent the afternoon swimming and laughing in the jungle. It was the last time they were all together.

27

RAMACHANDRAN

On the day of the parade, Thimma went with Arun and Gowda by jeep to Nalkere. The previous evening, Arun and Gowda, Thimma and Killahuntha, had all agreed that Hathi would not leave the jungle, but that for Thimma to completely disobey the wishes of a man like JCB Vijayan would be unwise. Thimma was very unhappy, but it was decided that the boy would go and help in whatever way he could without the blind elephant.

It had also been agreed that it was time to seek outside help. Kala's hunting had progressed to the point that she was making kills once in every twenty attempts. Soon she would be able to hold her own in the wild. Arun and Gowda felt strongly that it was time to invite Chinnappa to see. Gowda said that the ranger, with a few trusted reporters at his side, would be their best defense against anything Vijayan might plan against them.

By now they had gleaned a vague idea of the hysteria that the Hindu article had caused across south India. If they could harness that excitement and ensure outside world knew the true story, it could make it hard for anyone to cause Kala harm. Isha listened to these plans with tightly knitted eyebrows. It was hard for her to objectively discuss such things.

"So when you are in town, you'll talk to Chinnappa?"

"Yes, and I'll make sure it goes better," Arun said.

"This is a powerful list of reporters," Gowda said, scratching his pencil across a small pad that bent under the pressure of his thumb. "Arun, don't let me forget to ask Siddartha about that veteranarian."

286 · PAUL ROSOLIE

"I won't." Arun took the notebook to look it over. He nodded and handed it to Isha, who knew none of the names written on the page that was now mangled from Gowda's writing grip.

She handed the notebook back and folded her arms, her braid resting on one shoulder. Both men waited on her word. "Okay," she said, nodding. "Let's do it." She met Arun's eyes, and then Gowda's. "It scares me, but I agree it's time. Like you said, what can they do if the whole world is watching?"

Gowda's farewell was a rough hand on the head and a wink that made Isha smile. Arun delivered a list of final warnings and promises that made her roll her eyes. He said they would be back the day after tomorrow and begged her to leave the tiger be. Kala was well fed and roaming free in the forest. She was too large and dangerous to risk playing with while the rest of them were away. He hugged her before climbing into the jeep. As the doors closed, Isha nodded in a way that both men knew she would never listen. She told Arun to remember to mail the letters and to buy as much chocolate and chakli as he could find.

Thimma was already in the back seat with worried, distant eyes. As Gowda drove the Pajero out of the village, Isha climbed onto the step to ride along outside. She leaned in through the window as the car drove and punched Thimma hard in the arm. Before he could retaliate, she leapt off and hit the ground at a run. She shouted that she'd look out for Hathi while they were gone and wondered if Thimma heard her. She never saw him again.

An hour after they left the village, Gowda's Pajero emerged from the jungle and out the forest gate, to the dirt road that led along the boundary. For two kilometers, the road ran south along the forest edge, then turned left, away from the forest, onto a concrete bridge over the river and out onto finished road. As they climbed up the steep incline, there was a ruined section where the pavement was broken and eroded, and it took them nearly an hour to coax the jeep up the rocky gradient. From there it was only ten minutes to Nalkere, but they arrived forty minutes past eight, almost an hour late.

The town was already throbbing. People from all across the region had come for the parade. Gowda drove to the elephant yard, where he parked and they dismounted the jeep. Thimma went in search of the other mahouts. Arun went to find a phone, explaining that he was long overdue to check on the sanctuary.

Thimma could hear elephants in the distance as he spoke to a mahout from Mysore, who told him how the night before the mahouts had surrounded Ramachandran's cage and used a bow and arrow to fire ropes through the cage and through the elephant's legs. Four ropes had been cast, and each one had pulled in a chain. The chains had then been manipulated so that they held the legs taut and were locked in the center. This ensured that the violent elephant could not run, and in fact would just only be able to walk. He said that they had had a hard time of it and Ramachandran was furious. But everyone would be safer given the restraints.

The man went off on some work, and Thimma was moving through the yard when a voice called him by name. It was one of the men that had been in Vijayan's office the previous day.

"You please come," he said, beckoning with his hand.

Thimma hesitated, unsure.

"Come, ya! JCB must give directions to you, come!"

Thimma looked back toward the jeep for sign of Gowda. Something in him made him wish the old hunter was there. The thought of speaking to Vijayan alone made him queasy, but there was no time. They were already late.

"What is your name?" he asked the man.

"I am Chandan," the man said, wobbling his head. He placed a hand on Thimma's shoulder as he led him through the building door and into the long blue hallway. Thimma jumped when the door swung closed behind them. They walked in silence down the hall until reaching the heavy teak doors.

Inside Vijayan was waiting. His sleeves were rolled up; he was breathing hard. Chandan's hand moved to Thimma's back, guiding him forcefully. Thimma wanted to run, wanted to scream out. But he drew a brave breath and looked the politician in the eyes. Behind him, the teak door closed, the lock clicked. Thimma and Vijayan were alone.

Isha's arm was over Kala's back as sunbeams fell into the glade. They were lying beneath the giant old temple tree that stood over the pooja stone. She covered the tiger's eyes with her hands and Kala brushed them away with a massive paw. When she did it again Kala rolled. Isha was still at play when Kala suddenly went rigid as a sphinx. Her ears snapped eastward. The forest had become deathly silent. When Isha heard the first distant gunshot, she clipped Kala to the heavy rope leash that ran to the temple tree and made for the village. It took her some time, even at a jog, and when she arrived, men were running to and fro. People were shouting. Something was about to happen, but she did not know what.

Sudha ran up to her and knelt, putting her hands on Isha's shoulders. "Forest! Forest! Go!" Sudha said in English and hurried off.

Isha was no more than halfway to Kala when the animals began running. A stampede of guar was leaving the great field. The deer were nowhere to be seen. The air smelled of smoke, and the fruit bats were in exodus above the trees. The sounds of vehicles were everywhere, and curious if it was Ramana's Pajero returned early, she made for the main trail.

She ran down a game trail to return to the village. She was rock hopping down a stream—the fastest and quietest way to move. The first of them she saw were three men atop a tusker, coming around the turn. The elephant's tusks swung low as its great steps scattered the stream. Isha sank down into the ferns, her heart racing. The men on top had guns over their laps and machetes on their belts. One was smoking. They were filthy and rough with murderous eyes. The elephant they rode was a rageful, scared old bull.

She lifted mud from the earth and smeared it onto her face. As the great steps drew nearer, she slithered down beneath the leaves and closed her eyes. She thought of the fawn, so close to the wolves tearing apart its mother. *Do not move. Not even a muscle.* She thought of nothing as she lay there clutching the earth, praying.

In Nalkere the parade was starting. Arun had run backwards along the line of elephants as they left the stockade. Thimma was not with them. He trotted in through the cottages and called out the boy's name. The elephant yard was deserted. He stood in the scalding heat below gathering clouds, panting, thinking.

He had not slept well the previous night and had dreamed that his father was in the room with him. Several times he had woke and then slept, and each time his father's form was there in the corner, watching him. When finally he woke to light, he rubbed the sleep from his eyes with a headache that felt like a drill between his eyes. He had sat for some time to shake off what was surely a bad dream. But the feeling of it followed him into the day like a soft cloud of dread.

Unable to find Thimma, Arun came to the parade road. He floated through the churning mass of bodies as though in a terrible dream. His eyes narrowed, a mysterious black dread growing in him. The crowd was shoulder to shoulder, tuk-tuks and busses suspended. *Panipuri*, *charmuri*, and coconut vendors were working rapidly, their stalls made islands in the jostling, spitting, farting, crowd. Firecrackers blasted from the rooftops. The music was deafening, the amplifiers crackling.

The procession of businessmen and politicians came first. The crowd was a mix of labor class lungis and shy tribals peering about. The seductive chaos of India had come to the sleepy town.

Now it was all sweat and tension. The iron clouds held heat against the earth that could only be relieved by rain. Arun looked to the sky and wished for drops to hit his face. There was a stage to his right where the addresses would be made, hands shaken, token gifts exchanged, the future celebrated. The stage was opulently garnished in long strings of flowers, banana leaves, and woven palm fronds.

Speakers blared a pulsating treble tune above a grand and plunging bass that shook the air as the parade advanced. Next to come was a swarm of white clad men and boys. They bounced and flailed, dancing down the street to the tremendous beat of the music.

Arun stood in the jostling crowd beside the stage. His forehead was furrowed with concern and glistening with sweat. It was murderously hot out here where there were no trees for shade. Masala and armpits and paan juice filled the air in his nostrils as he anxiously awaited the second wave of the parade.

By the time the first Bollywood track had ended, the procession of dancing men and boys had passed before the spectators and fanned out before the stage. Behind them was a scattered legion of vehicles, mostly white Ambassadors with bayonet hood emblems, their sheaths removed so that the blades glinted on the hood of each car.

Then the jumbos rounded the corner. Elephants came down into the town: monstrous and colorfully gilded with bells and mirrors. Tiny human mahouts in orange turbans rode atop each neck. The elephants lumbered through the crowd, the humans dispersing like a school of fish before an army of whales to allow the passage of the elephants. He recognized Shanti and Gulabi and their respective mahouts from the forest. They were followed by two others he did not know. There was no sign of Thimma. Two more elephants came through. *Where the hell is Thimma?*

Ramachandran came like a black cloud on the street. The behemoth's eyes were pits of rage under the blinding color of his decor. Each curved tusk was larger than any man present. They touched at the cracked tips as he yawned and flexed. The mahout on his back nervously prodded him with the metal bull hook. He was experienced enough to be terrified of the elephant.

The pachyderm parade went nose to tail through the crowd. A man on a motorcycle, pushing through the crowd and swearing loudly and shouted at by everyone, got too close. Ramachandran veered toward him. Chains secured each leg tightly, bound in the center. They jingled as he went, pulling against the pink-and-black sores they had created on the skin they constricted. Ramachandran knew he had to be careful walking, for the chains could trip him.

The mahout's bullhook found the soft rear of his ear, coaxing him back to course. The giant's eyes bulged. He swung his trunk and shook his head, letting the anger wash over him. The patience drains out of an elephant with fewer words than it does for a man, and with far greater finality.

Men on the stage were speaking in grand gestures. The mahouts gathered the elephants into a line, perpendicular to the corner of the station. The area had been cleared earlier and guarded by fences and police officers; otherwise, the flood of bodies would have long ago filled every available crevice of the street.

Shoulder to shoulder the elephants stood. Ramachandran was a goliath even among giants. Parents pointed to him, children *aww*-ed, men stood with a lost and perplexed expression, trying to see through the paint and process the size, to figure if this thing could truly be real. His tusks hung heavy, thick bows on either side of his trunk. His ears flapped to dispel heat, the capillaries and veins swollen and clogged in the stifling warmth. His orange eyes scanned the crowd. There was Vijayan; he was at the podium, he was bowing, he was speaking loudly and with gesture. There also in the crowd was Arun.

Arun stood less on his on legs than by the shouldering pressure of the crowd. Hatred burned in his eyes as he watched Vijayan. Some local dignitary began a long-winded introduction on the stage. Arun looked left and right. The feeling of dread had percolated and spread throughout him, and he was left immobile with indecision, unclear what the sum of it all meant. The crowd erupted in applause and whistles. Arun came back from his thoughts as Vijayan took the podium. Arun's thoughts were racing, dread groaned in his stomach. Vijayan's speech entered his ears in a detached and distant way, choked by heat and worry.

"Bless you all on this beautiful day! ...we cannot let India fall behind! We are a nation of innovation! Of progress! There are those who would keep us in the gutter, in the past, but we must prosper! Projects... prosperity... the future!"

Arun rolled his eyes as the speech continued, but the crowd erupted with applause. Arun realized he was missing almost all of what Vijayan was saying. There was only one thing he could think: *Where the hell is Thimma?*

As the politician shouted on, Arun pushed through the crowd. Past the sweating bodies, the jostling, the grins, the sneers and crimson paan spit. Through the empty elephant yard, down the hallway to Vijayan's office. The sound of the microphone, of the parade, of the crowd, were distant now. He was alone. There was the sound of buzzing, an escalating droning.

An old, hunchbacked woman, gap toothed and mad-eyed, stood in the doorway to the office, her hand out before her.

"And I just cleaned this floor! Who will clean this now? Me, that's who!" She stepped back. On the floor before here was a pool of black-looking blood.

Arun peered around the large cabinet. The sight sent him back against the wall. Thimma's eye socket was broken and deeply purple, a black river of dried blood running down to the ear. His mouth was ajar, only a single tooth remained in the bloody gums. Flies fed at the eyes and inside the mouth, down in the godless darkness.

A bony hand gripped his wrist, and he whirled around.

"Who would do such a thing on this clean floor?"

He raised a hand to strike her but held it. She grinned, cackling as he withdrew. He went down the hallway and fell against one wall then the other. His legs became weak as grief and hatred that washed over him. *Is that what Anu looked like when they finished with her?* He wished he could reverse time. He wanted to back up, to leave, go back. But everything was hurtling forward. He stumbled forward and fell to his hands and vomited. In a side room there was a knife, which he lifted.

In the harsh inferno outside, he drifted among the muted throng of grinning contagious faces. He felt the blade in his sleeve and watched from the camouflage of the masses.

JCB Vijayan waved with both hands high above his head as he walked down the stairs of the stage. One at a time, the politicians of the region came to the line of elephants. One by one they knelt and touched their feet (not actually but symbolically from a safe distance) and then their own foreheads and lips, blessing themselves with the elephant's sacred magic.

Through the blaring music, ears like sails received the news on the wind. Over the din of the crowd, the shifting of feet and the thrumming of engines, the elephant's ears heard it. Ramachandran stood motionless. His ears ceased flapping. His grand tusks poised. It was a soft sound, distant and partial, difficult to discern at first. As he turned his head toward the sound, the mahout on his back coaxed him with the tip of the bull hook, urging his head back to the forward position. The elephant shrugged him angrily away. The mahout dug harder. Ramachandran strained to listen.

The sound he heard was of wailing, of gunfire. It was coming from the jungle. It was the sound of the herd. He could not hear what the elephants were saying, not at such a distance and through such a din of grinning faces, bouncing bodies, blaring music. He wanted silence to hear. He wanted to stamp out every little miserable human on the street.

JK Karunanidhi, chancellor of the province, came and knelt timidly at Ramachandran's feet, touching the ground and then his forehead and lips and standing graciously. He withdrew quickly. Then came Shankara Bhat from Mysore.

Ramachandran was in an auditory trance, engulfed in the distant sound, for he had heard it once before. It was the sounds of elephants in pain. Then one of the other elephants shifted, and Ramachandran knew the pose. The cement of the street thrummed with bass and motors and moving feet, but still there was another signal. It came up from the earth and through the concrete and up through the thick callused pads of his feet and up the bones of his tree-trunk legs.

When JCB Vijayan came before him, Ramachandran snorted and shifted his weight. The bull hook was suddenly at his ear, tugging in reminder, but he began to back up as the memory of the vicious beatings this man had dealt him played deep inside his skull. One step, then another. The crowd reacted audibly as the monster withdrew.

Vijayan stood with a grand smile on his face and spread his arms wide. "What is it my old friend? Do you fear me?"

The crowd applauded and cheered, for it appeared that even the great Ramachandran feared and respected JCB Vijayan. The politician stepped forward and reached up to put a hand on Ramachandran's trunk. For the first time there was no barrier between them.

Ramachandran began to shiver like a pressure cooker. Suddenly the thing that had been growing in him for years, clawing to get out, ruptured, filling the bones and muscle and pressing against the heavy armor of his hide. A low grumbling sound, a deep resonance of distant thunder, grew from the throat of the old tusker as if the last of his patience slipped down some vast, gurgling drain.

"We must not fear the powerful. They are here to help us!" Vijayan's smile was wide, his voice full of pompous, spurious sincerity. Ramachandran's trunk rose and curled around his wrist. Vijayan's head snapped round, his eyes full of terror. He forced the smile to return. "Ah! He is my friend after all!" The crowd applauded.

Ramachandran held him there. Then with the sweep of one leg, snapped the chain. People began rising, drawing back, pointing. Parents hurried away with their children. Vijayan pulled back against the immense power of the trunk that held him. He looked up to the back of Ramachandran, to a mahout he did not know.

"What do I do?" he said desperately in Hindi. The mahout only continued to stare, too terrified to speak. Then, in one sudden arcing motion, the elephant hurled Vijayan so that his body flew like some discarded toy through the air, crashing onto the roof of a white Ambassador with a metal-and-bone crunch that sent glass everywhere.

Panic bloomed in the scalding street. Men and women withdrew as Ramachandran advanced. Vijayan tried to rise and found his stark white humerus protruding from the torn flesh of his arm. He rolled off the roof and onto his feet. As Ramachandran bore down on him, the crowd vanished like receding water. Vijayan crawled in through the open window of the car, landing in a painful heap on the wide passenger seat. He propped himself up on his right arm. The window only showed colossal legs, wrinkled skin.

The elephant could feel his mahout stabbing at his skull but took no notice. He bowed his giant's head forward reaching his tusks beneath the car. One of the wheels fired out a hiss of air as it was torn. The car rose into the air and slid down his tusks so that the doors came against his forehead. His left eye was level with the man inside. The terror on his face was delicious to the elephant. Ramachandran took a monstrous step, and then another, easily carrying the car. Arun stood transfixed in the midst of the fleeing crowd.

The mahout on Ramachandran's back was shouting desperately, slapping the elephant's head, and laying hard downward blows with the bullhook. None of it mattered. The elephant hurled the car, which rotated, landing on its hood, the carriage smashed flat under the weight of its own metal, glass exploding out the sides. Policemen ran for cover with the other civilians, *panipuri* wallahs abandoning their stalls. The band dropped their instruments, and the mahout riding Ramachandran leaped down to the street, shattering his ankle.

Ramachandran came to the car and put a heavy foot down so that the metal groaned. He could hear Vijayan inside the twisted metal, screaming. Two shots rang out and Ramachandran felt a hot sting on his rump, like large fire coals. He snatched a fallen motorcycle with his trunk and flung it. The terrifying metal weight of the bike rotated through the air and came down on a policeman, killing him instantly.

The street had nearly emptied, and the two-story rooftops and windows were filling. Other elephants were stampeding in various directions, screaming. More gunshots rang out. When Vijayan crawled out from the upside-down car, Ramachandran turned. Another policeman raised his rife, but when the elephant took a

threatening step, the man threw the rifle and ran for his life. JCB
Vijayan dove for the firearm.

Arun had made his way up onto the stage, where he now stood
blinking, forehead tangled in lines disbelieving awe. Ramachandran roared and groaned and accelerated toward where JCB
Vijayan was lying on his back, holding the rifle. A sharp crack rang
out as he managed a shot.

The last thing JCB Vijayan saw was the colossal shadow
against the dark sky. As the calloused foot crushed his skull, a long
splash of blood and brain erupted from the neck where Vijayan's
head had previously been.

All was silent for a moment. Arun's own pulse throbbed in his
ears. Smoke and ash and paper swirled in the air of the street.
Wrecked cars and twisted metal motorcycles lay burning, alarms
blaring from their ruined metal bodies. The blood puddle from Vijayan's neck grew like a black hole onto the pavement.

Thunder rumbled from Ramachandran's great throat, the long
tusks sweeping before him. There beneath the leaden sky, the old
mammoth roared, streaked in blood with ears spread. Great pillar
flanks and wrinkled black skin flexed and accelerated, gaining
speed on a decided and unalterable course. The orange eyes of the
old pachyderm looked toward the distance, past the houses and
farms, to where plumes of black smoke were rising from the burning jungle.

Three guns fired almost in unison. The elephant roared so
loudly that Arun's hands went to his ears and he fell to his knees.
With a flip of his tusks Ramachandran sent a yellow Piaggio auto-
rickshaw rotating through the air, then fled down the street hauling
a train of downed phone wires and rubble behind him, his bells and
mirrors and decorative designs stark over the wreckage. The three
cops followed, reloading and taking aim. The elephant shouldered
and toppled a bus that sprayed glass and tinkling metal shards
against the pavement. Then hurled a motorcycle at the riflemen. As
he left the single-street town, two police vehicles pulled up in front
of him, blocking his way. They fired a cacophony of shots that
slapped into the elephant's flesh as he crashed through parked cars,
smashing the motors and windscreens. His flanks were pocked and
bloodied with the various bits of lead that continued to slice into
him like hot rain.

When he finally broke free of the town, he powered out down the road, a jingling, steaming, rampage of power. He accelerated to his fullest speed. In the distance, the screams of the herd continued. Only now he was certain: he could hear Hathi's voice among them. For the first time in decades, the sum of his unrestrained fury charged toward his family, toward home.

The hunter appeared beside Arun. "We have to go."

"Thimma's dead," Arun said lifelessly.

"I know it." Tears rushed into Gowda's eyes. "I've been searching for you." He closed his eyes against the pain in his throat and with monstrous hands clutched the head of Arun.

Arun's eyes swam past the world, staring at nothing, aghast and disbelieving. Gowda was saying something, repeatedly. His urgent words became shouting. The words came through to Arun in clips. *Vijayan. The jungle. Orders. Shikari.* The hunter's eyes were dire, but Arun could not focus. He was lost somewhere deep inside himself.

Gowda clutched Arun by the robes and hurled him against the wall of the stage. "*Listen to me!* The entire forest is on *fire*. There are fifty of Vijayan's hunters out after the tiger."

In the throbbing silence, dread broke in a wave in Arun's eyes: *Isha.*

He struggled out of Gowda's grip and ran, Gowda jogging beside him. He kicked the nearest bike to life, sending a skirt of gravel and dust as it turned and ripped into the distance. Gowda plugged rounds into his rifle and pulled himself heavily into the Pajero. The truck growled and reared like a charging bull, adding a second plume of smoke to the air as it peeled out of the yard.

Moments later they broke free of the town onto the open dirt road. The bike sped ahead of the heavy jeep, both at top speed and jolting violently on the uneven track. Arun's robes billowed behind him, and a trail of dust came from him like rocket exhaust. He leaned perilously low on a turn. Then came Gowda, fishtailing the jeep without slowing.

As the bare landscape descended gradually toward the river, they could see black clouds belched from the jungle canopy beyond. They raced down the road, first the bike then the jeep coming into their highest gear. One then the other hurtled past Ramachandran as the elephant went crashing forward down the road in his own plume of dust and crumbling costume. The elephant roared as they passed, shaking his great head in a billow of ears and trunk and tusk. They were all headed for the forest where a mass exodus of birds, millions of them, screamed into the sky. Terrified fruit bats circled up out of the trees, joining the black clouds of rising smoke.

Arun's bike left the ground entirely over the edge of the broken road. He skidded and fell and then regained balance and sped on. Gowda crashed down on the breaks, and the old shocks fully flexed in a violent metal *chunk* as the jeep came down. The impact sent rapid fractures through windscreen.

They crossed the bridge and turned right to race along the jungle boundary. Two kilometer's farther, Arun slid to a halt and dropped the bike. He ran and lifted the latch to swing the groaning forest gate open, and then leapt back onto the bike. As they vanished beneath the branches and vines of the jungle, shots rang out ahead. Screams floated in through the motor din. A topless woman ran down the road streaked in blood, her breasts flailing as she ran.

Arun prayed, willing God and earth and wagering all he could offer as bounty. *I offer my body, and all the moments of bliss I have left. But please God, do not take her from this world.*

28

NO HELP IS COMING

At the village Arun's bike fell to the ground, Gowda's Pajero skidded to a halt. They stood amongst burned huts and silence. The huts were broken, and all the living people were gone. The rest were corpses on the ground. Ramana Gowda scanned the wreckage with his rifle ready at his shoulder. The vegetable garden was trampled and the fence was broken. Sudha's dark regal body lay sprawled as if dancing, her right arm outstretched. For a moment they stood stunned in the violent silence.

"She's not here," Arun said.

"No. No, she's not. Most of the village isn't here, thankfully. And it looks like they put up a fight before they went." Gowda knelt down beside a dead man. "You're not using this, are you?" He pried the machete out of the dead man's chest and handed it to Arun.

They jogged out from the village through the forest. The path brought them to where the ground declined toward the yellow grass of the great field where Isha's Stand had played out. As they moved past the forest edge they could not yet see, wind carried the smell of dung and flames, the sound of drums and shouting. Above the distant canopy, out over the field, black smoke curled toward the sky.

Shoulder to shoulder, Arun and Gowda crouched at the forest edge. A monstrous elephant with great curved tusks lumbered across the center of the field, moving west. On his back were two mahouts. At fifty meters on either side of the tusker were pairs of men. In each pair one man carried a rifle and the other a flaming torch. The riflemen went with muzzles in the air, while the torchbearers bowed to the grass at intervals. The orange flames lapped

up to elephant height behind the hunting party. The parade of beaters, jumbos, and their mahouts traveled in formation through the
wobbled mirage air above the flames. The golden field eclipsed to
black as they went.

Gowda's eyes glowed with dread and wonder. "Devare!
Krishna! I didn't want to believe it—they're on a shikari! Like the
maharajas used to do. That one in the center there, he's the shikari,
the head of the hunt. That line will extend for several kilometers on
either side. The other men, the beaters, will go with the torches and
drums, burning gradually and constricting forward and in. They'll
draw together into a choke point. They fill the forest with men and
elephants, flushing out the tiger."

The mammoth tusker hurled its tusks to the sky and bellowed,
a guttural trumpet blast that drowned out the drums. An answering
roar boomed out from the east, then another from the west. Then,
much more distant, came other replies, these echoing in from kilometers away. Wind hurried across the field and the flames were
swelling with dangerous speed, popping and cracking the grass that
swirled toward the sky.

"Where the hell did he get so many men?"

"It's not the first time JCB Vijayan has cleared out a village.
He must have plenty of *goondas* salivating for the grandest blood
sport on earth."

"Vijayan's fucking dead," Arun spat.

"What?"

"You didn't see? At the parade?"

"I saw that street looked like a tsunami hit it."

"Ramachandran flattened his head."

A loud blast sounded, and both men startled.

"Was that a gunshot?"

"Exploding bamboo. That fire's growing fast. Just give me a
moment, ya, I'm trying to think where they're choking to."

"She's not in there."

"What makes you say that?"

"She can't be in there. She just isn't."

Ramana Gowda gave Arun a pitying look. Indeed, she
couldn't be in there. And if she was, she was on her own. Trying to
get in past the line of beaters would be pure suicide.

"Okay, let's go," Arun said, scanning the trees.

"Listen," Gowda said, clutching Arun's arm. "Wherever she is, she's whip-crack smart and she knows the forest. She'll either head up for the canopy or hunker down in a stream." He hesitated. "Or they have her."

"Well let's go!"

"What I'm saying is I need you to tell me you understand what we are getting into if we go in there. There's fifty men, and they have a job to do. And whatever happens, make no mistake: no help is coming."

"We have to go."

"I agree. I just want to hear you say it. That you know it. Not just about what could happen, but what you might see—"

Arun nodded with eyes averted and turned to go. The hunter clutched him at the shoulder. Arun turned on him with a dangerous, unhinged stare that shot a thousand miles through him. Gowda stepped back, suddenly sick with the recollection of the last time he'd seen it: *gasoline and burning bodies*. Arun nodded. His face was trembling, as if just below his skin the force of the hurricane was already lifting away the parts of him that had healed. The hunter swore and shoved him onward.

They agreed it was best to keep both the jeep and the bike, so Arun led ahead of the Pajero as they raced down the main trail that cut into the forest. It would bring them as far as the pooja stone, to the tree where Isha often stayed.

"Kala could protect her, no?" Arun said through the window.

"Don't be ridiculous, she's just a giant cub." *And they are trying to kill Kala!* Gowda almost said out loud.

They devoted themselves to haste. As they raced through the jungle, broken branches and ruined earth marked the wake of elephants. The jeep jolted and smashed through the deep elephant tracks in the road. With each bend they rounded, Arun's heart sank. Where the hell was she if not in the village? How far had the beaters gotten? He tried to push away the image of Thimma's ruined face.

Isha leapt out on the road before them so quickly that Gowda slammed on the breaks not to hit her. Arun dropped the bike and in two steps took her up tightly in his arms, looking to the sky in thanks.

"Isha, where were you?" Arun said.

"I saw all the men, I climbed a tree and then—"

"We need to get you out of here," he said, releasing her. He lifted the bike and swung his leg over to sit.

Her eyes filled with tears.

"Let's go, Isha."

"We can't."

"We have to."

"But Kala."

"She's a tiger; she'll be long gone by now with all this—"

"She can't run. They'll kill her."

Her sobbing confession froze him mid gesture. A dead second ticked by, then another.

"Isha, what are you saying?"

"She's tied. Kala is tied. I tied her to the tree. It's the last thing I did before everything started. I thought…"

Arun's hands covered his eyes. He turned so that his face was hidden from them.

Gowda's mouth was slightly ajar below his white whiskers, a scowl on his face. They could not possibly risk rescuing the tiger, but the alternative was unthinkable. The dominos of compassion had fallen to him: Isha could not bear that her mistake would end Kala's life, and Arun could not bear the pain she would feel if that happened. Neither of them would survive what came next without Gowda. When Arun met his eyes the hunter nodded, and all three rushed into the jeep.

As the hunting party moved through the jungle, the torchbearers set flame to what would burn. The drummers boomed on, and the mahouts called to one another. Out of fifty men, only ten had rifles; the rest were armed with machetes. They went slowly, cautiously, not knowing the true danger of their endeavor. Not a man among them had been on a tiger hunt in their lives. They had only heard the stories of their fathers or grandfathers, that what they hunted had the power to break a man's mind with its eyes.

The sweep was inevitable. Occasionally rifle shots rang out as men killed bears or boar or other hidden creatures. But no horns blew, no blasts of triumph were fired.

At four p.m., an unarmed beater on foot found Kala standing beneath the wide-spread roots of the enormous old tree that stood above the pooja stone. The tiger was poised listening, panting against the rope that held her. The man turned with a hand to his mouth, shouting *"Hai!"* And soon the clearing began to fill as the hunting party converged. Mahouts put fingers to lips, whistling to one another and forming. Elephants groaned and men chattered and crashed nearer. Everything was drawing in toward the tiger.

Isha and Arun sprang out of the Pajero and ran behind Ramana Gowda. It was another hundred meters the pooja stone. They could not go quietly in such dense green growth, but it did not matter because the forest was full of gathering commotion. Men were shouting. Rifles were firing calling in the other teams of beaters and burners.

Isha ran low beside Arun. Gowda waved back at them and all three crouched as an elephant crashed by. The men atop the elephant did not see them. The elephant, the slow giant above, did not bother with the humans below, for his trunk was already outstretched ahead to where the smell of tiger was sharply real.

"Stay here," Gowda hissed, leaving Arun and Isha huddled against a fallen log.

Gowda powered off and vanished into the green. As he went, he heard the men calling between shots the Malayalam word for tiger: *katuva*. He panted as he went, growling under his breath. *You've been in the shit once or twice but not like this. This is a mess.* A sickening sense of derailment held in his chest.

Something moved to his left, and Gowda turned, rifle ready, only to see a rock roll still. He had fallen for the second oldest trick in the book. Before he could turn his rifle, a blow fell on him, then another. He felt a rapid plunging as a blade slid into his back. They went down together in a mess of fists and legs. On the ground, through the rolling commotion of the fight, the old hunter saw two more coming.

At the edge of the pooja stone clearing, Arun gripped Isha's shoulder and shoved her to the ground. Out beyond the leaves, he could see the elephants and men gathering. Isha drew a breath to speak but Arun stopped her with terror in his eyes.

"Isha. I'm sorry, we are too late."

In the clearing, Kala was low in the grass and tangled vines that hung from the temple tree. Several men stood cautiously as the first elephant broke through the clearing, three men on its back. Heavy tusks swung scanning, ears flapped. Atop the elephant, mahouts were talking and motioning. Searching.

"Where is it?" one asked the men on the ground.

"Just there, see!"

Atop the elephant, one mahout pulled the other close so that they both look down his arm and pointed finger to the exact place—a fragment of panting orange fire. They were urgent and hushed as they prepared. One man passed the rifle to the other. At the fringes of the clearing, other men were arriving. They climbed trees to peer and crane and whisper. The shikari took the gun up, checked it over, and then aimed from atop the elephant. For a long time everyone was still: men, elephants, tiger. Then he shot.

At the fringe of the clearing Isha shrieked into Arun's hand, which was tight over her mouth. He pushed her down, pleading with her to be silent.

Kala snarled as the shot grazed her, gnashing at the invisible enemy in her shoulder, rising in furious circles and crashing down again. Elephants spooked and turned to run. Men on foot scattered. The mahouts worked to turn their elephants back around. Then there was a crescendo of voices as they realized she was tied.

"Kayar! Kayar!" Rope! Rope! they called, hardly able to believe it. They spoke fast, curt, and the lead hunter, the shikari himself, barked a command and his elephant raised its foot for his dismount. His bare callused feet hit the ground and he adjusted his lungi. Reaching up, he received the rifle from the mahout above. He took aim again, his black skin tight over his bare ribs, his eyes dark and determined beneath the bright orange turban. He fired.

Kala jumped as the hot metal hit her flank, just above the back left leg, and her body fell, though more out of shock than actual pain or damage. This time her eyes locked on and she understood without question from where the pain had come, who the inflictor was. Her head sank below her shoulders, her eyes laser focused, her neck straining against the line. Her voice was the sound of feline wrath, a blast and draw, a scraping, throaty shred.

The front-most elephant hugged the edge of the clearing while another tried to hide behind it. Men on foot hung partially out of trees, ready to climb or flee. The tiger snarled like the tectonic scrape of continents against the earth. She thrashed with all her mortal force against the line that held her as the man drew in.

Twenty feet from her, the shikari paused. He wanted to be closer for the shot. He wanted the men to tell tales of his bravery. But his body refused his will, held by the ancient limbic part of the brain that knows true danger.

"Be careful! That rope won't hold her!" came the warning from atop an elephant.

The shikari knew that this particular rifle was not such a heavy bore as to take down a tiger properly, and that if he was going to do this safely, he'd have to make sure the next shot went through her skull. He was too terrified to rush. Also, he had found his prize, the thing he sought, and it was wondrous and terrifying and could not escape. He savored the primal awe of the animal before him. The thrill of the hunt.

He moved the bolt open to check that a round was in the chamber, closed it, and then fit his finger around the trigger. Against the ancient tree, the tiger stood in the ferns with the full bristling arc of her neck flexed and trembling. The muscular front legs were spread, the black jowls pulled back behind the savage teeth. The eyes were unalloyed wrath; the ears peeled back flat against her skull. With the butt into his shoulder, the shikari raised the barrel to aim.

Isha trembled in Arun's grip. Her eyes filled with hot tears. With a wrench, she broke free of him and sprinted out into the clearing. Coming in around the great tree, she slid in on her knees, spreading her arms between the hunter and the tiger and screaming, *"Stop! Stop it now!"*

A dozen men and four elephants stood in grim bewilderment. The shikari let his rifle fall, cocking his head, then turned to catch the eye of his companions. What odds had brought both of their targets so conveniently before them? No one could fathom from where the girl had come. Nor would any go close enough to move her. Kala was pressed against the vast tree like a wounded gladiator on the wall of an arena, as far she could be from any human, snarling like a demon. There was a hurricane of hate and terror contained in her eyes as she panted and tried to understand what was happening. For a long moment the shikari stood calculating. Then he stepped in, taking aim at Isha's chest.

Arun swore and made the sign of the cross. Armed only with his prayer, he stepped out into the open.

All the men and elephants turned to him. As did all the rifles. He put his hands in the air. Somehow before that moment he had not noticed their eyes. Now that he did, the dread certainty of the moment flooded over him.

A short man with areca-red teeth and an old police rifle walked toward him. "You are making this easy, friend!" he said in crass Kannada through a mouth full of paan. He raised the old rifle to Arun's gut.

"Please aṇṇa, please brother, I am at your mercy. I am just here for the girl."

The man red-smiled and fired.

Arun snapped forward like he'd been punched in the gut and then fell to his knees. His face held a look of fading confusion. He simply could not believe the pace and finality of it all. He knelt, clutching his stomach, and when his hand came away, it was bathed in blood. Arun knelt, pleading with God for a miracle as the man took a step closer, rifle at his hip. Arun held his hands up and cowered, as if he could shield himself from what was coming.

The second shot echoed and Arun fell.

Isha watched trembling, far beyond horror. She was gasping but could not breath.

The attention of the men and elephants now shifted back to the tiger, to Isha. Shikari stepped forward and leveled the rifle on Isha. Her hysterical breaths had become convulsions as she remained frozen, fixated on the spot where Arun lay.

Isha's vision began to shudder and fade. Wouldn't it be nice to have lived for so much longer? Even in the wild rush of it all, there were so many thoughts and words flowing through her: the faces of her mother and father and sister, of Ajja and Ajji, and her sunlit room. How had it come to this? How could it be? How much would it hurt?

Tears ran down her face as she looked up the black barrel of the rifle. The world had blurred. That they would—that they *could*—kill a person had not occurred to her. There was no compromise in the shikari's eyes, no sympathy or hesitation—only cold resolve. In some distant universe just a few feet before her, the man was shouting at her to get up.

With his gun pointed at her, he shouted again for her to rise, but saw clearly that she was fading into shock. He looked back at the many men watching behind him. Execution was not something to be done before a crowd. It would be better out of sight. He stepped forward to grab her.

At that moment, Kala roared and sprang forward to the limit of the rope. The tiger's claws sank into Isha's shoulder and pulled her back and down. The shikari staggered backward off his feet. Isha hit the ground hard as the tiger's jaws fit over her neck. She spun and her hands clutched fur, and her legs flailed at the heaving chest as her throat was crushed. Her eyes shut tight. The tiger's mouth was over her neck, the long canines blunt wedges against her spine. The volcanic throat was a furnace blasting into her.

But the snap did not come.

Isha's eyes opened as her mind came online with dazzling focus. Vivid white whiskers and orange fur filled her vision, the soft yellow-green of the canopy in the unfocused distance above. Her arms wrapped around the tiger's head, and as they did the roaring tapered. The tiger inexplicably softened; the immense pressure of tooth and jaw ebbed. Panting and trembling, an agonized howl rose from within Kala. Something inside the tiger was breaking, being born.

The shikari regained his feet, and the men in the clearing stared, captive to the suspense. The tiger's eyes were circles of demonic wrath, her whiskers raising as each wave of savage staccato boomed from her throat. The girl's body, frail and insignificant beneath the muscular stripes. A frightened elephant shuffled, and the shikari raised a hand in the air for the others to hold, but it was meaningless as not a man among them could move. They watched as the law of wild was demonstrated before them, the ancient constitution enacted. Like a car halfway off a cliff, the tiger was teetering between the road and the abyss, and not a man could look away.

Isha tried to struggle free, and the snarl intensified terribly. The tiger bore down on her; the teeth pressed onto her throat and her spine with supreme power. The tiger fought inwardly the urge to kill her and the urge to protect her. Then Isha's hand found Kala's ear. She rubbed the ear with her fingers and thumb the way she had when Kala was just a kitten. The jaw loosened a degree further, just enough for her to draw a desperate breath and choke-whisper: "Kala!"

The tiger softened, as though remembering some sweet past, though the snarl continued. Isha whispered urgency and love, and slowly and with great effort of spirit, the tiger's jaw loosened. Isha drew a trembling gasp. For a sorrowful moment the tiger bowed so that the side of her great skull rested on the girl's. Kala's *kajal* eyes closed; the growl became a howl, for in that moment the cub wished she were safe, wished there were some way to go back and hunt and play in the sunlit fields and streams.

Isha's legs fell from the striped, heaving ribcage to rest on the ground. For a moment everything was silent. She drew a breath, savoring the scent, the touch of her tiger, for the last time.

Then she pressed the lever with her thumb and there was a sharp metal *clack* and the belt fell from Kala's neck.

The tiger's roar erupted with unspeakable force that shuddered air and timber and bone. The volume and depth of the blast were paralyzing and forced men and elephants back like an explosion. In one bound, the tiger slashed across the shikari's stomach. The man had no time to lift his rifle. In the time it took the men to process what they saw, the tiger traveled through the air—extended, then drawing up like a spring, back legs overtaking the front paws, and then exploding out again. A mahout threw up his hands as the tiger rose up on her hind legs and with one swipe opened his neck.

Vanishing and materializing through the foliage as if by teleportation, she flashed through the jungle. By now men and elephants were screaming. One tusker reared, spilling men and gear from its back. Shots fired in all directions, always to where the tiger had been and never was, until the air was thick with blood and bullets and falling leaves. Gunshots cracked as the tiger flashed away through the forest.

Isha lay panting on her stomach as the thrashing tumult of the chase raged off into the jungle. The shikari before her was on his hands and knees, where his dry, dark exterior had birthed an aggregate of vivid moist interior. He was trying to gather slippery pink entrails from the ground.

Another man at the edge of the clearing was rolling back and forth on the ground clutching his neck. Four deep lacerations ran from his ear to his opposite shoulder. His windpipe and artery were opened, and ribbons of flesh draped from the wound. He was moving rapidly now, as if anything could stop the crimson life from flooding out of him onto the leaves. Unseen in the forest, the elephants were bellowing and stampeding, knocking down trees, the cries of agonized men echoing amid the gunfire.

At the far end of the clearing, two men descended from the trees. The right arm of one was soaked in blood; the other was shirtless and wore a great assortment of necklaces and beads. Their eyes were full of excited opportunity. She struggled to rise as they rushed in and came down on her. Isha resisted, but they struck her and pulled back her arms. A brutal hand clutched her hair and shoved her face into the moist soil. She gasped and choked as he mashed her face against the earth. She could not breath, and her nose and mouth filled with soil.

A tremendous gun blast ripped apart the air. When the first body hit the ground beside her, a brief spray of atomized brain matter was fading in the ringing air. Ramana Gowda snarled out from the jungle, haggard and mad, dangerously exerted. His formerly white shirt was stained with sweat and mud and several men's blood. A brass shell went spinning over his shoulder as his trigger hand worked the lever, the barrel smoking. The butt of the Winchester was firmly in his shoulder, and his eyes were slits of gray ferocity below his disheveled white eyebrows. He scanned left and right with corresponding grunts.

Isha ran to Arun. He was lying on his side holding his gut. Isha threw herself on him.

His hand went to her cheek. "Are you hurt?"

She pushed back and looked at his face. Was *she* hurt? She would have shouted at him, slapped him for asking such a thing at such a time. But all she could do was fall into him, sobbing.

Gowda spat and nodded toward Isha and Arun. They were alive; that was all he needed to know.

The remaining beater hurled his machete at the hunter and ran, but a second heavy blast from Gowda took him off his feet.

"Cover her eyes," Gowda said. He worked the lever and put the rifle practically to the man's head before firing.

Next he went to the shikari. The hollow man lay curled around his organs, which had spilled out of him onto the ground. Like a mother beside her child, eyes wide, mouth moving involuntarily. The hunter squatted and stared into the eyes of the living dead man as if disenchanted by his own corporeal workings, inexorably hypnotized by the elemental truth before him.

At Arun's side, Gowda fell to one knee. He placed his gun on the ground. "Where are you hit?" The hunter took Arun's hand in his own.

Arun's left hand had deflected the shot that would have hit him square in the face. The bullet had entered between the ring and middle fingers, cut through the back of the hand, cleaving it almost in two, and exiting at the wrist in an ugly mess of tissue and bone. Blood was flooding out of the wound.

"There's your bloody miracle," Gowda growled as he worked to tear cloth from Arun's robe. "Finally the blasted robes are good for something." He wound the fabric around Arun's hand and cinched it. "Where else?"

He raised Arun's robes up to search his stomach. The warm black hole near his navel was a perfect circle. Isha's vision grew dizzy at the sight of it, and she sunk to her knees. Gowda bent and turned the younger man, searching his lower back for signs of exit. There was none. As Arun moved his arms, the hole in his abdomen vomited a slow stream of thick read blood. *Blood from a black hole.*

"One in the wrist, one in the gut," Gowda said neutrally. "Take a breath" Arun drew a shuddering breath and blew out. "Did that hurt?" Arun shook his head. "Good. Your lungs aren't hit." Gowda knelt still lower and sniffed the wound. As his nostrils confirmed what he had feared, he looked up to meet the priest's eyes. "Can you smell that?"

Arun nodded subtly enough that she would not see.

"I'm sorry. I came as fast as I could. There were three of them..."

Arun shook away the apology: *I know.*

The hunter turned to Isha and held her shoulders with urgent tenderness. "Are you okay? You look okay." He wiped mud from her face.

"I'm okay."

"Let me see your back."

She turned and lifted her kurta over her shoulder, revealing four long lacerations. Kala's claws had cut to the scapula, and the meat was showing—a serious wound that she would survive.

"You're fine. Those will need stiches."

Gowda stood and winced with involuntary pain.

"Uncle, you have a knife in your back!"

"I know that but couldn't reach it. Isha, could you just..." Gowda bent so she could reach the small dagger embedded in the musculature of his back. "Quickly please." Isha reached up and slid out the blade. Gowda gave a bear's roar as the pain washed over him.

Arun laughed and then winced, and Gowda leaned down to help him up.

Isha was his support, his uninjured arm around her. His eyes firmly locked on Gowda, waiting for the plan. The hunter rose with the rifle in one hand, Arun's arm over his shoulder. He scanned the jungle.

"Let's go!" he said, and as they left the clearing, Isha looked once more to where the hollow shikari was trying to crawl, his organs dragging behind him.

When they reached the jeep, Gowda leaned Arun against the side and Isha stepped in to steady him. Arun put his arm around her, her head cupped in his hand and pressed to his chest. She was crying quietly. He rubbed her head reassuringly, and she could feel him trembling. Gowda was on his knees below them, tearing lengths of robe into strips. Isha tried not to stare at the hole in Arun's stomach, and the streams of dark blood that ran from it. Gowda worked fast.

"Hold this here." He handed Isha a length of fabric and ran a knife downward. He wrapped the length of fabric around Arun several times to dress and pressure the wound.

"What are we doing?"

"We need to wrap him around the waist, pressure the wound. Lean him forward. Isha, listen to me. We need to get him out of here fast. Really fast. Okay?"

She nodded.

"I want you to talk to him in the car as we go, make sure he doesn't get bounced around too much, okay?"

She nodded but he was working and did not see.

"Okay?"

"Yeah."

Gowda cinched the dressing, rummaged through the back of the truck, and found a western button shirt with a collar that he fit over Arun's arms and buttoned for him. "Now…"

"Uncle, hush!" Isha pointed to her ear, eyes wide. Her hands made deer ears to better hear. The sound of a motorcycle came from the distance. Gowda lifted his rifle and aimed down the road just as a motorbike appeared. Riding it was an unusually large man, who skidded to a halt just before the jeep. Isha stood beside Arun, looking up at a red-faced and frantic Chinnappa.

"Don't fucking move!" Gowda snarled.

"Please, please!" His hands went up. "You have to help me."

"*Help you*? This man has two holes in him, and the girl's got an army after her! And what are you doing riding this direction?"

"I recognized your tire tracks and followed them. My men. There are five of them. One gun. Three of Vijayan's men all have guns. Please, you have to help me."

"No deal."

Gowda lifted Arun by the armpits so that he stood leaning against the car.

"You can't do this," the ranger said, tears welling in his eyes.

"Oh, can't I?"

"They are good men and they will die if someone doesn't help them."

"This boy's hit in the stomach," Gowda said in Malayalam.

"You cannot let them die!" Chinnappa bellowed. There were tears coming down his face, his hands trembling. He wiped his forehead, looking in either direction, cursing or praying to himself, Isha couldn't tell.

"This never would have happened if you all hadn't come!" Chinnappa screamed.

"He's right," Arun said, eyes closed, breathing. "You have to go."

"No, he's not right and I don't have to go. We need to get you back *now*."

Arun held up a hand. "Listen, I can drive. I can drive. You go. Like you said, I have some time. Blow their fucking heads off, save the men, and catch us up on the bike. I'll be okay."

"Please, Ramana," Chinnappa hissed. "Please, by God, I beg you."

Arun did not wait for more dialogue, but opened the driver's door and slumped in. Isha climbed in through the back window and forward to the pillion seat. Gowda shut the door and held a finger up through the window.

"I don't like this," said Gowda.

"I'm asking you to go."

"Drive like hell on wheels, you hear me?"

"Okay. Come fast."

"I will."

Arun tested the pedal with his foot. Gowda leaned in through the window to clutch the boy's head. Forehead to forehead, he held him there in a fierce embrace.

"You good?"

Arun nodded.

"You good?"

Arun nodded harder.

The two men held one another in a moment of candid, ferocious intensity, trading growls to rally above the fear. "You are fine. Don't worry. Gut shots take time. I'll be right behind you." He kissed the boy's head roughly and released him.

"Promise you'll be safe," Isha called out as Gowda climbed on the bike and blazed off with the ranger.

Arun keyed the ignition but had not yet shifted into gear. The car started and died. Arun's split left hand went for the clutch, sending waves of pain over him. Isha watched as he winced and then braced to try again. But he could not grasp the shift. The cloth bandage was leaking red rapidly. He tried to grip the gear, but the bandage and the pain prevented it.

"Shit. I can't hold it!" He pushed harder on the shift and blood came in a stream out of the bandage.

"Let me do it. I can do it."

Isha took the knob, slick with his blood, and commanded him to push the clutch. She slid the shift left and then forward into first. "Okay then, let's go!"

They sped off as shouting rose behind them and another blast of Gowda's gun sounded. Isha moved the gearshift to second and then to third and to fourth. As they drove through the jungle, Arun called out gears above the motor-din. At times he would decelerate before puddles or holes, and Isha scrambled to first or second, her eyes wide with concentration.

The trees and dark iron clouds, the long road—it all seemed like a horrible nightmare. Kala was gone, the jungle burned, the dream ended. The seat was awash with the dark red blood from the black-hole wound in Arun's stomach, black like the skin had been broken, reality torn, and the cold blackness behind it all was showing through.

Arun glanced at Isha working, and her silence worried him.

"Good! Very good! Down to second!" Isha moved the gear-shift to fourth and the engine shrieked.

"Sorry!"

"First gear! Listen, Kala is a tiger. She has probably run as far as she can away from the noise and men. Don't be worried. *Third!*"

Blood dripped steadily off his hand.

"You're shot," Isha said quietly, unable to keep her eyes on the road.

"It is nothing if thou art safe." Arun winced, working the wheel.

Isha smiled tears, which she wiped away quickly. Then in a quiet voice, "Are you going to die?"

"No, I'm not going to die," he lied. The seat was saturated red. "No, we are going to drive out of here and to the hospital. And a year from now, we'll drive this road and laugh as we track Kala and her cubs. How does that sound?"

Isha nodded dazedly. Her eyes stayed on the road.

The road was nearly un-drivable, and the car jolted and shook in and out of muddy trenches and over fallen tree branches. In places the air was so choked by smoke that the sun eclipsed, and they were forced down to second or even first gear. The jungle was burning. Isha tried not to watch the blood pool that grew between Arun's legs and covered the floor. It was coagulating into sickening gelatin, ropes of crimson that trembled and broke.

"Good," Arun told her as she began shifting without instruction. The road turned along the top of a sharp promontory that fell to the left. The river ran below, vivid turquoise amidst the muted green and smoke. So much of the forest was burning. On one of the beaches they could see the forty-strong herd pouring out of the forest and onto the gravel beach. At the front of the pack was Ramachandran, leading them to safety of the river. Behind him was

Hathi, holding his tail. Arun slowed the car just for a moment to
see. The scorched herd plunged into the blue water, quenching their
long trunks and soothing their singed ears.

The road turned and they lost view of the herd below.

Arun was silent now, his lips pale. *Keep pressing the pedal.
You don't have long. Shake it off, just a little longer. No, don't look
down.* But he did. *There is so much blood. Who would have known
you had so much blood in you. Stop looking. It's scaring the shit
out of you. Don't pass out. Just keep driving. All that matters is
that you keep it going just a little longer. Nalkere is less than an
hour away. Just keep going till you run out of blood.*

Isha's voice came from far away. "How are you feeling?"

"I'm fucking cold," he said and tried to laugh.

"You're doing good and we're almost there," she said reassuringly. But he wasn't.

The gearshift and dashboard were stained black and red. The
window was streaked pink. Isha herself was streaked and soaked in
blood, some of hers, some his, some of tiger. She stole glances at
him as she worked the shift. As it flowed out of him, the interior of
the car warmed with red as his lips became increasingly blue. An
hourglass of blood with no bottom. She wished the road would end,
but every turn revealed more jungle. They drove for twenty
minutes as fast as the road would allow. On a straight stretch, she
sat up and looked out the back window.

"What if they come?"

"Then nothing. Go to three."

She worked the shift. "What do we do if they do come?"

"They wont. Back to four," Arun said, his eyes were distant.
They drove in silence.

"There!" Arun said without pointing. The forest gate was in
view and Gowda was waiting there on the bike. The bike was
idling and one leg was down on the ground for support. As they
drew near, he waved for them to keep driving and accelerated. Together the Pajero and the bike sped out of the forest boundary and
onto the road that ran along the forest until the bridge. Gowda
came up beside them.

"There's no time to stop. Almost there!" Gowda shouted.

Arun nodded. His lips were blue, his eyes sunken.

"Is Chinnappa safe?" Isha shouted over Arun and out the window.

Gowda nodded and made a triumphant shooting motion with one hand, then blazed ahead of them. In the distance was the concrete bridge where the road turned over the river.

"Fifth!" Arun wheezed, and as she did, he brought them to a speed that Isha found terrifying. They crossed the bridge and then tilted upward with the road. Arun swore as Gowda's bike struggled up the cliff-like portion they had so violently descended on the drive in.

"Down to first!" The car came skidding to a halt. With great effort Arun tried the incline but was pulled back. With his wrist, he shifted to four-wheel drive for maximum power and tried again, but the wheels spun on the dry earth. Up ahead Gowda put down a leg and turned to watch them as they struggled. The jeep wasn't climbing.

Gowda froze, staring west toward the jungle gate. Isha turned to see a truck loaded with half a dozen beaters. They were piled on the roof and hanging out of windows. Their hands held bars and blades and guns. Their vehicle was coming fast along the forest line toward the bridge with a plume of dust billowing behind its rocket speed. Her eyes dilated as she searched for some escape.

Arun swore bitterly at the obstacle before him and then tried again. He had not yet seen. Gowda dropped the bike and ran shouting toward them through the field, arms in the air. Now Arun checked the rearview mirror and when he saw, swore bitterly. In moments the death squad would be at the bridge. Sweat was dripping off Arun's nose as he worked frantically, willing the jeep up the sharp incline one last time.

Even with the pedal down, the jeep could not climb. As they came to a dusty halt, Ramana Gowda fell against the hood of the car. The ferocious confidence that had been his eyes in the forest was replaced by undisguised panic.

"Get out! You can't climb it! I'm out of ammo!"

For a bewildered moment, the two men held a look of understanding through the fractured windshield. There was no debating the physical truth of it. Vijayan's hired killers would cross the bridge and reach them in moments. There was nowhere to run or hide, nothing to hold them off with. It was certain. Their thoughts ran tandem: there was only one thing that could be done.

"Send it down alone," Gowda growled.

"It needs to be steered and timed if it's to work. *I can't lose another.*"

"Then I should go. I'm an old man."

"I can't ride like this, just get her out of here!" Arun snarled, his face pale with oncoming shock.

Isha's heart was pounding like it would break her ribs, but there was no time for crying. Gowda's eyes moved over the blood-soaked interior of the car, and when Arun, speaking Malayalam, gestured to his stomach, the hunter leaned in and sniffed. The smell of shit made him grimace. He turned to look down the road, in the direction of town, trying to think of some alternative. But there was none. The hunter drew a breath and nodded solemnly, and then rallied himself. *Don't leave him with despair.*

Gowda smiled in such a way that the boy would know everything, the full extent of it and the depthless truth of it. For a moment he smiled it all into him, reached in and grabbed him and kissed him roughly on the forehead. The hunter turned and rushed around the back of the jeep.

"Isha, neutral," Arun said quietly.

"What?"

He turned to her with a wounded smile, and for a confused moment she almost smiled too. Before anything else could be said, Gowda's hand came in and clutched her by the shoulder, lifting her through the window. She grasped and kicked and fought.

"No! No! Stop it!" Isha railed against the hunter's grasp. "Stop it! *Stop it!*" Gowda squeezed violently, tight enough to hurt, so her hands came undone. He pulled her out of the window over his shoulder, and ran. As they went, in jolting terror tear-vision, Isha saw Arun wincing to work the shift.

Inside the cabin of the jeep, he grimaced and swore and made the sign of the cross. With his foot on the clutch, he threw his wounded arm over the pillion seat so that he could watch over his shoulder and released the break. The jeep accelerated backward as momentum carried the carriage to a dangerous speed. Arun's eyes narrowed in focus so that tears gathered.

The beaters skidded around the turn onto the far side of the bridge. Arun swore in pain as he rotated the wheel and swung the jeep around and pushed the pedal to the floor to accelerate forward—on course to hit the mouth of the bridge just as the beaters exited. He knew it, they knew it, and neither slowed. The two cars spit plumes of dust as they tore toward the end of the bridge. At seventy kilometers per hour, one of the beaters, then another, leapt from the side of the speeding vehicle to roll to their deaths.

At the top of the hill Gowda kicked his bike to life, clutching Isha captive to his chest so that her legs wrapped about his hips. The front wheel of the bike leapt off the ground as they sped in the direction of Nalkere.

Arun's jeep rushed toward the bridge at dizzying speed. For Arun, the world slowed. He would reach the mouth of the bridge just as the beater's jeep finished the span. In that final moment of hurtling sacrificial action, he felt wondrously alone with God.

At the mouth of the bridge, the two jeeps collided with a fantastic force. Earth and men and metal and glass filled the air as the two trucks twisted into each other and were lifted up and over and apart.

Over the hill and rapidly away, Gowda had the bike's throttle open full. He squinted his eyes against the rushing wind but could not stop the tears from streaking back toward his ears.

29

NIGHT

In the jungle dark, Hathi stood by where Ramachandran lay dying. The other elephants took turns touching him with their trunks. They lay flowers and palm fronds over him. Hathi held his tail, weeping. From Ramachandran's mouth, a slow river of blood ran onto the leaves, urged on by the deep thump of his limping heartbeat. Soon his body would be still and rejoin the jungle.

He lay in the dark among the old herd, drawing great labored breaths, curling trunks with various old friends and new young bulls that he would never have the chance to abuse. The old matriarch of the herd, Hathi's mother, came and tasseled his bullet-holed ears. She thanked him, in her way, for they all would have burned had he not come and led them to safety through the river. He was dying. She knew that too. The ants were already coming in quiet lines, ferrying away the first parts of him to rejoin the jungle.

The elephants would be busy. It wasn't the first time the jungle had burned. It would not be the first time it regrew. In the jungle dark, the host of elephants was silent beside the old tusker.

Deer came in timidly from the grass and slipped into the stream near where the elephants stood. The elephants permitted them to pass, for no creature could survive the inferno of the forest. Once the deer were all in, they huddled tight and watched everything. Birds had come to roost on the antlers of some of the deer. On one stag's antlers, a young python was inconspicuously curled. They all waited as the forest continued to smolder and glow. Then the bison came down to join the elephants and the deer in the river. Later in the night, a family of wild boar came. Then another. Monkeys came respectfully and with averted eyes onto the broad bison backs. Two scorched and smoking sloth bears shuffled clumsily in as well. The fire had made a truce in the jungle.

The tiger Kala was limping. She walked through the darkness where the embers glowed beneath her paws. The jungle burned and snapped and crackled around her as she went. In places the sixty-foot-tall bamboo clusters had become pillars of swirling flame that reached far above the canopy. Here they raged upward, hurling fire against the heavy sky. The flame was so hot that she winced from it even at fifty feet away. She watched these with the supreme disdain she watched all things. The air was hot. She wished for water.

In the black of the forest, the flame's glow reflected on her orange coat, flickering green in her savage eyes, so that the tiger seemed herself to burn through the night. When she reached the stream, she paused. The great heads of the elephants swung toward her. The bison watched her with large sorrowful eyes. On their backs, monkeys clung to one another or to bison horns; babies peered from the armpits of their mothers. Various others—birds, bears, and red-eyed crocodiles on the fringes—watched as the tiger stood panting.

The deer were all clustered together shaking, but the tiger had not come to kill. She was scorched and bloody, nearly black, as she came into the water with the others. Dropping to her stomach she lowered her head, eyes glowing above the water. Not an animal moved as she dipped her chin down and drank with her eyes closed as if in prayer. Long drawing gulps. Then without standing, she too slipped into the water. Blood of her own and the blood of men bled out into the black water. Not a creature moved. Everyone stayed the night in the cool current as the fires raged on. The reflection burned in a thousand eyes through the night like votive candles in the darkness.

Isha woke without any inkling of where she was. Instinctually she knew it was the very depths of night. Everything was silent. There was a soft light coming from table in the corner where Ramana Gowda was sleeping in a chair, hands folded over his stomach, chin on his chest. In the bed was a figure wrapped in tubes and bandages soaked with blood. The soft beep of machinery told her that they were in some kind of hospital. She went in barefoot silence to the bed. Arun's right hand was one of the few parts of him un-bandaged. She took it.

"We both owe our lives to this man," Gowda gravel-whispered, peering out from half-opened eyes. "He's lost a lot of blood."

"But how...?"

"You faded out on the bike before we got to town. I left you and took an ambulance back to the bridge. There was already a whole pile of cops and medical folks around after the parade went bad."

"What about the other car?"

"Most of them died."

"And the others?"

"I'm going to need a real priest soon. I have a lot to confess."

Isha was still for some time. Then, "What did he mean, 'I can't lose another'?"

"Thimma is dead," Gowda said. "He couldn't bear..."

The hunter never finished, for emotion caught in his throat. Isha felt dizzy as she wept. For a long time they were silent. Her left hand explored the bandage on her right shoulder blade. The wounds had been stitched as if by magic. She would bear the scars, the mark of the tiger, the rest of her life.

Gradually she calmed. Everything felt surreal in the dark room, as though it were an isolated world floating in the blackness of space. Sleep was taking her again, and she wished that she could find something to eat. Her stomach felt hollow, her lungs burned.

"I think it would be good if we stay with him, Isha. Spend time with him. Tell him what you need to."

"Can he hear us?"

"That's not what I mean." Ramana Gowda rubbed his eyes and down over his face.

Isha looked over Arun's body. Tears welled in her eyes. "If I hadn't run out there, he never would have been shot. It's all my fault."

"No. It's not. And I'll tell you why. If we had arrived and those men had executed that tiger, we would have been next. There's no question. It was only time before they all filled that clearing and found you hiding there. He distracted them just long enough to let what happened happen. If it had gone any differently, we'd all be dead for certain. But it didn't happen that way. And Kala! Those fuckers were so focused on her that it all fell apart."

Isha touched Arun's cold hand.

"But at the bridge…"

Gowda spoke gently. "At the bridge he saved us a second time."

For nearly an hour they sat quiet.

At length Isha dropped off to sleep and then woke. Gowda was snoring in the chair.

"Uncle?"

"Erm, yes?" he said, waking.

"Is there a loo here?"

"There is, just down the hall," Gowda said. He shifted on the spot in his back where the knife wound was becoming hard and painful.

"Uncle?"

"Hm?"

"Will you walk me?"

Gowda cracked an eye. "The girl who was halfway down the throat of a tiger is scared of a hallway?"

"I keep seeing that man… the shikari… and what came out of him."

"Ah, that. Yes, I think I'll also need someone to walk me to the loo for a time."

They held hands down the hallway in the dark stillness of the night.

30

THE END

In the morning they took leave of Arun. Gowda drove Isha out of Nalkere and through the jungle to the village where the people had reclaimed what they had deserted the previous day. The sky was white in a way that made you squint. Isha wished for Arun's sunglasses. But Arun was in bed with blue lips, barely breathing.

Isha was still cold. She hadn't been able to shake the cold and walked through the village beside Gowda with a blanket over her shoulders. By now the news had spread far and wide, and the villagers, as they finished the funeral pyres and cleaned their nearly ruined homes, turned to pause and gaze at her like she was a spirit.

Gowda spoke to a man who told him that earlier in the morning, the mahouts had brought Thimma's body and laid it on the pyre. He said that Hathi had come out of the jungle up to the pyre where Thimma's body lay. Everyone had run as the elephant charged in out of the jungle and grabbed Thimma's wrist. He pulled his body out of the pyre wailing the most heartbreaking sound anyone had heard. The men had come with rocks and fire then to chase Hathi back into the jungle. He ran off, they said, crying and with his ears flapping. He was "full wild now, full fury and wild."

Isha stood beside Gowda and said nothing. Her eyes were slanted and puffy, her scowl set in against the unjust white sky. The villagers milled about finishing the many pyres. Men and women with loads of timber on their heads came from the jungle and dumped their loads, then others would build up the piles. The bodies of Thimma, Sudha, and the dozen others who had died were wrapped in cloth and vines and leaves and flowers. They would

sleep in the embrace of the forest before flying up above the leaves
and out over the jungle to rejoin the rivers.

Isha sat mutely beside Ramana Gowda as the flames took to
the pyres and the snapping and smoke came. A shirtless monk
waved flame before a black stone idol, chanting and weeping at
once. Killahuntha and the hard mahouts stood in a line; behind
them the elephants were sullen and still as cold mountains. Women
and men sang as the flames grew, and many people wailed and
cried and Isha wished that she could cry. Beside her Ramana Gowda held his eyes with thumb and finger.

Chinnappa the ranger and several of his men in torn forest uniforms had not left the village since the fighting. They were
unkempt and dazed from the violence. They sat amongst the tribals,
or helped carry wood for the pyres. It was the bond of those who
had run for their lives and bled together. They had lost loved ones.
And now they were all united in the ceremony of grief.

Chinnappa came up behind Ramana Gowda, his decades-old
enemy. Both men were silent, and in their silence was truce.
Throughout the day, forest guards would come to Gowda and touch
his feet. What he had done with his rifle was a story that Isha
would hear for years to come. Good men would see their families
again only because of his intervention.

When the fires had consumed the bodies that lay on the pyres,
Chinnappa was on his radio, the one he wore around his waist. Isha
watched him hold it for a long time to his ear. Then move it to his
mouth to give a monosyllabic order. Then he replaced it at his
waist and came toward her. As he did so, he nodded respectfully to
Ramana Gowda. He asked permission to speak to her. Gowda nodded, and the ranger spoke.

"Would you both take a ride with me?"

Isha was staring at nothing at all.

Ramana Gowda scowled.

"It's about the tiger," Chinnappa said.

They drove for an hour. The ranger's radio barked and crackled.
Men reported things in Malayalam. In Kannada. In Kuruba dialect.
His eyes moved over the forest. Isha sat dead faced and mute.

When they came to a turn, there was a guard waiting for them. Chinappa slowed the jeep just long enough for the man to jump on, then accelerated. They parked at the edge of a small clearing where a stream ran through an open field below. As Isha climbed down from the cab, there were several Forest Department men in the distance standing around something beneath a blanket.

Ramana Gowda held her hand.

Chinnappa knelt. "Do you know how a tranquilizer dart works, Isha?" They both looked ahead and not at each other. Isha said nothing. "It works like this. Essentially it is a syringe, a needle, like at a doctor's office. This is a ballistic syringe loaded with an immobilizing drug. We shoot it out of a gun with compressed gas and it is stabilized by a special puffy tailpiece that works like a badminton shuttlecock. In order to knock down an animal safely, you need expert veterinarians to correctly guess the weight of the animal—otherwise the dose might not be powerful enough, and the animal could run away. Or if the dose is too much, it could die. Once you are finished working, the vet administers an antidote that reverses the immobilizing drug and wakes the creature back up. But that is not all…"

"What are they doing?" Isha said, not taking her eyes away from the men below.

"Your Kala was found with serious injuries, Isha."

Isha understood now. The men were standing around where Kala lay. A camouflaged blanket had been spread over the tiger. A clear plastic tube ran down from an intravenous bag that one guard was holding to under the blanket where Kala lay sleeping. The ranger looked at her from the corner of his eyes.

"Isha, you must understand that this tiger has killed men. She now may even have a taste for men now. Which makes her a problem tiger."

Isha's eyes were stones as the wind whipped black hair about her face.

"You have a decision to make. A decision only you can make. This tiger is a killer, which means she can no longer live in the wild. There are only two options. One of those options is that we send her to a zoo where she can live out her days. The other option is…we euthanize her here and now."

The ranger looked up to the hunter. Ramana Gowda shifted and closed his eyes. Isha didn't move.

"I won't let her rot in a zoo."

Chinnappa nodded solemnly.

Isha tried to feel something, or rather wondered if she ever would again. All she could feel was the cold wind. The men were standing now, drawing away from the place they had been working.

"What are they doing?" she asked in a whisper.

"They are preparing to administer the euthanizing agent."

Isha was a statue as tears gathered in her eyes.

The ranger's phone rang and he opened it, holding out a finger to excuse himself. He grunted, grunted again, and thanked whomever it was. Then he turned to Gowda, sighing heavily, and said something in Malayalam.

Ramana Gowda's hand went to his eyes and sobs shook him. He stepped away, breathing heavily, trying to remain composed. She turned now, as Gowda sank down holding his face as tears fell from under his hand. Chinnappa was looking guiltily at her, waiting for her to understand, and when she did, her face went wide as if she had been plunged into freezing water. Her breath came shuddering, and she sat down and wept.

Gowda would later say the words that Fitzgerald had written, which were one of Arun's favorite quotes: "It's so much darker when a light goes out than it would have been if it had never shown." But the words were useless to Isha. What she knew was that she had never met a single person whose view of the world was so close to her own. Nor had she met anyone she had laughed with and learned from in such a way.

Guilt rushed over her and was quickly followed by a frigid emptiness. It was her fault that he was not alive, she was certain of it. A windy century seemed to pass on the sad silent hill. When, at length, she lifted her head, her eyes were red and lifeless, her hair wild. Ramana Gowda was on one knee watching as the men worked below. He came up beside her and put a thick hand on her shoulder. She hugged his barrel chest and they cried for a time together, silent in the wind.

The ranger watched them miserably. He had a sick feeling in his stomach and a war inside his mind. Looking at the girl and the old hunter, he shook his head in acceptance some internal argument. With two fingers in his mouth, he whistled to the men below and they looked up to him. He stood and held up his left hand. One man nodded, and then knelt down to continue working. Their posture was confused, and then crackling came in from the radio. Chinnappa lifted the set and held it close to his ear. Below a forest guard held the other set, speaking into it. Chinnappa walked some paces away so that he would not be heard. He gave an order and then when they asked, he repeated the order.

Men knelt where the tiger lay, and even from a distance, Isha could see the syringe. Everything was ending. She watched as it went out of view and could see the concentration of the veterinarian as he depressed the plunger into Kala's veins. Isha closed her eyes and wished she could leave this place, the world, and sleep for months.

The ranger came and took a knee beside them. He placed the radio set on the ground and watched as the men moved about the tiger's body.

"Isha, I want you to listen to me very carefully. I have been protecting this forest for a very long time—decades before you were alive. I have walked with the wild elephant herd, I have hunted man-eating tigers. I have hunted the men who hunt tigers. There are many people who would say I have done things that no one else could. And to be honest, they are right. But the reason I tell you this is to say I know the lonely path you walk. I know some of the secrets that you think only you have learned. I too have a connection to these creatures."

Isha was hardly listening.

"You are courageous, to do what you did. And I am so terribly sorry..." He looked at her now, shivering and miserable. "You said something that day in my office, when you came with Arun, God rest his soul. It was about how you belong here, and how you know things no one does, and how one day you would learn the language of this place so well that I myself would be in awe."

The men below were packing gear now, gathering the blanket to reveal a crumpled collection of stripes in the grass. Kala's body was still. But the men were moving quickly away. As they reached the jeeps, closing car doors echoed in the clearing. Then it was still.

Chinnappa's fingers were rolling a piece of grass. "Isha, what I am trying to say is that after what you have been through for this place, for these creatures... It has never been before, and I believe it will never be again. You are one of them."

She looked at him now. The slightest sad smile moved over his face, like the hint of sun behind clouds. He leaned in closer and pointed to the clearing.

"Watch."

For a long time, she saw nothing. Then Kala's paw moved. The tiger's body curled and her head rose. She looked drunkenly around the clearing and rolled upright onto her stomach. Her whiskers were a mess. Isha's mouth opened ever so slightly. Her eyes grew with wonder. She looked to the ranger.

"You made the right choice," he said, his eyes never wavering from the tiger in the distance. "Not the easy choice, but the right one. That tiger belongs nowhere but the wild. It would be better for her to die than to live in a concrete cage. That is the truth. I was not joking or testing you with what I said. My responsibility only does allow those two options. But after hearing," he motioned to his phone, "there is only so much a person can take in one day. Isn't it?"

He shook his head. "If that tiger kills anyone it will be my ass. I'll be sacked for sure. But then, there is no guarantee. After what you have gone through, after what...*he* paid for this, it is worth it to give the time and see. We will monitor her, study her movements. And, when you have time, in the months to come—years to come—I'd like you to be a part of that effort."

"But?" She was reeling to keep up.

"I had them administer the antidote, not the killing solution. She is waking."

Below, Kala had risen on shaky legs. She bristled and shook off the haze and turned now to see them there above on the hill, watching her. With lips peeled back, she snarled at them. There was no recognition or love in her eyes any longer, only hatred. She moved off through the grass and out into the leaves and was gone.

EPILOGUE

THREE YEARS LATER

The mist is a blue ghost river through the silhouettes of the forest. Broad paws are soundless as she moves over the wet stones, and then along a trail. Elephants stand like dark mountains in the muted gloom, waiting for the warmth and the sun. Their trunks hang idle, ears pressed to their heads for warmth. The young drink from their mothers. She watches with wide, alert eyes, and moves on. At the edge of a clearing the deer turn their ears towards her. Countless dew-laden spider webs are laced amongst the still grass, and below, the fawns are curled tight in cold slumber. Not a stag or doe moves. They simply watch at attention. The treaty of the jungle is by now firm: a tiger seen poses no threat. She passes in silence.

It is the start of the monsoon, and the sound of the hunter's heavy jeep grumbles through the distance. With the rains the girl has come, just as she has each year. She is taller now. Her hair is longer. She is fully grown. The tiger watches unseen as she climbs out of the jeep. The girl smiles and hugs the crowding villagers, lifts the new children.

At midday the girl walks to the boundary of the village and steps out of her chappals, entering barefoot into the temple of the forest. She travels far and spends long hours up in trees watching the deer graze and the elephants wallow in the warm mud. She smells of city and stress, but these things lift from her like the morning mist.

The day passes without the sun breaking the heavy clouds. As evening comes the tiger follows from a distance as the girl walks silently through the vaulted spaces of the jungle. Though she cannot see the tiger, the hairs on her arm know it is close. She pauses often, looking behind her and peering into the far-off spaces. As darkness comes, she runs the trail with swift steps, hopping roots and dodging vines. When she finds the soft paw impressions she crouches. Her fingers trace the shapes in a knowing, longing way. When she stands her breaths are deep, her eyes wide. For here still burns the light of life, between the stripes and shadows.

A Note from the Author

Many novels and movies take great care to state that any resemblance the story or characters have to people living or dead is purely coincidental. I cannot make such a claim. The story of *The Girl and the Tiger* is less my own creation and more a collection of moments, truths, and legends I found over the years in the Indian jungle. It is a necklace of a book, a series of seeds and teeth, stones and bones, gathered like beads from the forest floor; I only added the string. It is the result of following elephants, searching for tigers, sitting late into the night around campfires, and becoming acquainted with the tribes of the forest, both human and animal.

I have spent most of my adult life in some of the last truly wild places on the planet. The Amazon rainforest, Kalimantan Borneo. I first traveled to India in 2008 on a study program through Ramapo College, where I was finishing a degree in environmental science. Originally, as a lover of wilderness and solitude, I was hesitant to go to a country with over a *billion* people. But a professor swayed me with two words: tigers and elephants. I met my wife, Gowri Varanashi, on that study trip—in fact, we met when we were trying to rescue the same snake under a banyan tree. Years later, we were married beneath that same tree, and Gowri has been my business and conservation partner for our company, Tamandua Expeditions.

India has changed my life. I found a new family, a new and vibrant country, and I began searching fruitlessly for a moment I had dreamed of since I was a child: to be walking in a forest and see a wild tiger. It was a far more difficult task than I knew.

That India still has as many Bengal tigers and Asian elephants as they do is testament to the devoted and tenacious work of India's citizens, conservationists, Forest Department workers, and scientists who refuse to see the country's wild places be cut down and paved over. The vastness and persistence of the mining projects, roads, dams, and various other projects is dizzying. It is helpful to imagine a flood that has risen to cover the landscape, making islands out of the forests. Concentrated on these islands of forest are the tigers and elephants, deer, birds, snakes, and thousands of other forest folk. These islands are also the refuge of India's tribal cultures.

Few groups on earth have drawn a shorter stick than the tribal people of India. Caught between the march of industrial "progress" and the public pushback to protect wild nature, the tribal communities have often found themselves with no allies. The road and dam projects want them pushed out of resource-rich forests. Today, tribal people live a tenuous life in which they are persecuted, threatened, and at constant risk of forced relocation that is as brutal a process as I've ever seen. Long before this book began forming, I spent time with Adivasi communities who had been displaced from their forest homes and were suffering greatly. I also spent time with communities that still lived within the boundaries of the jungle.

While exploring near a tribal community inside Nagarhole National Park in south India, I was in the care of a man from a tribal community named Thimma. It was he who first took my wife and me tracking tigers, running from elephants, and exploring streams so beautiful they defy description. It was his deep knowledge of the forest and its animals, his strong condemnation of the treatment of tribal people, that inspired the character of Thimma. He says that the Forest Department should hire tribals to protect their own forest. And it was in his village that I saw the night watchmen in machans, the deer that entered the village of small cow-dung-and-mud huts, and the lives of the beautiful tribal community Thimma is a part of.

Just as in *The Girl and the Tiger*, the relationship between tribal people and the Forest Department is infinitely complex. The tribals accuse the Forest Department of logging, stealing honey, timber, and hunting. The Forest Department accuse the tribal people of poaching deer (the primary food source of tigers and the key to their survival), setting fire to the jungle, and bringing in plastic and livestock to ecologically sensitive areas. Neither side is wrong every time, and neither side is perfect.

My time with real life Thimma has been countered by time with the committed and courageous men of the Indian Forest Department who risk their lives to protect the incredible natural wealth of India's wild. Real life Chinnappa is very tall, very harsh, and I once saw him shout at a gaggle of tourists, lecturing them mercilessly for casting a piece of trash on the forest floor. He roared on to explain how the water they drink comes from the very jungle they had come to see. He told them that the ground they stood on was sacred. His influence inspires as much fear as it does respect. Forest Department rangers, scientists, tribals—they all know his allegiance to the earth. He is one of the few people who can approach a wild herd of elephants and speak to them.

Ramachandran really is the name of a giant old tusker that is kept in a temple in Kerala. He really does stand eleven feet tall and really has killed numerous people, other elephants, and even a few cows. His incarceration, his rage, and the abuse inflicted on such a magnificent creature were things that kept me up at night. In the story, his violent outburst on the street, when he finally decides to run for the forest, is only a slightly embellished version of an actual event. A friend showed me the video of a bull elephant that had had enough and began lifting and throwing motorcycles and rickshaws all over the street. He lifted automobiles on his tusks the way you or I would lift a wooden chair. It is footage I have watched hundreds of times. The strength of the elephant is awe-inspiring. The rage behind the power is heartrending.

Kala is the name given to a female tiger that was found by villagers inside of an irrigation canal duct in 2011 in Nagpur. While trapped and frantic to escape, she injured herself badly enough that she was rescued by the Forest Department. They had to give her forty-five days in an enclosure to heal. Once healthy, she was fitted with a radio collar and freed.

In the coming months, she showed us a side to modern tigers that had never been seen before. She would spend weeks on the move, occupying a range between 720 and 920 square kilometers. She was surviving off whatever she could scavenge in a tamed landscape. During the day she would pass time in the shade of bushes, sometimes just at the edges of farm fields where farmers were laboring. She was in between the lives of millions of people. The region she traveled contained over 409 people per square kilometer. People working, playing, living beside a tiger, and no one knew.

Her incredible story made her globally famous and an ambassador for her species. She proved that a tiger, even without a home or food, wants nothing more than to be left alone, unseen by human eyes, to raise her family, hunt, and be happy in the way tigers ought to be.

I chose the name Hathi as homage to Rudyard Kipling's king of the elephants in *The Jungle Book*. In real life, a blind elephant lives with a very young boy at the jungle frontier in south India. I met them both in 2016 and was completely floored by how such a tiny boy could be so intimate and vital to such a mountainous creature. The elephant needed the boy to help him navigate even the simplest of terrain. Without the boy, the elephant would surely die within weeks. And the boy, with no other family, depended wholly on the elephant as his source of wealth in the world. We spent time together, and I observed them working, washing, and playing together. It was one of the most incredible things I have ever seen. In the case of the real-life elephant-boy duo, the elephant was blinded by another male elephant in the wild and was taken in afterwards.

There are other characters and events that are true. For instance, in a great forest fire, the animals will all come to the rivers. And a tiger really can kill an animal by the brute force of a swipe alone. I've seen what villagers do to bears caught out in daylight. In the months I've spent in the jungle in India, I have been charged by violent bull elephants and nearly killed. I have seen leopards in the night. And after seven years of searching, I have even stood in the wild before a full-grown wild female tiger.

But of all the tidbits of truth and great stories, the one who truly set off the spark that became this book is undeniably Isha.

For most of my twenties, I worked as a researcher, guide, and naturalist in the Peruvian Amazon. When an Indian family came for a weeklong tour of the Amazon in 2012, I was unaware of the effect it would have on me. By that time, although I have always been a conservationist at heart, I was perhaps a little calloused and used to the harsh realities of the Amazonian backcountry. Every year the forest is cut back. Every year the nomadic tribes and loggers exchange arrows and buckshot over timber. Living with Amazonian-Indian communities, I see all manner of animal suffering; many a campfire dinner has cooked monkeys. And so I was used to a certain level of brutality between species.

All that changed when Isha set foot in the forest to spend a week at my field station. Isha and I rescued butterflies out of the kitchen, followed lizards into their holes, and even caught a boa constrictor. She had a sense of justice and determination that was startling. She had the effect of turning those around her into more compassionate people. I found myself no longer killing mosquitos (partly to avoid her lectures). I became a vegetarian. She was wild spirited and when told she couldn't swim across the river, she did. When told she couldn't jump out of a thirty-foot tree into piranha-infested water, she did.

On the last day of the trip, we ran into poachers who had caught an ancient yellow-footed tortoise. They had him tied up and headed for the pot. I tried to tell her that there was nothing we could do. That didn't fly with Isha. She insisted that we save the tortoise, and in the end, I bargained with the poachers. The following day, with Isha on the back of my motorcycle, we took it somewhere safe and set it free.

There I was, a seasoned explorer, rescuing tortoises and butterflies and treating the forest in a whole different way. The effect lasted long after Isha and her family had left the jungle. In the years to come, I was certain that this child's great compassion for other creatures needed some lasting memorial. It was a compassion that needed to be told. And I was naturally curious to see where such a unique spirit would take her in life. We kept in touch after her initial visit to the jungle, and every few months Isha would update me on the wild things in her life: a barbet they were rehabilitating, the black leopard she had found tracks from at school and was hoping to see.

One morning, just a few years after we first met, I was about to embark on a six-week expedition in the Amazon. Perhaps it was nerves, but I woke at four that morning, long before it was light. I checked my email to find a message from Isha, then thirteen.

It read: *I am sending you this email to ask you about a tigress and cub but first I must tell you the story...*

She said that in her hometown on a coffee estate, a fallen tree had revealed a den with two tiger cubs inside. The mother tiger was missing. She had written to me as her jungle guide, asking how to protect them, what tiger cubs eat (should she have to care for them), and what she should do.

Please reply soon because I need the answers to these questions so that the cubs can be helped.

If anyone else had sent that message, I might have brushed it off. And if I hadn't had so many people and so much funding on the line, I would have gotten on a flight that very day and made for

India. It will endure as a regret that I didn't. But what stayed with me was Isha's startling devotion and willingness to act, and what came after.

And so this book is a necklace of legends, the result of years spent trading stories like seeds to better understand what I have seen. As the human ocean rises, steadily making islands out of natural spaces and threatening to drown some of our most vital species, it is my own plea for remembering. At a time when half of the people on earth live in cities, the numinous complexity of ocean and forest has become distant behind glowing screens. Our familial dependence on other species is little more than a legend. But there are corners of the world where the rivers run clean and the trees are kings. Where life is everywhere.

GLOSSARY

aazaan—Islamic prayer call
achha—*Hindi.* good
akka—older sister
anna—older brother
bai saab—Sir
beedi—cheap leaf-rolled cigarette
butha—spirit or lesser god
chakli —savory treat
chappals—flip flops
chutiya—fucker
crore—100 lakhs
devare (Oh devare)—"Oh god!"
devathe—female god
Ganesha—elephant Hindu deity
ganji—the flesh of a tender coconut
goonda—thug, gangster
haadi—hamlet within a village area
halli—village
Hanuman—monkey deity
hegidira—how are you?
hejjenu—big honey bee
hōgu—go
Huli-devathe—tiger goddess
idu—this thing
jenu—*Kannada.* Honey
kaddi—*Kannada.* stick, often used to describe
    small, skinny girls
kaddi jenu—*Kannada.* type of honey bee (literally small bee)
katte—*Jagali.* bench built into the side of a house.
katuva—*Malayalam.* tiger
kiddu—kid or kiddo (slang)
kurta—short tunic
laddus—sphere shaped sweets
lakh—100,000 rupees

lungi—sarong

machan—a tree platform to keep watch over crops in case ele
    phants come in the night.

machhu—sickle machete

magale—daughter

mosaru—curd

naaga devaru—the cobra god

naagarahaavu—spectacled cobra

namaskara—Hello in south India (Namaste in north India)

neeru—water

nyaya panchayithi—tribal council

ooru—*Kannada.* Hometown; not a specific place,
    but an ancestral home

paan—araca nut and leaves with tobacco and lime.

pooja—blessing or ceremony

pukka—proper

puttah—daughter/little one

rangoli—floral patterns drawn each morning by Indian
    women outside of their doors.

rotti—bread

soo-soo—pee-pee

Thika muchkondu hōgu—Shove it in your ass and go

thorsu—show, give

thumba—very, a lot

ulta—backward, inside out

vana—sacred forest patch, often at the fringe of a village

wallah—a seller of, for example, chai, coffee, or paper

warli—a style of Indian stick figure art.

zid—*Hindi.* determination (slang)

ACKNOWLEDGEMENTS

Firstly, to my wife Gowri, for all our adventures in India. Our jungle adventures and long road trips through elephant country were how I encountered so many of the experiences that would grow into this book. More than once we fell asleep to the sound of tigers roaring in the distance, and together we saw our first tiger up close. Gowri's amazing ability to connect with local people, whether tribals or Forest Department officers, and make them smile, was the magic thing that opened so many doors and encouraged people to share their stories and take us places. Her ability has made all of my work here possible.

My parents, Ed and Lenore, spent countless hours reading to us when we were kids. Every night. *Lord of the Rings*, *Sherlock Holmes*, *White Fang*, and so many others. They instilled a love of stories in me that has shaped my life. My sister Michelle was the first person to read early chapters of this book, and it was her encouragement and counsel that pushed it forward. She was crucial as a creative consultant and editor of this book.

I owe a tremendous thank you to my talented friend and agent Lindsay Edgecombe. I can always count on her to give me the hard truth. Thank you to Emma Nelson, Hannah Smith, Caroline Geslison, and everyone at Owl Hollow Press for believing in this book and taking this journey with me. Especially Olivia Swenson, who is a fantastic editor and a pleasure to work with (any editor that must sift through my dyslexic spelling attempts, fragments, and various other flaws has my respect!).

To my parents-in-law Sathya and Vishala Varanashi, for welcoming me to India and sharing so many amazing experiences. Vishala was crucial in correcting the Kannada translations, spellings, and otherwise India-proofing this story.

Neeti Mahesh is one of the most dedicated and talented conservationists I know. In our time in various forests of south India, she has taught me so much about the forest, and remains one of the most authentic, tough, and all around best people I know, even in the face of pure evil. If more people had her character and fierce dedication to nature, the world would be a drastically better place.

Trent Schroyer at Ramapo College for convincing me to join his study abroad to India (and in doing so, changing the entire course of my life!). Mike Edelstein, my professor and friend, who read the early drafts of this book and spent long hours on Skype with me editing and thinking through the story, just as he did for my first book. Neither one would be as good without his wise counsel. To Lorain Thomson for early editing and careful thoughts on narrative, and for always supporting my creative pursuits. Thank you to Chris Cimmorelli for seeing past all the rough errors and sharing your wise counsel on the earliest drafts.

To Prajna Chowta and Philippe Gautier for the incredible work you have done for elephants. You allowed me a rare glimpse into a beautiful world that helped polish and focus the details of this story. Dharma will forever be a part of my heart. Thank you.

Shonali and Anil Chinniah for letting me into your family. I think you know that this book book would never have been possible if you weren't the amazing adventurous people (and parents) that you are.

Lastly to the Indian Forest Department, so many of whom work so hard at a thankless job, holding back the tide of millions to protect the last slices of authentic nature left in this incredible country.

PAUL ROSOLIE is a naturalist, author, and award-winning wildlife filmmaker who has specialized in rainforests and endangered wildlife for over a decade. His work has helped protect over 6,000 acres of wildlife habitat in critical areas of The Amazon and India.

As an author Paul's mission is to explore the relationship between humans and nature, wild animals, and our vanishing wild places.

Rosolie has written for *National Geographic, published Mother of God: An Extraordinary Journey into the Uncharted Tributaries of the Western Amazon,* and had shows on Discovery Channel and Netflix.

Find Paul online at paulrosolie.com.

#TheGirlandtheTiger

CPSIA information can be obtained
at www.ICGtesting.com
Printed in the USA
FSHW010145020919
61564FS